St John Fisher

Bishop and Theologian in
Reformation and Controversy

VINCENT NICHOLS is the 11th Archbishop of Westminster. Born in Liverpool, he studied at the Venerable English College in Rome before his ordination to the priesthood in 1969. He prepared his thesis on John Fisher as a postgraduate student at Manchester University between 1970 and 1971. He was appointed Auxiliary Bishop to Westminster in 1992, Archbishop of Birmingham in 2000, and Archbishop of Westminster in 2009 following the retirement of Cardinal Cormac Murphy-O'Connor. Pope Francis created Archbishop Nichols a cardinal on 22 February, 2014, granting him the Titular Church of '*Santissimo Redentore e Sant'Alfonso in Via Merulana.*'

KEVIN EASTELL is a Professor at the Institut Catholique d'Etudes Supérieures at La Roche sur Yon in the Vendée, France and a priest of the Westminster diocese.

St John Fisher

Bishop and Theologian in
Reformation and Controversy

Vincent Nichols

Afterword and textual
editing by Kevin Eastell

alive publishing
Publisher to the Holy See
www.alivepublishing.co.uk

First published in 2011 by Alive Publishing Ltd.
Graphic House, 124 City Road, Stoke on Trent ST4 2PH
Tel: +44 (0) 1782 745600. Fax: +44 (0) 1782 745500
www.alivepublishing.co.uk
e-mail: booksales@alivepublishing.co.uk

©2014 Alive Publishing
British Library Catalogue-in-Publication Data.
A catalogue record for this book is available from
the British Library.

Cover image: John Fisher, Bishop of Rochester (1469-1535)
engraved by Francesco Bartolozzi (1727-1815) (engraving),
Holbein the Younger, Hans (1497/8-1543) (after) © Private Collection /
The Stapleton Collection / The Bridgeman Art Library

ISBN 978-1-906278-17-5

Contents

Introduction

There have been a fair number of surprises in my life. Three of them concern this book.

The first came in the summer of 1969. To my surprise I was asked by Mgr Thomas Worden, on behalf of Archbishop Beck, to go to Manchester University when I had finished studies in Rome and had been ordained. It was to be my first appointment. Mgr Worden was the Dean of Studies at St Joseph's College, Upholland, the senior seminary for the Archdiocese of Liverpool. However, he assured me that a period of lecturing at the seminary was not what the Archbishop had in mind. That was a relief, for I had never thought of myself as an academic. The appointment was for a more immediate purpose: Manchester University had, at that time, accepted the Licence in Theology of the Gregorian University as a first degree. Mgr Worden, who had brokered that understanding, wanted to consolidate it with a further post-graduate student. I was to be that student. I was free, he said, to pursue any line of post-graduate studies in the Faculty of Theology.

At Manchester University I made contact with Professor Basil Hall, a renowned Calvin scholar. A two-year course of study was put together under his guidance. I remember his main point to me when I expressed an interest in the theological debates of the Reformation. He said that seven years study in Rome had given me a strong foundation in philosophical and theological methods and it was time to move on to something else. So he urged me, and then introduced me, to the disciplines of historical study, pointing out that history is the most speculative of disciplines, as long as evidence is produced to support a thesis. My course, then, was made up of lectures on John Calvin's Geneva and a thesis on 'Saint John Fisher: Bishop and Theologian in Reformation and Controversy'.

Professor Basil Hall supervised the work, encouraging me always to look for the wider historical setting of the work of John Fisher. Professor Jack Scarisbrick was a great help and also acted as the external examiner when the work was complete.

As I recall, working on this thesis was a real adventure, taking me to primary sources in libraries that I would never have expected to enter. There was a thrill in handling manuscripts and very early printed books which, in all likelihood, had lain undisturbed for hundreds of years. I think particularly of the work of Edward Powel, tucked away in the Bodleian Library until I asked for it to be brought into the light of day.

The second surprise concerning this work was very recent. It was the suggestion, made by a number of people, that the text should be published, and the willingness of *Alive Publishing* to take it on. It reminded me of the words of G.K.Chesterton that the best of all pleasures comes with surprise. ('By asking for pleasure he lost the chief pleasure; for the chief pleasure is surprise.' '*Orthodoxy*'). But the wisdom of Chesterton applies also to dismay: that which truly surprises us can also dismay us the more. And my pleasure was mixed with dismay for I knew that this text is now outdated and incomplete.

But it must stand as it is and in this I ask the reader's understanding. This book is not yet another biography of St John Fisher. Rather, it is an attempt to trace his intellectual and spiritual development from the time when he went up to Cambridge as a young teenager to the years when, by now an accomplished theologian who had been deeply influenced by Renaissance humanism, he took up the pen against Luther and other early Protestants. It does not deal with the heated argument concerning the identity of Mary Magdalene in the New Testament, on which Fisher had spent much time and ink, nor with the remarkable pieces he wrote later in defence of the validity of the marriage between the king and Catherine of Aragon, and then in defence of the Church in England against royal assault. These topics have been well treated by other writers.

Nearly forty years have passed since I wrote this thesis. In that time, scholarship in this period of English history has abounded. I have not kept up with it in the least. Nor could I do so now. Any attempt to revise this text is beyond my capabilities in time and, I suspect, effort. So in this publication the text is presented as it was written, with the exceptions that Latin quotations have been translated into English and medieval texts put into contemporary script. A few corrections have been made to the inevitable errors that crept in.

However, further work has been done and I am grateful to Fr Kevin Eastell for undertaking it. He has kindly written further material related to each chapter. Through his efforts, my work is brought into the context of subsequent research and publications. He shows where new light has been cast on these topics, correcting or elucidating my work of nearly forty years ago. His work is an important part of this publication and a necessary complement to my own.

Introduction

The publication of this text is also a moment for me to pay tribute to my father. The work was done at a pace, as I had only two years to complete it. As a newly ordained priest, I also wanted to be playing a part in the pastoral life of the Church. My father understood and offered to help as much as he could. He typed the entire work for me. He did so, of course, without the assistance of electronic typewriters or computers. He used an old typewriter, carbon paper for a copy and lots of tipex. He painstakingly worked out the layout for every page, allowing for the many footnotes on each of them. It was a work of great love, without which this thesis would probably never have been presented, nor this book published.

The third surprise has come most recently. On February 22, 2014, on the Feast of the Chair of St Peter, I was created a Cardinal by Pope Francis. It was a wonderful moment, filled with deep emotion, feelings of trepidation, of profound unworthiness, of heartfelt willingness to do my best. But through them all there also came the awesome realisation that I was now standing even more closely in the shoes of St John Fisher. One sharp difference stood out. As is well known, such were the times and challenges in which he lived that, echoing the wish of the King, St John Fisher had no head on which could be placed his cardinal's red hat.

I thank God that we live in different times. I thank God that so many people, from many walks of life, from many parts of society, from many different religions, expressed delight at the appointment of a new Cardinal in our land. It was a sign of the widespread acceptance of the positive contribution made by our Catholic faith in contemporary society.

Yet, in matters of our faith, times are never entirely different. Today hostile voices are raised and social trends and legislation move against our faith as well as protecting it. Witness is to be given today, in a manner suitable to our times and with a courage similar to that of this great saint. I pray that I may be as faithful as he. And for this I ask your prayers, too.

One of the aims of this thesis was to site John Fisher more clearly in the context of his age. As a great Saint, he has tended to be seen standing alone, distanced from the perception of failure around him. What emerged from my study was a clear conviction that while John Fisher was a man of outstanding abilities and achievements, he did not stand alone, nor even as one of a very small company. Through a study of materials drawn from the late fifteenth century, a picture emerged of both parish life and academic life which is far more positive than popular impressions.

Introduction

Now this aspect of this study has been strongly affirmed by many subsequent publications. The state of the Catholic Church in this country on the eve of the Reformation was not as lax, corrupt or inept as many had thought. While the contribution of this work to the correcting of these perceptions is slight, I am pleased that it can now be seen in the context of much subsequent and more distinguished academic work. I think, in particular, of the work of Professor Eamon Duffy and I am grateful to him for the encouragement he gave for the publication of this text.

John Fisher was certainly a man of his time. This we see in many ways: in the upbringing he received; in his academic formation; in his style of thinking and writing. This identification also emerged in other ways, one of which I remember vividly.

In following up a reference to the statement that John Fisher had held the benefice for the Church of All Saints in Northallerton from 1491 to 1494 – a statement which, in fact, is not true – I came to learn that he had held the benefice for the little Church of St Oswald's in Lythe, Yorkshire, from 1499 to 1504. This was quite a wealthy parish benefice. Yet, interestingly there is no record of John Fisher having ever been present in it. As was the custom of the age, he appears to have taken the benefice and from it appointed a parochial chaplain to act in his name. One more surprise awaited me when I visited the Church of St Oswald's, on the hills north of Scarborough harbour. There in the Vestry was a portrait of St John Fisher. Nobody seemed to know why it was there and there was delight at the explanation I brought.

As a man of his time, who carried many of the strengths and weaknesses of his age, John Fisher might appear distant from us today. Yet that need not be so. There are many themes of his thought and writing which carry strong echoes for us in this age. These have come across strongly to me on rereading this work.

Throughout his life, John Fisher had a deep concern for the well-being and ministry of the clergy. He realised that the health of the Church depended largely on the health of the parish and, in turn, this depended on the work and presence of the clergy. Many of his initiatives, especially during his years of academic life, were aimed at the support and improvement of the priests of his day.

Fisher's concern was of the hard-headed variety. He did not hesitate to point out the failures of the clergy. Indeed he did so at times with vigour. Perhaps his most famous phrase in this regard is to be found in his Sermons on the Seven Penitential Psalms, printed in 1509. Preaching on Psalm 102, he said that whereas in the past there had been 'no chalices of gold but there was many golden priests, now there be many chalices of gold and almost no golden priests.' What is clear, however, is that this kind of admonition had been very much in fashion for some time. Indeed this very phrase use by Fisher had been taken from an Advent sermon of the Florentine Dominican Friar Savonarola. Many standard sermons and exhortations listed the failures of the clergy in a manner which changed little over a great number of decades.

Yet the evidence of parish life, as far as we can tell, did not support such an entirely pessimistic outlook. There was real hardship among the clergy. Also there was real support given to them, at least in the publications and handbooks available to them, sound advice about pastoral practice and clearly focussed help for their weekly sermons.

All of this has some resonance today. It is again popular to criticise the clergy. Has it not always been so? Of course now as then some of the criticism is justified. But its generalisation is not. Now as then there is much evidence of the untiring work of the majority of priests and those who assist them. There is ample evidence of the on-going formation for priests, of the resources and opportunities available to them. There is a need today, as then, to look at the facts of parish life rather than the popular impressions.

It might also be a consolation to recall that in the fourteenth century too the question of clerical celibacy was contentious and its abolition proposed as the solution to many of the failings attributed to priests.

Fisher's main effort in support of the clergy was in the area of education. He wanted a clergy that was better educated, thereby better able to inform and form itself for its important ministry. And in that ministry the task of teaching the faith was uppermost in his mind. He wanted his priests to be able and ready to study. He wanted them to bring the fruits of that study into their preaching. He wanted a laity that understood their faith and not be led astray by erroneous opinions and error. This was behind his initiatives at Cambridge.

Together with Lady Margaret Beaufort he pushed forward the priority that academic work in the University should be at the service of the parochial clergy. This was to be seen most clearly in the foundation of St John's College. For this College both the vision and purpose of education were crystal clear. The vision was one of faith, uprightness of life and education coming together in the closest harmony. Its purpose was the formation and support of the parochial clergy. Nor was this a narrow or backward-looking enterprise. Fisher worked hard to integrate the best of the new learning that was beginning to come into English University life. This consisted in the study of the Biblical languages themselves and a new attitude and use of the Scriptural texts as a source of inspiration both academically and spiritually. Fisher was not afraid of innovations. Rather he firmly believed that they could serve the greater good of the Church and revitalise its traditions and practices.

What would be Fisher's view of similar matters today? He would be dismayed at the public failings of even one priest. He would be adamant about the need for personal renewal and discipline of life. He would look to us bishops and priests in particular to give a clear and helpful account of the truths of faith in a manner which spoke to people of today. I think he would be delighted at the richness of resource available to us, embracing with enthusiasm some of the potential of contemporary means of communication while always on guard for the way in which these same means can be used to circulate misleading or corrosive views. In short, he would recognise a similar pattern of strengths and weaknesses and would offer to us today the same example of steadfast study, disciplined self-application, courage of expression and faithful observance of duty, not least the duty of personal prayer and devotion.

As a reformer, then, Fisher's stance was clear. Reform was not a matter of radical change of structure or teaching of the Church, but rather an issue of personal lives being reformed to the age-old wisdom of the Church in each contemporary setting. I cannot believe that his stance would be any different today.

He understood well that structured efforts were needed in patterns of education and in its content so that the best of academic work could be brought to serve the ministry of the Church. This, after all, was the real purpose of research: the greater service of the truth of Christ proclaimed in and by the Church. Such reforms were matters for those who carried academic responsibility and oversight. Fisher would be dismayed, perhaps even astonished, that theological academic effort today has, for the most part, moved so far from its origins and its definition as faith seeking understanding. But this would not turn him away from such effort. Rather it would reinvigorate his determination that theology again finds its traditional '*raison d'etre*'.

For me, there is something very appealing in the life of Saint John Fisher as a diocesan bishop. I was delighted, for example, when Cardinal Hume invoked his memory in his homily at the Mass of my Episcopal ordination. He said:

Introduction

Your model must be St John Fisher. You were once closely involved with the study of this great bishop. He, in return, is surely taking now a quite special interest in you, at least in accordance with my understanding of the role of heavenly patrons in our earthly affairs. St John Fisher died to defend the rights of Peter and thus for the unity of the Church. This bishop of great scholarship, this man of prayer, this lover of the poor was a true man of the Church, humble, faithful courageous. Those are qualities to esteem and to make our own.

There are many accounts of the exemplary nature of John Fisher as a bishop. Perhaps the one which appeals to me most readily is the account given by Henry VII to his mother Lady Margaret, in 1504, when he was announcing to her his choice of Fisher for the vacant see of Rochester. In it he praises Fisher 'for the great and singular virtue that I know and see in him as well in cunning and natural wisdom and specially for his good and gracious living.' The King hoped that by promoting Fisher others would come to follow his example.

Records tell us that Fisher made official visitations throughout his diocese in the years 1505, 1508, 1511, 1514, 1517, 1520 and 1529. This is evidence enough of his systematic dedication to the bread and butter work of Episcopal responsibility. Indeed I have the impression that Fisher was one of the first to establish such a pattern in this land. Many of us today do our best to follow it.

There is another small incident of Fisher's life which discloses his love of the Church and which would find an echo in many bishops today. As Chancellor of Cambridge, he was called upon, in 1521, to pronounce a sentence of excommunication against an unknown person who had defaced copies of the Papal bull against Luther posted at all the college gates. The contemporary accounts tell us that Fisher failed to persuade the culprit to confess. Then it adds that when he came to the point of proclaiming the sentence, 'after he had proceeded a space in the reading thereof, he stayed and began again to consider in his mind the great weight of his grievous sentence which so much pierced his heart that even before them all he could not refrain from weeping.' There are surely few bishops who would not share this sentiment and who would not go the extra mile rather than turn a person away from the Church, even in such a solemn manner.

At the heart of this study, however, is the figure of John Fisher, theologian and bishop, in a period of profound controversy. Here too there is much for us to learn today.

As a first step, it is important to remember that the first controversy to envelop his life was not that of divorce of Henry VIII and his subsequent break with the Holy See, but that of the proclamations of Martin Luther. This is the context in which we first see Fisher at work in defending the teaching of the Church and engaging with those who were opposed to it. Here the central issue was that of the Lutheran claim of the priority and authority of Scripture alone. In his defence of the Catholic position, Fisher did not concede any ground at all. He used every argument from the tradition of the Church, as well as from Scripture, to insist that the views being expressed by Luther were erroneous.

This appeal to the weight of tradition and to the voices of the Fathers of the Church, while being thoroughly traditional, also bears more modern resonances. This is the pathway also taken by John Henry Newman as he struggled to come to terms with the need for continuity in the teaching tradition of the Church alongside the development of that teaching. Newman's study of the Church Fathers convinced him that there was, within the Catholic Church, an unbroken line of teaching which was discernable within a proper development. This was essentially Fisher's argument, too, although put forward in conflict with the Protestant reformation of Luther.

A similar application of this same principle has come to lie at the heart of what is known as the 'ecumenical method', adopted by the Anglican/Roman Catholic International Commissions. In their work these Commissions decided to go back beyond the divisions of the Reformation to study again, and together, the common inheritance of the Fathers of the Church and the other ancient voices which gave witness to the faith of an undivided Church. Although the motivations in these two cases were entirely different, there is an interesting converging of convictions that there is unanimity of witness to be found to the essentials of the faith in the traditions of the ancient Church.

In the context of his conflict with Luther, Fisher's intentions and method were not shaped for dialogue. He was interested in defeating Luther's arguments, not in engaging with them. Not all his contemporaries shared that same perspective. There was one, a Welshman Edward Powel, who set about the task of defending Church teaching in a rather different vein. At the opening of his work he explained that his intention was to answer Luther by the use of Scripture alone, not because he agreed with the principle but because he realised that only Scriptural arguments were acceptable to Luther. He did this, he said, in the hope that Luther might thereby return to the true path.

Edward Powel failed, not only in regard to Luther himself but also in his attempt to meet Luther on his own grounds. But at least he tried.

This contrast between Fisher and Powel casts some light on the challenge facing the Church today. The issues facing the Church today are very different from those of Fisher's time. The challenge which was the focus of this study is that of the acceptability of the Church as a divine instrument. The challenge today is about the reality of the divine itself and the relevance of faith to the project of modern living. In facing his challenge, Fisher called on all the resources of Church tradition and of his learning, but he found it difficult to leave that frame of reference and embrace that of Luther. Edward Powel attempted to do so. Today there is a similar challenge and choice facing us.

During his remarkable Apostolic Visit to the United Kingdom in September 2010, Pope Benedict came face to face with the realm of secularity and the secular institutions of a State. Of course, this was not a new encounter for him, for this interface had been explored by him often during previous years, not least in academic settings. But in London, on Friday 18 September, in Westminster Hall, Pope Benedict addressed the relationship between faith and reason directly. In doing so he posed the questions as perceived by his secular audience. He entered that frame of reference, started from that perspective and unfolded his argument in terms which all could accept.

He said: 'The central question at issue then, is this: where is the ethical foundation for political choice to be found?' The question he presented was a shared one.

The reply he gave did not simply appeal to Catholic ethical teaching, arguing from its coherence and foundations in revelation. Rather he said this: 'The Catholic tradition maintains that the objective norms governing right action are accessible to reason, prescinding from the content of revelation.'

In developing his reply he maintained a careful openness and mutuality between the perspectives of reason and those of faith, willingly stating their mutual dependence. He explained how, on the one hand, faith illuminates reason and how, on the other, reason has a 'purifying and structuring role within religion.' He was not prepared to overstate claims for the contribution to be made by faith alone, as expressed in the teachings of the Church. Rather he established a ground of mutual interest and concern which enabled him to make his fundamental and lasting appeal:

Introduction

'I would invite you, therefore, within your respective spheres of influence, to seek ways of promoting and encouraging dialogue between faith and reason at every level of national life.'

One of the conclusions of this study was that Fisher's long and arduous efforts in theological controversy may not have been closest to his heart. He was, in many ways, an academic, but only when understood in its contemporary sense: one who wished above all else to pursue the deepest riches of faith in a setting of prayer and community life as experienced in the University colleges of his day.

This deepest longing emerged again in his prison cell in the Tower of London as he awaited trial and execution. During this time his writing turned again to the quest of the soul for God. His final end came after a year of imprisonment. We are told that on the morning of his execution, 22 July 1539, he was awakened by the prison officer at 5.00am and told that his execution was to be at 10.00am. He promptly asked to be allowed to sleep a few more hours!

Herein lies his true greatness: peace before God and within himself. May his example continue to inspire us today.

Cardinal Vincent Nichols
Archbishop of Westminister
March 2014

Childhood and Youth

The crisis of John Fisher's life put him at the heart of the most involved and emotionally charged incidents in the history of this country. It is little wonder, then, that biographies and commentaries on his life have tended to display as much of the allegiances and sympathies of their authors as of the well-founded historical facts of Fisher's life. Examples of this are easy to find. Reginald Pole (1500-58) in his *De Unitate Ecclesiae* lib. iii observes:

> *What other have you, or have had for centuries, to compare with Rochester in holiness, in learning, in prudence and episcopal zeal? You may be, indeed, proud of him, for were you to search through all the nations of Christendom in our days, you would not easily find one who was such a model of episcopal virtues. If you doubt this, consult your merchants who have travelled many lands; consult your ambassadors, and let them tell you whether they have anywhere heard of any bishop who has such love for his flock as never to leave the care of it, even feeding it by word and example, against whose life not even a rash word could be spoken; one who was conspicuous not only for holiness and learning but also for love of country.*

More recently Fr Vincent McNabb O.P. opened his book *Saint John Fisher* with these words:

> *Dear reader! You are about to take part in perhaps the greatest tragedy of an age that wrote Hamlet and Macbeth. Greater even than the writer's part will be yours, the reader's and the hearer's part. Only your hearing ear and your seeking eye will bring the tragedy to its own. But your seeing eye and your hearing ear must first recognise that a greater than Hamlet or Macbeth is here. They are but splendid fiction.*

And brings it to a climax thus:

> *The headsman struck one blow at the outstretched body, and the head of the first canonised Cardinal Martyr, like the Baptist's head he had so long honoured, had won its title to a place for ever on the altar of Sacrifice.[1]*

---

[1] V. McNabb, *Saint John Fisher*, (London: Burns & Oats.,1935) pp. 9 & 129.

Meanwhile, at the other extreme, R.S. Arrowsmith includes John Fisher in his list of reforming bishops with these comments:

> *while John Fisher, Bishop of Rochester, with all his credulity, narrowness and reactionary views, commanded universal esteem for his learning, piety and courage. If, as a later prelate once wittily remarked, the good are not so good as they think themselves, it is certainly true that very often the bad are not so bad as the good think them.* [2]

Study of the Reformation, then, is fraught with the danger of overflowing emotion. In excess these lead either to a distortion of the balanced picture or, at least, to an interpretation of the facts which contributes another shield to the armour of an entrenched position. All efforts must be made to avoid such a damaging course of action. Constant vigilance is required of those studying this period to ensure that statements are as free as possible from distortion arising from misguided loyalty, for the desire to serve one's cause can eventually defeat its higher purpose if it gives rise to any divergence from truth, or from an honest search for a truth as yet unknown. We need to refer continually to established facts and firmly to establish newly uncovered facts; only on these foundations may we begin to pass comment and evaluate.

The basic facts of John Fisher's life are available to us in the various biographies that have been written. On the whole they are reliable in outline, for this has been established mainly by the extensive research of Fr F. Van Ortroy. After making a survey of the manuscript sources, he has produced the definitive version of the original biography of John Fisher. On other counts, however, the biographies, for the most part, have been written from a confessional point of view and accordingly require critical appreciation. [3]

But biographical detail is not our primary concern. Rather our attention is directed first and foremost to the times in which John Fisher lived. We intend to use a study of his life and works as an opportunity to explore some of the varied aspects of the life of the Church in England in the years before the Reformation. What can we say of the Church into which John Fisher was born? What was the level of spiritual life? What

---

[2] R.S. Arrowsmith, *The Prelude to the Reformation*, (London, 1923,) p. 15.

[3] This biography is based on MS Arundel 152 f. 248-264 and on sixteenth and seventeenth century copies made from it before it was damaged by fire in 1865. Ortroy writes: 'We believe then that we have demonstrated that the MS Arundel 152 is the original of the English text and that it served as a model for all the others.' P. Van Ortroy, *Vie du bonheureux martyr Jean Fisher, Cardinal Évêque de Rochester (ob. 1535). Texte Anglais et Traduction Latine du XVI siècle. Analecta Bollandiana.* (Henceforth Van Ortroy, *Vie*) Vol. X (1891) pp. 121-365 and Vol. XII pp. 97-287. Cf. Vol. X p. 130.

do we know of its clergy, its bishops, its parishes; whose contribution to the age would be so important? What can we state about the system of education in which John Fisher was formed and in which he spent the first thirty years of his life; for its influence must have been far-reaching, not only in his life but also in the lives of his contemporaries?

In what ways are we able to develop our picture of the life of the Church in these decades? These are the vital years. The mental and spiritual equipment gradually acquired during these years was brought by bishops, theologians and clergy to the first conflicts of the great Lutheran debate. Skills and abilities mastered in these decades are all that traditional Roman Catholics had at their disposal in the defence of their faith. What were these skills and abilities? Which gifts once possessed had been lost? Was the Church impoverished spiritually and intellectually? Can we find evidence of a broad range of learning, of attention to intellectual developments which later can also be seen to have been employed by Catholics in their defensive manoeuvres? Can we, faithful to an honest search for the truth, contribute in any way to an understanding of the state of Catholicism in England at this time? Indeed we must remember the difficulty of understanding this period, for often it is approached as a period of transition from one era to the next, and not fully appraised in its own right. As H.A. Oberman writes:

> *When one attempts to sum up the views of late mediaeval spirituality which have been current during our century a very bleak picture emerges. To be sure there are some redeeming features, but these are usually described as 'the dawning of a new age' and, therefore, dissociated from the 'real state of affairs', or limited to stubbornly persisting traces of the flowering High Middle Ages.* [4]

A.G. Dickens offers the ability to 'inspire lively art and craftsmanship' as the most important mitigating feature of fifteenth century religious life in England. Men such as Thomas More and Henry VIII must somehow be removed from such an ill-becoming context: 'people who sing the same creed are not necessarily practising the same type of religion.'[5] The popularity of quotations from Simon Fish, as representing Pre-Reformation England, is another symptom of unsympathetic study.[6] Fish's *A Supplicacyon for the Beggars* should be appreciated as a 'rabble rousing piece of anti-clericalism', which understood the temper of the times and how to appeal to people's prejudices and the King's avarice,

---

[4] H.A. Oberman, *Forerunners of the Reformation*, (London: Lutterworth Press, 1967) p. 4.

[5] A.G. Dickens, *The English Reformation*, (London: B.R. Batsford, 1966) pp. 9 & 4.

[6] Eg. A.G. Dickens & D. Carr, *The Reformation in England*, (London: Edward Arnold, 1967) p. 15.

but not as providing a reliable report of the facts.[7] D. Fenlon also writes of the Church in general:

> *At the close of the Middle Ages the condition of the Church was nowhere healthy – a Papacy preoccupied with politics and taxation, ... an absentee episcopate; and ignorant clergy; and uninstructed laity; a widespread indifference to the spirit of Christianity beneath the forms of established, though sometimes irregular observances: everything combined to reduce the spiritual life of Christendom to a state not far removed from bankruptcy.[8]*

Although he later admits that 'bankruptcy is not the same as intent to defraud'; clearly this negative assessment has to be measured carefully against the known facts. However, since the late 1960s, a number of historians have reviewed the period with a more balanced perception, and their work continues.[9]

So, as the successive stages of John Fisher's life are unfolded, being attentive to the pitfalls which surround us, we shall be studying the period's circumstances and its environment. We shall be seeking to know more accurately the quality of the theological and ecclesiastical life of the times so that we can appreciate the contribution made by Fisher, not in isolation, but in the context of its formative influences and his contemporaries.

John Fisher was born in 1469 in the town of Beverley in Yorkshire, of a large family of merchants.[10] His father was Robert Fisher, and the evidence of his will suggests that he was a man of some standing in a town dominated by trade. Dr. J. Lewis reports the will of Robert Fisher,[11] who died when John was eight years old, and we may reasonably assume that, as the eldest son, he was left in a position of some responsibility. His mother married again, and the sixteenth-century biographer comments that despite this she did not abandon the children of her first marriage, but secured for them a good education from the wealth left by their father.[12] These were adverse conditions for a young boy. The later

---

[7] Cf. S.W. Hass, 'Simon Fish, William Tyndale and Sir Thomas More's Lutheran Conspiracy', *Journal of Ecclesiastical History*, Vol. XXIII, No.2, April 1967, p.125. Also, H. Maynard Smith, *Pre-Reformation England*, (London: Macmillan, 1938) p. 14.

[8] D. Fenlon, *Heresy and Obedience in Tridentine Italy*, (Cambridge University Press, 1972) p.1.

[9] Numbered among the scholars who have revised the perspective of the early 16th century are: J.J. Scarisbrick, E. Duffy, J. Guy, A.A. Chibi and R. Rex.

[10] M. Macklem, *God Have Mercy*, (Oberon Press: Ottawa, 1967) p. 210.

[11] J. Lewis, *The Life of Dr John Fisher, Bishop of Rochester in the Reign of Henry VIII*, 2 Vols, (Joseph Lilley: London, 1855) Vol. II p. 253.

[12] Van Ortroy, *Vie*, Vol. X, p. 203f. Also E. E. Reynolds, Roper and Harpsfield: *Lives of Thomas More* (New York: Everyman's Library, 1963), p. 2.

life of Fisher points to a strength, a confidence and a self-sufficiency of character that may well have been rooted in these early days.

Records of Church life in Yorkshire give us the impression, sufficient for our initial comments, that Fisher grew up in a Church that was loyal to the old traditions and statements of faith, loyal to the style and patterns of spirituality, and loyal also to the traditional struggle for local autonomy in administrative matters. Throughout the fifteenth century relations between the provinces of York and Canterbury were often tempestuous, while communications between diocesan bishop and local chapter were marked by strict formal courtesy. G.R. Elton notes 'The first thing to understand about the English Church in the Middle Ages is that it never existed. There was no one authority in ecclesiastical affairs coterminous with the King in secular affairs.'[13] More particularly, Beverley is recorded as having been involved in conflicts between local chapters and deaneries and the central diocesan administration.[14]

The loyalty of the Yorkshire Church in matters of faith and practice, however, emerges as a major characteristic of this age for it is clearly to be seen in many features of Church life. Even when traces of Lollardy appeared in various parts of the country, there is little evidence of it in Yorkshire.[15] Rather the old faith is presented as having been enthusiastically maintained: churches were rebuilt at Tickhall, Rotherham, Harewood, Thirsk and Bolton Percy; churches were given large extensions at Wakefield, Halifax and Silkstone; churches and chapels were founded at Skirlaugh, Catterick and Cowthorpe. Henry VIII's commissioners, when they visited St Nicholas' church in Doncaster, made this report:

> *there are 2000 communicant people and above within the said parish, whereof the said incumbent and other 7 priests now resident in the said church can barely hear the confessions of the said parishioners from the beginning of Lent until Palm Sunday, and then administer the blessed sacrament all the said week.*[16]

---

[13] G.R. Elton, *England under the Tudors*. (London: Methuen, 1956) p. 84.

[14] A.H. Thompson, *The English Clergy and their Organisation in the Later Middle Ages*, (Oxford; Clarendon Press, 1947) p. 9.

[15] See Dickens, *The English Reformation*, p. 30. Also P. Janelle, *L'Angleterre Catholique à la Veille du Schisme* (Paris, 1935), p. 28.

[16] In 1535, Thomas Cromwell compiled a survey of the assets of the Church of England: the *Valor Ecclesiasticus*. W.J. Sheils, *The English Reformation*. 1530-1570, (London: Longman, 1989) p. 26.

They added that every day Matins, Mass and Evensong were sung in the choir, and there were six Masses celebrated on the hour from 5 am until 10 am.[17]

Continuing further, in general terms only, we can see that in this period, unlike subsequent periods, there was a total integration of religion and daily life. Just as the edifice of the church dominated the skyline, so too the presence of the Church in its preaching and liturgy, its pageantry and learning, formed the patterns of the laws, schools, habits of travel and of entertainment; even the language used by the people and the way they dated their correspondence were fashioned and coloured by their membership of the Church.[18] The Sunday attendance at church would often be extended to include a meal in the church hall; and entertainment, archery, wrestling and dancing followed Evensong.[19] The Church, with its traditions and practices, was closely knit into the lives of the people, and the secular clergy were undoubtedly loved and respected by their parishioners.[20] That is not to say that everything was well, but it is to assert that the picture of a people loyal to the faith and doctrines of the Church yet dissatisfied and opposed to the clergy, takes too little account both of facts and human psychology.[21]

Turning to matters of spiritual practice, the will of Robert Fisher provides us with an excellent starting point. As we shall see in greater detail, a constant emphasis on the need for forgiveness from sin, brought to a crisis point by a meditation on death, was a feature of the spirituality of this time. A flurry of activity in old age, a hurried effort to satisfy an uneasiness of mind and heart were commonplace and practical works of charity were the popular expressions of the hopes and fears of the ageing testator. The results were to be seen in practically every town in England and to this Beverley was no exception. There were in the town at least six hospitals founded and supported as works of charity, in which care of the sick and poor was carried out in the context of a strictly observed religious life. The Hospital of St Giles was the most important of these. It had been founded in the thirteenth century and by 1274 it had an officially appointed rector and four or five chaplains, 'who by their example of life might have a wholesome influence over others,

---

[17] W. Page (ed.), *Victoria History of the County of York* (Henceforth *VCH Yorks*) (London: Constable, 1913), Vol. III, pp. 41–2.

[18] P. Hunt, *Fifteenth Century England*, (Oxford Univ Press: 1962) p.5.

[19] Maynard Smith, *Pre-Reformation England*, p. 119.

[20] J.R.H. Moorman, *A History of the Church of England*, (London: Black, 1953) p. 115.

[21] H. Maynard Smith, *Pre-Reformation England*, (Macmillan: London, 1938) p. 51.

honourably maintain the property of the hospital, continually celebrate there and preserve the observance of the hospital.'[22]

Most prominent in the will of Robert Fisher is his desire to be remembered in the prayers and Masses of his fellow Christians.

> *In like manner I give and bequeath to the alms-houses of Beverley 20 pennies. In like manner I bequeath to the fabric of the Collegiate church of St John, Beverley, 20 pennies. In like manner I bequeath to the fabric of the Cathedral of St Peter in York 8 pennies. In like manner I bequeath to both the Franciscan houses of Beverley 3 shillings and 4 pennies. In like manner I bequeath to the chapel of the Trinity that they may pray for my soul 13 shillings and 4 pennies. In like manner I wish that one of the Chaplains will appropriately pray for my soul for one year. In like manner I bequeath to Robert Kirk, Vicar of the church of the Blessed Virgin Mary 6 shillings and 8 pennies. In like manner I bequeath to John Plumber, Chaplain, 11 shillings and 8 pennies. In like manner I bequeath to the Conventual Abbey of Hawnby in Lincolnshire commending the celebration of 30 Masses for my soul 10 shillings. In like manner I bequeath of my own free will and of my responsibility 53 shillings and 4 pennies...*

To this end he set aside almost half of his wealth. In this he illustrates a major feature of the age: the practice of charity bequests. This religious generosity had been observed by King Henry VII, following his death in 1509. [In his will he left funds for the foundation of hospitals and for the celebration of 10,000 Masses with an offering of 6d each (double the normal offering) within three months of his death. To every parish church and friary that was equipped with only a wooden pyx he bequeathed a pyx of silver gilt emblazoned with the royal arms.][23] This practice rests firmly on traditional Catholic teachings such as the efficacy of prayers for the dead and the merit of the sacrifice of the Mass, and so its popularity in Yorkshire at this time attests the traditional nature of local spirituality.[24]

Wills such as Robert Fisher's must have been welcomed by the many young and un-patronised curates of the times who were

---

[22] *VCH Yorks,* Vol. III, p. 301. Of the lesser hospitals in Beverley, Trinity Hospital had been founded c.1400 and in 1402 John Kelk founded the Leper Hospital.

[23] J. R. Lander, *Conflict and Stability in Fifteenth-Century England* (London: Hutchinson, 1969), p. 121.

[24] A token table of the growth of Chantry foundations, from Page, *VCH Yorks*, Vol. III, . 43:

Deanery.	13th Cent.	14th Cent.	15th Cent.
Ainsly	1.	2.	7.
Doncaster	1.	11.	11.
Pontefract	1.	5.	13.

dependent for their livelihood upon chantry and other bequests.[25] As we shall see, contemporary social critics pointed to gross negligence in admitting candidates to ordination as the main cause of the many problems concerning the clergy, but it is clear that the financial position of many clerics was far from satisfactory for their stability was seriously undermined by the appropriation of benefices by religious houses. This practice led to the appointment of parish vicars, upon whom the responsibility for the parish was placed in return for reduced tithes, while the rest of the tithes and other revenues went to the religious. Furthermore, sometimes the religious order, or the vicar, would appoint a non-beneficed curate or chaplain who would receive only a small annual salary without any security. With its large number of religious houses, Yorkshire appears to have had a major problem with this practice at the end the end of the fifteenth century: of the 622 Yorkshire parishes, 392 were appropriated by religious houses and of these one hundred or so were served by poor removable curates.[26] A further indication of the conditions is given by Archbishop Edward Lee (1482-1544), when he wrote to Thomas Cromwell (1485-1540) in 1535, observing: '…we have very few preachers as the benefices are so small that no learned man will take them.'[27]

Under such conditions, the life of a priest working in a parish cannot have been an easy one, financially at least. Yet closer attention will reveal that the spiritual life of the clergy was not totally obstructed by these circumstances. Though simple and poorly educated, the parish clergy were by no means illiterate or grossly immoral. The number and type of books emerging from the printing presses of William Caxton (c.1422-91) and Wynkyn de Worde (?- 1534) are firm evidence of this. [Pierre Janelle notes that between 1470 and 1500 about 23 lives of the saints, 15 books of piety and 26 prayer books were published. A.G. Dickens counts 29 books of piety among the 74 works produced by Caxton between 1470 and 1490; and 30 religious books among the 54 publications of Wynkyn de Worde.[28]] Significantly, Thomas More could write this of the English clergy in this period: '…in learning and honest

[25] A. Tindal Hart, *The Curate's Lot*, (London: John Baker, 1970) pp. 33 and 46.

[26] D. Knowles and R. Neville Hadcock, *Medieval Religious Houses* (London: Longman, 1971); cf. maps. Also Dickens, The English Reformation, p. 47, and E. M. Thompson, *The Carthusian Order in England* (London: SPCK,1938), p. 115.

[27] *VCH Yorks*, Vol. III, p. 46.

[28] Janelle, *L'Angleterre Catholique à la Veille du Schisme*, p. 21, and A.G. Dickens counts 29 books among the 74 works produced by Caxton in his book *The English Reformation*, (B.T. Batsford: London. 1966).

Chapter One

living they were well able to match number for number the spirituality of any nation Christian.'[29]

Turning from priest to bishop we can state that the Church which cared for the young John Fisher was not blessed with the total and undivided attention of its episcopacy. The absenteeism practised by Archbishop Thomas Rotherham (1423-1500) of York did not cease after his death, but was carried to a climax by his three successors: Thomas Savage who was never publicly enthroned, Christopher Bainbridge who spent five of his six years archiepiscopate in Rome and Cardinal Thomas Wolsey (c.1473-1530) whose record is now quite famous. However, it was often the conflicting duties of Church and State that gave rise to these situations and for this the accusing finger may be pointed at the system of episcopal appointments. All too often a bishop was appointed because of his service to the State and not because of his spiritual dedication. The call of State duties was often strong and irresistible. It must be said, however, that as their Church responsibilities continued to clamour for attention, the diocesan bishops often took care to provide representatives, as did Bishop Rotherham.

During the fifteenth century successive bishops of Dromore were suffragans to York. One of these consecrated churches for Archbishop Bowet in 1424 and dedicated Holy Trinity at Hull in 1425. Three chapels were consecrated by the bishop who helped Rotherham: Middlemore in 1484, Wentworth in 1491 and Hook in 1499. Ordinations were also conducted by him. Various bishops '*in partibus*' aided this Archbishop during the fifteenth century and the Bishop of Negroport consecrated Huddersfield Church for Archbishop Savage in 1503.[30]

Records show that an absent bishop was not always a negligent bishop. This is confirmed by their often expressed desire to return to their pastoral duties, so long neglected, as soon as the duties of State had ceased. In 1513, Bishop Richard Fox (c.1448-1528) wanted to return to his diocese of Winchester not 'to hunt or to hawk, nor to take more worldly pleasure, nor for the ease of my body, or yet for quietness of mind' but 'to do some satisfaction for xviii years of negligence.' Archbishop William Wareham (1450-1532) of Canterbury expressed a similar hope.[31]

[29] T. More, 'A Dialogue Concerning Heresies.' *Complete Works of Thomas More*, (Yale University Press: New Haven and London, 1961-1997,) Vol. 6, Part 1, (1981) Book iii, Ch. 11, lines 15-20, p. 295.

[30] *VCH Yorks*, Vol. III, p. 44.

[31] J.J. Scarisbrick, *Henry VIII*, (London: Penguin, 1971) p. 67, quoting the letters of Richard Fox,83 and 32, and Rogers. *The Correspondence of Sir Thomas More*, (Princeton Univ: 1947,) p. 86. On the issue of residency see: A.A. Chib, *Henry VIII's Bishops*, (Cambridge: James Clarke & Co. 2003) p.76.

In fact it was such a rare event for a bishop to be chosen on grounds of his spiritual qualities that when it did occur, as with the appointment of John Fisher, it finds a special mention in a letter from Henry VII to his mother: 'I have in my days promoted many a man unadvisedly, that I would now make some recompense to promote some good and virtuous man which I doubt not should best please God.'[32]

Such a predominant involvement of the bishops in affairs of State cannot have been to the benefit of the Church and we can be sure that the picture of the hierarchy first observed by Fisher was far from satisfactory. Significantly, when Fisher himself became a bishop, far from accepting the status quo he strove by word and example to bring a higher level of spiritual ambition and achievement to the brotherhood of the episcopate.[33]

A further conclusion to be drawn from this state of affairs is that the influence of the Papacy in the appointment of bishops had worn thin.

The *Calendars of Papal Registers* show, beyond a shadow of a doubt, that during the second half of the century the Pope could hardly appoint a clerk of his own choosing to any English bishopric or even a lesser benefice. In theory his right to make such an appointment remained intact, in practice he was quite unable to exercise it. In the thirteenth year of the reign of Pope Sixtus IV, from 1471 to 1484, he nominally provided or translated 20 bishops to sees in England and Wales. Of the seventeen clerics involved, sixteen were the King's trusted councillors.[34]

We must not then suppose that there was any papal stranglehold over the *Ecclesia Anglicana* for other factors had far more immediate influence over the life of the Church than the sway of distant Rome. Certainly, popular understanding of the Church must have included the central position of the Bishop of Rome but, as we shall see later, it was a teaching which received neither nourishment nor explanation at the hands of the preachers.[35] Nor could the position of Rome have been readily strengthened by appeals to emotions: faith in Rome was not a lively or loving faith, for in many respects Rome was unlovable and the behaviour of her representatives in England was hardly endearing. Rather, it was a duty accepted, not a movement of the heart. This surely

---

[32] C.H. Cooper, *Memoir of Margaret, Countess of Richmond and Derby*, (Cambridge: Deighton, Bell and Co. 1874,) p. 95.

[33] For example, Fisher remained faithful to his diocese, one of the poorest in England in terms of revenues. This may be compared to Fox who successively occupied Exeter, Bath and Wells, Durham and finally Winchester, reputedly the richest diocese in England. S. Thompson, *The Bishop in his Diocese*, B. Bradshaw & E. Duffy (Ed) *Humanism, Reform and the Reformation*, (Cambridge Univ: 1989) p. 70. Fisher may have been offered and declined Lincoln and Ely.

[34] Lander, *Conflict and Stability in Fifteenth-Century England*, p. 137.

[35] Scarisbrick, *Henry VIII*, p. 317, and Thompson, *The English Clergy*, p. 38.

meant that the eventual loyalty of men like Fisher and More must have been cold and stubbornly intellectual, in strong contrast to the natural warmth they showed for Henry and their country. Loyalty to King and country was often the sentiment expressed by such men, particularly in their final words. In Fisher's case, 'I pray God save the King and the realme and hold his holy hand over it and send the King a good counsel.' In More's case, 'I die the King's good servant and God's first.' – an allusion to Matthew 22:21.

These general observations about the state of the Church in its spiritual life, its clergy and its bishops will suffice for now. Already a picture of the age is taking shape. In Yorkshire we see a Church of deep loyalty to the traditional faith in its spiritual practices and attitudes. We see a piety expressed in terms of practical charity, and a clergy often left struggling to keep itself financially viable. Equally clearly some startling weaknesses emerge, most notably the worldliness of Church leaders.

In the days of Fisher's youth the town of Beverley was dominated by the Minster of St John, the Collegiate Church of Beverley that still stands today sentinel over the compact town centre and over the surrounding countryside. It played the part of the cathedral church for that section of the largest diocese in England and, together with Ripon and Southwell, was one of the three major centres of the Archdiocese of York. It symbolised the autonomy that was enjoyed and treasured by local churches, and gathered round itself the stable and deep-rooted parish life of the region. Its history is long and colourful, a typical combination of tale and fact, reflecting the qualities of the religious life of the times, enriched as it was by the contributions of many centuries; embracing all aspects of human life, admittedly uncritical, but totally sincere. Legend assigned the origins of the Minster to the middle of the second century and a monastery was certainly founded there in the later seventh century by St John of Beverley. The canons of the town received their first charter from Edward the Confessor, and from the thirteenth century the Minster records are well documented.[36] Its basic structure was that of a college of seven canons, holders of the seven prebend benefices. Each canonry had its own altar: SS. Andrew, James, Martin, Mary, Michael, Peter and Stephen. The yearly value of these, according to the 1535 *Valor Ecclesiasticus,* ranged from £48. 16s. 1d. for St Andrew's to £31. 8s. 4d. for St Michael's. An eighth canonry had been added, that of St Katherine, but it was never accepted as possessing full

---

[36] A.F. Leach, *Memorials of Beverley Minster; the Chapter Act Book of the Collegiate Church of St John of Beverley, A.D. 1286-1347,* (Surtees Society) p. xxvii, xlvii-xlix.

capitular title. The Minster was, in fact, a well-established, prosperous and influential establishment, impressive not only for the size of its building, but also for its tradition and status.

It was to the Collegiate School of St John's that Fisher was sent as a young boy:

> *His mother...caused her two sonnes John and Robert to be put to learnings at the expences of such goodes as theyr father had left them; and to that ende she committed them both to a priest of the Church of Beverley, a collegiate church of priests, richly endowed of auncient time with landes and possessions, by whom they were amounge other children instructed and taught their first letters and rudiments of grammer.*[37]

The effect of being in close association from an early age with a place of such well-established and traditional Catholicism must be understood as substantial.

Even though the Chapter Acts books are missing for the period 1456-1525, we may still form fairly clear ideas about the type of schooling received by Fisher. The school conformed to the long-standing pattern of Cathedral schools or Collegiate Churches as established by the Lateran Council of 1179.[38] An integral part of the founding of every Cathedral or Collegiate Church was the setting up of a school to provide education primarily for the clerks of the church, but also for poor scholars and boys of the neighbourhood. Accordingly the school master was appointed and licensed by the Cathedral or Minster Chapter and received a stipend for all pupils on the foundation. The full force of ecclesiastical authority supported the school, even to the extent of forbidding rival establishments under pain of excommunication. For example, in 1486 James Sheffield was given the 'teaching and keeping of the grammar school in the City of York' and a special clause forbade rival schools or masters within a radius of ten miles.[39] In Beverley too, this was the nature of the school and undoubtedly the pupils were imbued with a sense of identity and pride at being so closely associated with the heart of ecclesiastical authority and power.[40]

---

[37] Van Ortroy, *Vie,* Vol. X, p. 204.
[38] J. Lawson, *Medieval Education and the Reformation*, (London: Routledge Keegan Paul, 1967) p. 12.
[39] A.F. Leach, *Early Yorkshire Schools*, Yorkshire Arch. Soc. Record Series, Vol. 27 and 33 (London,1899-1903) p. xxix.
[40] *VCH Yorks,* Vol. 1, p. 425f.

Rigour and discipline were the predominant features of the educational system of Beverley School, as was vividly portrayed in the degree ceremony of the graduates of grammar. Each was solemnly invested with a rod and birch and a victim was at hand to undergo a symbolic flogging. Comfortingly, the victim was later rewarded for his pains.[41] Fisher took part in this ceremony in 1483, and so we may presume that his basic training had been thorough and severe.

Latin was the subject that would have occupied his time and energies during these years. It was not only the language of the Church, but also that of trade and administration; for most business and legal transactions, records, minutes and accounts were written in Latin. The aim in education was the speaking, reading and writing of Latin, and in this Fisher certainly became proficient: the methods used being dictation and memory work. The standard text books employed were Donatus and Priscian, with Aesop's *Fables* and the *Disticha* (a volume of moral maxims) providing readings.[42] At the same time, the basic prayers and statements of faith were used for parsing and construing, and we find frequent references to Archbishop Pecham's 1281 programme for religious education. As we shall see, this proved to be the basis of much preaching, but it is significant that it found its way into the grammar school curriculum too, demanding that attention be given to the articles of faith, the ten commandments, the two precepts of charity, the seven virtues and vices, the seven works of mercy and the seven sacraments. So, from his earliest years the young cleric, such as John Fisher, would have become intimately familiar with the basic statements of Catholic belief in their simplest form. He would hear the same themes enriched and developed in various fashions from the pulpits, read the same manuals and handbooks as a parish priest and, if such was his lot, continue his study of them in the halls of the Universities. His grounding in them started with the first moments of his education and so it is not surprising that the first public reaction we find to Lutheran theology is in terms of a general re-statement of the simple traditional tenets of faith.

John Fisher set out for Cambridge in 1483. He left behind him a childhood spent in the bosom of the Church, where contrary influences must have been negligible. The religious life of Yorkshire, the influence of the Collegiate School gave him a profound initiation into the traditional patterns of Catholicism which were to remain at the centre of his life. Yet his early experience may also have exposed him to some

---

[41] Reynolds, op. cit. p. 6.

[42] Lawson, *Medieval Education and the Reformation*, p. 24.

of the weakness of Church life; the inadequacy and hardship of some of the parish clergy, the lack of single-minded dedication in the bishops and, comprehensively, the need for greater detachment from the hold of this world's affairs. Certainly in his own life Fisher strove mightily to improve the state of the Church on all these matters. His Yorkshire temperament and his privileged background of economic stability, together with his comparatively exalted schooling, would have made him sure and steady of character. He is portrayed as slow in giving affection and loyalty, unafraid of challenges and able to take his stand and make his opinions known when called upon to do so.[43]

His early catechetical training, as his piety, was along the well defined lines of a simple exposition of traditional Catholic doctrine. What his later theological studies were to build upon these foundations we have yet to see but we may presume that he set about his years of study with that single mindedness of purpose and that strength of character which dominated his whole life. Those of lesser sympathy interpret these traits as narrow mindedness and obstinacy: the characteristics are the same.

---

[43] Reynolds, op. cit. p. 8.

Student and Lecturer

Twenty one years of John Fisher's life were spent in the university town of Cambridge. During that time, links were forged which identified him forever as a man of that university town. He first arrived in Cambridge in 1483 as a youth of fourteen, and left in 1504 when he was appointed Bishop of Rochester, having already been chosen as Chancellor of the university one month previously. Clearly, an understanding of the events and influences of this period are essential; not only to our presentation of Fisher as a man, but also to our understanding of the period in which he lived, for apart from the barest outlines very little is known or sure about the pattern and content of university life in those years before the Reformation.[1]

University life in Cambridge, then as now, centred round the College which, in the definition of Lawson, is described as: 'an endowed self-governing corporation of Scholars living in common life of study, and in return for the founder's charity offering perpetual intercession for his soul.'[2] An applied commitment to study and serious attention to college life along with a corporate spirituality were the characteristics at this time for the majority of colleges, since a major concern was the preparation of men for the priesthood. John Fisher joined the company of scholars at Michaelhouse and within fifteen days, as the statutes laid down, he had entered himself under the tutorial supervision of William de Melton, who at this time was working on his doctorate in theology.[3] He was later described by Fisher himself as 'an eminent theologian'.[4] The college at Michaelhouse has been variously described. Mullinger states that it was 'one of the most monastic and conservative of English Colleges' and couples this with Fisher's early intensively ecclesiastical

---

[1] Since this was written, Damien Leader has published a history of the University, and John Twigg has also written a history of Queen's College that provides information on the curriculum of the University at the Pre-Reformation period.

[2] J. Lawson, *Medieval Education and the Reformation* (London: Routledge Kegan Paul, 1967), p. 41.

[3] *Documents relating to the University and Colleges of Cambridge*, Published under the direction of the Queen's Commissioners, (London: Longman, Brown, Green and Longman, 1852) Vol. I Sect. 42. Henceforth referred to as 'Documents'. See also Reynolds, p.5-6 and A.B. Emden, *Biographical Register of the University of Cambridge to A.D. 1500.* (Cambridge University Press: 1963) p. 400, (henceforth referred to as Emden, *Biographical Register*).

[4] Reynolds, op. cit. p. 3, from the Proemium of *De Veritate Corporis Christi.*

training as accounting for his later conservative attitude.[5] However, Stamp, who has written a full account of the foundation and early history of Michaelhouse, conveys a different impression. He presents Michaelhouse in these terms:

> *It was wealthy and enjoyed a very considerable position in the eyes of the University. Its clerical but non-monastic character made it a favourite recipient of donations for those who would insure for themselves prayers and masses without having the means to endow chantries on their own account. Its wealth and prosperity were continually increasing until in 1546 it suffered the same fate as other religious houses and was compelled to surrender all possessions to the king.[6]*

Taking up the well-documented evidence offered by this author, we can present a concise portrait of the College which became Fisher's Cambridge home.

Michaelhouse was founded in 1324 by Henry de Stanton, Chancellor of the Exchequer, who, on approaching his last days, turned to a work which he hoped would ensure his remembrance in the academic and spiritual life for posterity. The inspiration for the foundation is known to us, for the original Statutes laid down by him are still extant.[7] The College was originally established in honour of the holy and undivided Trinity, of the Blessed Mary ever Virgin, of St Michael the Archangel and all the Saints; and its expressed aim was the promotion of learning and zeal for the Christian faith. The Fellows of Michaelhouse had to be priests or at least in *sacris ordinibus constituti* (placed in holy orders), intending ultimately to devote themselves to the study of theology.[8] Their communal life was ensured by a common table, a uniform dress and a sharing of stewardship responsibilities, though their foundation avoided overburdening the members with excessive religious obligations. The College had a duty to provide and attend religious services in the neighbouring church of St Michael, but the obligations were laid down with great detail so as to ensure they did not clash with the duty of study.

In fact, throughout their length, the Statutes endeavoured to grant a remarkable degree of autonomy to the Fellows. It was they who were the

[5] J.B. Mullinger, *The University of Cambridge from the Earliest Times to the Royal Injunction of 1535.* (Cambridge University Press: 1873) p. 424.

6 A.E. Stamp, *Michaelhouse*, (Private printing: 1924) p.37. In 1546 Michaelhouse and the neighbouring King's Hall were amalgamated to form Trinity College, Cambridge.

[7] Mullinger, *The University of Cambridge*, p. 234, and Stamp, *Michaelhouse*, p. 24. The record of the college muniments from 1427 to 1433, known as the 'Otryngham Book', is still in existence. This record, started by John Otryngham, Master, is still kept up to date and at present is in the keeping of the Bursar of Trinity College.

[8] Stamp, *Michaelhouse*, pp. 13, 42, 45.

true recipients of benefactions and donations made to the College, and questions finance and administration could not be decided by the Master alone, but in conjunction with the Fellows.[9] This certainly reflects a more liberal spirit than was common in contemporary Statutes and is possibly a measure of the inaccuracy of Mullinger's remarks.

This was the College that Fisher joined. It was privileged by reason of its economic stability and autonomy; it was comparatively democratic and unhampered by any excessive religious obligations, though unquestionably disciplined and purposeful. In contrast, its neighbouring College, King's Hall, was a royal foundation supported by public funds and designed for laymen studying civil law. The Master of King's Hall was liable at any moment to be called upon to give an account of his charge, whereas Michaelhouse was overseen by means of an occasional visitation by the local Bishop or Chancellor of the University.[10]

Such a stable and dedicated environment must have helped Fisher considerably. We may speculate that during the opening years of his study the support and encouragement of the community was quite essential, for his first seven years from 1483 to 1491 were passed in arduous study of the *Trivium and Quadrivium*. These two courses, which carried the student to the stage of Master of Arts, must have been a formidable period of study; working from early fifteenth century sources we are able to reconstruct a working outline of their content.[11] Fisher graduated as a Bachelor of Arts at Easter 1488, and as a Master of Arts in 1491.[12] He consequently had undertaken the following courses.

The first year of the *Trivium* was devoted to Grammar, using the text book of Priscian; the second year consisted of the study of Rhetoric, using Aristotle (384-322 BC.), Boethius (c.480-524), Cicero (106-43 BC.), Ovid (43 BC. - 18 AD.) and Virgil (70-19 BC.). In the ensuing year the subject was Logic with works by Aristotle and the *Summulae logicales* of Petrus Hispanicus (1210-1277) being the most commonly mentioned texts in use. The fourth and possibly fifth years were given over to Aristotle's philosophy: natural, moral and metaphysical. Throughout this study of Grammar, Rhetoric, Logic and Philosophy the

---

[9] Expenditure undertaken by the Master had to be ratified by a majority of the Fellows. He had to present quarterly accounts of 'receipts and expenditure and all surplus benefices were to be divided equally among them'. Stamp, *Michaelhouse*, p. 28.

[10] Stamp, *Michaelhouse*, p.1. A.B. Cobban, *The King's Hall within the University of Cambridge in the Later Middle Ages*. (Cambridge University Press: 1969).

[11] The main sources are *Documents: Grace Book A*, ed. S.M. Leathes, (Cambridge: Deighton Bell & Co. 1897) *Grace Book B*, ed. M.Bateson (Cambridge University Press: 1903-5). C.H. Cooper, *Annals of Cambridge*, (Cambridge, Warwick & Co. 1842) Vol. I. Commentators include G. Peacock, *Observations of the Statutes of the University of Cambridge*, (London: J.W. Parker, 1841).
[12] For the B.A, *Grace Book A*, pp. 211-215. For the M.A., *Grace Book B*, pt. I, p. 25-26.

main educational technique in use was public discussion (or disputation), for efficiency of argument both in speech and in writing were held at a premium. As the student progressed he was able to take an increasingly active part in the public disputations which were the highlights of the academic system.

The Statutes of the University give us further details of the structure of these studies. Statute 139 lays down that no one could apply for the B.A. status, the culmination of these studies, before the end of the fourth year. There were then detailed steps necessary to gain official University recognition.[13] Following enquiry about his age, character and academic status, the student was allowed to present himself as a 'questionist' on payment of a fee of twelve pennies.[14] This involved a formal questioning by the Master of the College involved, the inception of his B.A. and followed a period of 'determination', during which the questionist had to stand in the Schools from 1 pm to 5 pm each afternoon (Sundays and holidays excepted) accompanied by a younger student, defending three given questions in Logic and Philosophy.[15]

To proceed for the Master's degree, three more years of study were required that were devoted to the subjects of the Quadrivium: Arithmetic, Geometry, Music and Astronomy; and to undertaking major roles in public debates. Apart from this study, the student was expected to make a contribution to the life of the University. He had to give 'cursory' lectures which consisted largely of the public reading of text books, in order to make their contents available to larger numbers of people. Appropriately, this type of lecturing declined with the growth of printing and the availability of mass produced books.[16] The concluding stages of the study of arts were laid down in Statute 86. The student entered the state of inception in Arts by obtaining a licence from the Chancellor or Vice-Chancellor, with a charge of twenty pennies, having already been recommended by five Masters of Arts on the grounds of personal knowledge and by seven others on the grounds of reputation.[17] The first act of actual inception to the degree of Master of Arts was a solemn service of Vespers, followed the next day, always the first Tuesday

[13] *Documents*, pp. 382 & 384.

[14] For Fisher see *Grace Book A*, p. 211. Dated 1488.

[15] *Grace Book A*, Introduction, p.xxii.

[16] *Ibid.*, p. xxiv, 'He is expected to read the Posterior Analytics…' I did not find that any lectures except these are mentioned in the Register. See also Peacock, *Observations*, pp. 30-31.

[17] *Grace Book A*, p. xxv. *Grace Book B*, pt 1, pp. 25-26. Also *Documents* Vol. I, p. 360. If there were less than 12 M.A.'s present in the College, the candidate had to have at least half the company to testify on his behalf.

in July, by a public disputation and solemn lecture of inception.[18] As a Master of Arts, the individual entered a period of 'regency', which bound him in the service of the University as an ordinary lecturer, and obliged him to attend Masses, congregations and convocations for that time.[19] The lectures which he now gave commanded fees, and he was in fact forbidden by Statute to give lectures freely; he also received a stipend from his College.

However, it was not the financial security offered by the degree of Master which gave the most satisfaction, but the fact that the way was now open to a place in the higher faculties: Theology, Canon and Civil Law, and the student was now eligible to become a fellow of the College and so enjoy the fuller facilities of its library and accommodation. As for John Fisher, once elected a fellow of Michaelhouse, he was able to be ordained a priest to the title of the College. This he did on December 17, 1491, having obtained a Papal dispensation for ordination to Major Orders while still under canonical age, for he was but 22 years old.[20]

This outline of the seven-year course of study brings to light only its rudimentary features. The emphasis is heavily on preparing the student to think clearly and to speak precisely. But can we know in any greater detail what the content of these years of study was? How was this pattern, taken as it was from sources, which came from the main period of the fifteenth century, applied in the years of Fisher's residence in Cambridge? Can we bring some precision to these most general terms? There is a great lack of evidence concerning this topic, though Erasmus provides us with one very precise starting-point. Writing in 1516, he remarks in a letter to Henry Bullock: 'About thirty years ago nothing was taught at Cambridge but Alexander, the Parva Logicalia, as they are called, those old 'dictates' of Aristotle and questions from Scotus.'[21] This was part of the letter of Erasmus which formed his *Apologia* for the *Novum Instrumentum* and was intended for public circulation in Cambridge. Erasmus was answering his critics and characteristically used any weapon which came to hand, including a somewhat mocking assessment of the achievements of the past. In this mood he is not to be read as an objective reporter of facts; but considering the lack of

---

[18] Peacock, *Observations*, Appendix A. xxii.

[19] The period of regency varied from one year in Fisher's day to two years after 1537 and five years under Elizabethan Statutes.

[20] Emden, *Biographical Register*, p. 229.

[21] P.S. Allen, *Opus Epistolarum Des Erasmi Roterodami*, (Oxford: Clarendon Press, 1926) (henceforth Allen, *Opus Epistolarum*) Vol. II, Ep. 456, p. 328, also F.M. Nichols, *The Epistles of Erasmus*, (London: Longmans Green & Co. 1901-18) Vol. II, Ep. 441, p.324.

alternatives we must make this our starting point, assured at least that there must be some basis of fact in his remarks.

The first author mentioned by Erasmus as receiving the attention of the students of John Fisher's era is the French Franciscan Alexander de Villa Dei (1175-1240). His work on Grammar is described for us by Lupton: 'His treatise was in rhyming hexameters; each verse of which was made the text of laborious comments and each line of these comments itself painfully annotated.'[22] Lupton also gives us an example of this process. The first line of the *Doctrinale Puerorum* of Alexander was 'To clearly write a new preparation for learning' and working from a 1487 edition, Lupton describes that opposite this was printed the gloss or commentary, the 'intention of Alexander', which had been further annotated by a student according to the lecture he was giving or hearing.[23] This text became a handbook of Logic at Cambridge.

Next, Erasmus refers to a book of logic, the *Parva Logicalia*. It is not recognizable as any well known work, though attributable to the same Alexander, but Thomas More leaves us in no doubt about his considered opinion of it: 'This book of the small logicals is thus called I suppose because it has very little logic, how little is for all the world to see.'[24]

A well-known and well-used work on Logic was the *Summulae Logicales* of Petrus Hispanicus, for this reigned supreme in the Logic Schools of the University for two and a half centuries after the death of its author in 1277, who by then had been elected Pope John XXI. It conveyed to all who used it 'the content of the school logic up to the close of antiquity',[25] for it was in fact a Latin translation of the Greek work of Michael Constantine Psellus, a professor at Constantinople towards the end of the eleventh century. It was he, then, who was largely responsible for giving the west its basic intellectual tool, Byzantine logic, which, as we have seen, was held in the greatest esteem by the University in the fifteenth century.[26]

Erasmus also makes mention of Aristotle and Scotus. The remark 'those old dictates of Aristotle' leaves us without any precise reference, but Lupton comments:

[22] J.H. Lupton, *An Exposition of St Paul's Epistle to the Romans by John Colet*, Published and annotated by Lupton, London 1873, republished in London 1965. See Introduction p. xv.
[23] There is a British Library copy marked 12933.1
[24] Thomas More, *Collected Works* (London, 1563), p. 379. Also Lupton, *An Exposition of St Paul's Epistle to the Romans* by John Colet, p. xv.
[25] Mullinger, *The University of Cambridge*, p. 176.
[26] The practical emphasis on logical ability is seen in the subject matter of the course. But logic was also at the heart of one of the most persisting academic debates: was logic a tool or a science? For Hispanicus and significantly for Scotus it was a science in its own right, concerned with necessary non-contingent subject-matter.

> *It is not easy to determine exactly what these might be. There are many textbooks from which such texts might have been given. The number of them is quite bewildering and the real difficulty in this case, as in that of Grammar, is to convey by any brief citations, an idea of the enormous labour spent in cultivating a field so barren.*

He describes the books as: 'Detached lines of Latin text by Aristotle, heading solid masses of commentary in smaller type, both alike assiduously annotated by the student.'[27] So, while we can be certain of the popularity of Aristotle, we cannot be at all sure of the value of the study of his writings to the extent in which they were indulged.

The *Quaestiones Quodlibetae* and other works of Scotus concerned with Logic and Philosophy are well known for their complexity and precision of thought, and for their outstanding display of mental power and for their high metaphysical subtlety. But they are equally famous for the futility of much of their intellectual endeavour, for their habit of arguing over details of words and expressions, and of dividing everything into a multiplicity of parts. Consequently, the name 'Scotist' became a recognized term of abuse, and symptomatic of much that was unsatisfactory in the pre-Reformation period.[28]

Accepting these as the main topics of study, it is easy to appreciate the profound inadequacy of the subject matter and style of this seven-year course of study. Without further enumeration of books and authors which were used, we can see the foundation of the charges made against this age of academic barrenness, or lack of stimulating and imaginative thought, paucity of subject matter, of excessive concentration on mental agility and a preoccupation with verbal exactitude. However, we must not underestimate the capacity of such a course of studies to produce a disciplined and well trained mind: the ability to think clearly and argue cogently, to avoid ambiguity and vague generalizations, to work methodically and present findings with precision. Further, there was a choice of teaching methods to be used in the ordinary tutorials and lectures which reinforced the training potential of these courses.

---

[27] The General Catalogue of the British Library up to 1520 shows 36 titles of Aristotle under Logic alone.

[28] Writing to his friend Watson in 1516, Erasmus says that though he was versed 'in the mazes of Scotus' he can still appreciate the *Novum Instrumentum*. See Allen, Opus Epistolarum Des Erasmi Roterodami, Vol. II, Ep. 512, p. 429. Nichols, *The Epistles of Erasmus*, Vol. II, Ep. 494, p. 454). In his reply Watson accepts the encouragement, but recognizes that Erasmus was also 'giving me a cuff at the same time to prevent my growing proud, for when you call me Scotist you obscurely charge me, if I am not mistaken, with ill-directed study. I frankly confess that I am not such a Scotist as I should like to be.' Allen, *Opus Epistolarum*, Vol. II, Ep. 576, p. 552; Nichols, *The Epistles of Erasmus*, Vol. II, Ep. 555, pp. 549–50).The charge was not at all obscure.

Student and Lecturer

An analytical method of teaching could be used which would involve the breaking down of a treatise or statement into its constituent parts until progress was made by dealing with each successive statement independently. In this form of treatment terms were defined, objections presented, the statement demonstrated and objections answered, and only then would the next statement be considered. As is quite clear from the achievements of Thomas Aquinas (1225-1274), the result, if grasped in its entirety, is one of considerable strength. But it may remain suspect of inadequate and disjointed understanding when individual topics are considered in isolation. The alternative method was dialectical: here the aim was to train the students to formulate their subject-matter into questions which could then be debated. Public disputations and participation in lectures were clearly the order of the day, all serving to underline the importance of Logic and the precision of thought and expression.

So we cannot overlook the positive potential of this course of study as a medium for rigorous intellectual discipline. Indeed, drawing upon the fruits of centuries of systematic studies, the student at the later medieval universities had at his disposal many of the means necessary for undertaking a disciplined study of theology and law. However, fuller consideration of these seven years of learning leads us to the conclusion that this was small profit to take away from such effort. The aridity of the material presented to him and the apparent lack of vitality and imagination in the construction of the courses must be seen to outweigh the advantages gained there. If the student was not already overawed or numbed by the demands of these studies, then he must have welcomed with open arms the move into the higher faculty in which he could employ his hard earned intellectual methodology and, hopefully, direct his attention to more fruitful and rewarding subject matter.

Thus equipped, Fisher made the move from Arts to the study of Theology in 1491. On that day in July when he emerged from the solemn lecture of inception as a Master of Arts, Fisher was at least able to commence his theological studies and enjoy the benefits of a Fellowship at Michaelhouse. It must indeed have been an emerging from the shadows. The sixteenth-century biographer, reflects upon this episode:

> in which space according to the ancient laws and statutes of his college, he received the holy orders of priesthood, he fell to more profitable learning; and leaving all his former study, betook himself to the high and heavenly philosophy. In which according to the order

> of the school, he kept his disputation with great laud [praise] and
> commendation so that in short space he grew to such profoundness
> as he was easily accounted the flower of all the university, and at his
> due time proceeded to the dignity of bachelor and after of doctor of
> divinity, which degree of doctor with no small praise he achieved in
> the year of Christ 1501.[29]

So it was then that for ten years, from 1491 to 1501, John Fisher was studying theology. During this time the formation of his theological opinions and learning, which gave such massive support to his faith, was taking place. Yet we know so little of his academic activity in this most formative period that Reynolds in his biography of Fisher devotes but one sentence to this period: 'After taking his Master's degree, John Fisher began the study of theology which normally lasted ten or twelve years, and took his doctorate in 1501, the earliest year in which he could have done so.'[30]

We cannot let the matter rest here. John Fisher became one of the theological spokesmen of the Catholic Church in England. His theological education and preparation are of great importance, and despite the lack of detailed information we must try to reconstruct as far as we can the studies and activities of this period in his life.

Relying on the same sources that we have already cited, we can take an initial stride by outlining the requirements for qualification as a Doctor of Theology. Statute 124 lays down these conditions:

1. *The candidate should have been a regent in arts.*

2. *He should have attended lectures at Cambridge for at least ten years.*

3. *He should have heard lectures on the Bible for at least two years.*

4. *He should have lectured cursorily on some book of Scripture for at least ten days in each term of the year.*

5. *He should have lectured on the whole of the Sentences and*

6. *Subsequent to his lectures, he should have responded and opposed in all schools of his faculty.*[31]

Contained in these conditions is a structure of learning leading, first of all, to the position of Bachelor of Theology. The first four years of this course appear to have been given over to lectures on the Bible, on

<hr>

[29] Van Ortroy, *Vie, Texte Anglais et Traduction Latine du XVI siècle. Analecta Bollandiana* (1891), Vol. X. p. 206.
[30] Reynolds, op. cit. p. 7.
[31] *Documents.* Vol. I. p. 377.

the *Sentences* of Peter Lombard (c.1100-1160) and to public lectures. The fifth year demanded that the active part of 'opponent' in the public disputations was taken, and then, supported by the recommendations of one Master *de scientia* and all others *de credulitate,* the student was admitted as a Bachelor of Theology. John Fisher reached this position in 1496.

Consequent upon this was the course leading to the doctorate in Theology. Opening with two years 'cursory' reading of the Sentences, the course then carried the student into further study of the Bible. Pastorally-centred demands were incorporated at this point in the form of a number of public sermons.[32] One had to be preached by the student at St Paul's Cross, and another to the clergy. Finally, at least three years after the completion of the Sentences, by the usual disposition of the doctors of the faculty and on taking the customary oaths to obey the Statutes, the student was allowed to incept by licence of the Chancellor or Vice-Chancellor and so became a Doctor of Theology, having at last completed his long and arduous course.[33]

On 5 July 1501, John Fisher became a Doctor of Theology.[34] The course of theological studies which he completed followed this outline and all possible details of it will be examined later. However, the record of the *Grace Book* about Fisher's doctorate, not only assures us of the thoroughness of his fundamental training in theology, but also reveals that his industry and application had reached out in other directions too, attracting the approbation of his examiners. So we must understand that 1501 saw not only a highlight of Fisher's academic life but also a recognition of his administrative potential. In fact, throughout those ten years of theological studies Fisher had taken an increasingly active part in the administrative life of the College and the University.

He first made an appearance in administration when, along with Thomas Cowke, he was elected as one of the university proctors for the period 1494-5.[35] Each year two of the regents were chosen by the Fellows to attend to many of the practical sides of the university's life, and Fisher's election to this post is a measure of the esteem in which he was held. The functions of the proctors are described by Peacock:

> *They regulated absolutely the time and modes of readings, disputations and inceptions in the public schools, and the public ceremonies of the university; they superintended the markets, with*

[32] *Documents, Vol. I,* p. 337.

[33] *Ibid.,* pp. 397, 378. Statutes 167 & 125. Also *Grace Book* A, p. xxvii.

[34] *Grace Book B,* pp. 143, 145, 162.

[35] Emden, *Biographical Register,* p. 229.

> *a view to the supply of wine, bread and other necessities for the scholars, and to the suppression of monopolies and forestallings and those other frauds in the daily transactions of buyers and sellers which furnished our ancestors the occasions of such frequent and extraordinary legislation: they managed the pecuniary affairs and finances of the university; they possessed the power of suspending a gremial from his vote and a non-gremial from his degree, for disobeying their regulations or resisting their lawful authorities; they collected the votes and announced the decisions of the house of regents, whose peculiar officers they were; they examined the questionists by themselves or by their officers, the bedels; they administered the oaths of admission to all degrees, and they alone were competent to confer the important privileges of the regency.[36]*

It was no mean task to undertake this function and we may well wonder how there was any time for academic pursuits if the function was performed competently. The position demanded the strength to accept and exercise authority, attentiveness to detail and efficiency in organization; there is evidence that Fisher was good at the job. Thomas Baker, a Fellow of St John's College in 1730, compiled information about the university, known as Baker's Manuscripts, and included in the collection a transcript of the proctor's records of Fisher and Cowke. To this particular record Baker added his own comment:

> *All of these are written in Fisher's own hand, a neat hand given that it was a hard time, which I have truly known and therefore have transcribed literally; in order that that they should not perish, so that the minor and small things should also not perish.[37]*

This awareness to detail and conscious effort at precision were the emerging characteristics of Fisher. They are to be seen in all his theological writings, as we shall see, as evidence of the efficacy of the training he received.[38]

It was in 1494, when he was on a business trip to London as proctor on behalf of the university, that Fisher first met Lady Margaret Beaufort, the mother of Henry VII.[39] Their friendship developed in later years and was productive of many contributions to university life, but in its initial

[36] Peacock, *Observations*, p. 24.

[37] M. Macklem, *God Have Mercy*, (Oberon Press: Ottawa, 1967) p. 210.

[38] Baker, *Manuscripts*, Vol. 24, fol. 8. A different manifestation of the same characteristic is found in the closing moments of Fisher's life. On his way to execution he asked his jailer for his fur tippet and, in response to the latter's amazement he said: 'I pray give me leave to put on my furred tippet to keep me warm for the while until the very time of execution for I tell you... though I have a very strong stomach...yet I will not hinder my health in the meantime not a minute of an hour but will preserve it in the mean season with all such discreet ways and means as Almighty God of his gracious goodness hath provided for me.'

[39] Reynolds, *op. cit.* pp. 9–14; M. Macklem, *op. cit.* pp. 8–10.

stages it was a personal, spiritual association that brought them together. Fisher was appointed her confessor in 1497 and it appears likely that for a time from 1499 to 1500 he actually took up residence in her household.[40] That such a friendship should be established, despite the great difference in ages may indicate something of Fisher's own reputation in spiritual matters. Lady Margaret was outstanding for her dedication, her strength of purpose which had sheltered and prepared Henry throughout his long exile, for her profound and largely traditional spirituality, as evidenced in the type of spiritual books she used,[41] as also for her loyalty to and active concern for the Church, witnessed by the endowments to both Oxford and Cambridge universities. Fisher undoubtedly supported her in these interests, and it is clear that considerable initial sympathy must have existed between them. Elton, describing Henry VII, observes:

> *Some of the austerity which hangs about him must have been due to the school of exile; more, one suspects, came from the influence of that formidable old lady, his mother, Margaret Beaufort, who ruled his court with a rod of iron.*[42]

We can learn much about a man from his friends.

The next phase of Fisher's administrative career was his election to the Mastership of Michaelhouse in 1496, when William de Melton left to become Chancellor of the Diocese of York. Fisher held this post for two years and, in the light of our reading of the College Statutes which make the Master *primus inter pares* rather than overall ruler, it is not surprising that during this time Fisher was also able to give a course of ordinary university lectures, for which he received a stipend.[43] As we have seen, on completion of his course of studies in 1501, Fisher was appointed to the highest administrative post, that of Vice-Chancellor of the university and his services to the university were officially recognized when he was named Chancellor in 1504 through 1514, the latter appointment being for life.[44] Clearly he had served Cambridge well, always performing his tasks conscientiously and efficiently, and the special nature of his appointment for life is testimony of the public recognition of his great work.

---

[40] Reynolds, *op. cit.* p. 13; Mullinger, *The University of Cambridge*, p. 435.

[41] Examples include: Walter Hilton's *Scala Perfectionis*, F. Siler's *Sermons on the Seven Penitential Psalms*. She herself translated the *Mirror of Simple Souls* and Book IV of the *Imitatio Christi*.

[42] G. R. Elton, *England under the Tudors* (London: Methuen, 1956), p. 6.

[43] *Grace Book B,* i. pp. 104–5 for 1495–7. Also Emden, *Biographical Register,* p.229.

[44] Emden, *Biographical Register,* p. 229 and ch. 2.

We do not know the extent of his term of office as Vice-Chancellor, for the next recorded event of his life was his appointment as Lady Margaret Reader in Divinity by September 8, 1502.[45] This was a position which was not consonant with being Chancellor or Vice-Chancellor, so we can say that by September 1502 Fisher was no longer Vice-Chancellor and, on his appointment as Chancellor in 1504, he vacated his Readership. The post of Reader in Theology appears as the first of many fruits arising from the relationship with Lady Margaret, for it was established for the first time in both Oxford and Cambridge in 1497, the year Fisher became her confessor.[46] However, it was not until 1503 that the Cambridge endowment was finally formulated and executed. It was a generous settlement of £13. 6s. 8d. a year and bound the incumbent to give his lectures gratuitously, a major innovation in the theological life of the university.[47] The Reader was obliged to present such works as the faculty (the Vice-Chancellor and the doctors) should judge necessary for one hour every accustomed day every term, and during the summer vacation until September 8. The office was held for a period of two years and the election of the Reader was carried out by the Vice-Chancellor, all the doctors, bachelors and inceptors of divinity, secular and regular, who were to swear to choose the most worthy 'without favour, partiality, reward, fear or sinister affection'.[48]

Unfortunately, there is no record remaining of what were considered to be suitable topics for these lectures, and it is difficult to estimate the direction of this innovation. However, it was clearly a major drive at improving the standard of academic theology and is a measure of Lady Margaret's concern for and devotion to the Church. It is hardly surprising that we find Fisher appointed to this position in Cambridge, and it is evident that the responsibility for such lectures would have given him the opportunity to consolidate his theological study and to apply to it the rigorous demands made by university lecturing. The years after his qualification as a doctor, then, must have been spent in continuing theological enquiry, which left John Fisher with considerable ability and

[45] Emden, *op. cit.* also Cooper, *Annals of Cambridge,* p. 271. Mullinger, *The University of Cambridge*, p. 437.

[46] Cooper, *Annals of Cambridge*, Vol I, p. 247. At Oxford, Edmund Wilsford was first appointed in 1497. He gave a series of lectures on Scotus. He was followed by John Colet who presented his famous *Exposition of St Paul's Letter to the Romans.*

[47] This was more than three times the amount of the Rede Lectureship founded twenty years later, and considerably more than the average parish benefits.

[48] Mullinger, *op. cit.* p. 437. Cooper, *Annals of Cambridge*, Vol. I, pp. 271–2.

a growing reputation. We will attempt to clarify the exact nature of this
theological activity a little later; sufficient for us now is to realize that by
1504 Fisher was totally immersed in the life and activity of Cambridge
and the fruits of this engagement are to be seen in the rest of his life.

There is, however, one further biographical detail of this stage of
Fisher's life that has been overlooked by most of the biographers. While
not effecting any great change in the understanding of his life, it forms
a link between Fisher and the parish life of his time; a link which is not
only interesting from a biographical point of view, but also gives us the
opportunity of increasing our own understanding of life and learning in
the parishes of England.

In the *Athenae Cantabrigiensis* it is recorded that John Fisher held
the benefice of the Church of All Saints in Northallerton from 1491
to 1494.[49] This statement is also found in Langdale's *The History of
North-Allerton in the County of York* and in subsequent histories of
Northallerton.[50] However, the register of the Prior of Durham, to
whom the advowson belonged, states clearly that the incumbent during
these years was John, Bishop of Ross and not John Fisher. A possible
explanation of this mistake is that 'Ross' was misread for 'Roff', but
this displays not only careless reading but also slipshod history, since
Fisher was appointed to Rochester only in 1504.[51] In fact the Statutes
of Michaelhouse preclude this possibility, for if a Fellow of the College
received benefice with a yearly value of more than £5. 0s. 0d, he must
either renounce the Fellowship or forego the benefice.[52] The parish of
Northallerton was valued at £17. 10s 0d in the *Valor Ecclesiasticus* and
Fisher was a Fellow from 1491 to 1495.[53]

It is quite clear, nevertheless, that Fisher did hold one such parish
benefice and that from 1499, when he relinquished the Mastership of
Michaelhouse, until his episcopal appointment in 1504. On March 28,
1499, he was admitted to the benefice of the church of St Oswald at
Lythe in Yorkshire, a fact still brought to mind by a copy of the Holbein
portrait of him which still hangs in the vestry of the church.[54] The parish

[49] Cooper, *Athenae Cantabrigiensis*. (Cambridge: Deighton, Bell & Co. 1858) p. 530.
[50] A.B. Cobban, *The King's Hall within the University of Cambridge in the Later Middle Ages*, (Cambridge University Press: 1969) p. 146.
[51] For this information I am indebted to Miss Margaret McCollum, Assistant Keeper of the Prior's Kitchen at Durham. Her reply to my enquiry was so full that it included the identity of this John, as one John Hornse, suffragan bishop of Ross in Ireland, who appears to have spent some time in Durham. Mrs. K.M. Gurney, Director of the Borthwicke Institute in York, provided confirmation of this from Institution entries of the Archbishop's Register.
[52] Stamp, *Michaelhouse*, p. 43. A. B. Cobbam, *The King's Hall within the University of Cambridge in the Later Middle Ages* (Cambridge University Press, 1969), p. 146.
[53] Ingledew, *The History and Antiquities of North Allerton in the County of York*, p. 171.
[54] *The Register of Archbishop Rotherham*. Vol. XXII, fol. 165v.

of St Oswald came under the patronage of Sir Francis Bigod of Mulgrave Castle, both he and this region being noteworthy for their part in the later Pilgrimage of Grace. It was a parish of considerable wealth with a yearly value of £34 4s 2d, and it was no doubt due to Fisher's reputation both at Cambridge and at the royal Court that he was presented to this living.

The significance of Fisher's holding this benefice is hard to calculate, as we cannot establish whether he ever took an active part in the life of the parish. As there is no Proctorial clause in the Institution Register he was presumably present at the induction ceremony, but since this took place at Scrooby in Nottinghamshire, it does not indicate Fisher's presence at Lythe. Surviving parish records betray the fact that wills were witnessed by non-parochial clergy or by a parochial Chaplain and there is no positive evidence that Fisher ever took up residence or activity in the parish. We are left to conclude that pressure of work at Cambridge made Fisher an absentee rector. This was quite the normal custom and in no way reprehensible behavior on Fisher's part, provided that adequate arrangements were made for the care of the people of the parish. Rather, it gives us a point of contact between Fisher and the existing parish system, indicating clearly that Fisher was a man of his times, accepting the ways and habits of his contemporaries. In such matters he is not to be divorced from the realms of historical reality, despite his later heroism and subsequent canonization.

These are some of the details of the Cambridge period of John Fisher's life. His appointment as Bishop of Rochester did not end his connections with the university, but merely raised them to a different level. As a student, his life had followed the well-worn tracks of many generations; as an administrator, Fisher showed more of the efficiency and dedication that later characterized his term in episcopal office. Of the first stage of his academic career, the Arts studies, the best we can say is that it afforded him considerable training, giving him certain basic abilities which were manifested in later life. It is now our task to examine more closely the content of his theological formation, and this must be done at the levels of both the parish and the university.

Parish Life

One of the starting points for many studies of the Reformation in England has been the lamentable state of the English clergy at the time. General statements about their lack of genuine piety, the absence of high moral standards, the neglect of pastoral duties and their preoccupations with the affairs of this world are supported by quotations from contemporary observers and critics. Further, contemporary analysis of the situation pointed to the preparation and ordination procedures of the clergy as the root cause of the troubles; reform in this area was a constant call. Our assessment of parish life at the time of John Fisher demands that we take account of these comments and attempt a balanced appreciation of them.

The only surviving work of William de Melton, Fisher's first tutor at Cambridge, is a *Sermo Exhortatorius hiis qui ad sacros ordines petunt promoveri*.[1] (Discourse concerning the improvement of holy orders) In it he writes about the dignity of the priesthood, of the humility required of candidates and of the intelligence demanded by their vocation. He gives an exhortation to ordinands to avoid vice, especially luxury, anger, avarice, drunkenness and vanity. His hope is that England would be freed from the numbers of the 'ruined and useless clergy', and the remedy he suggests is that no-one should be admitted to Holy Orders: 'who has not arrived at the teaching of good letters to the level at least of a moderate knowledge.'[2] His emphasis on learning, both in criticism and recommendation, no doubt reflects his interest as an educationalist, but his diagnosis is followed by that of Thomas More: 'Now if the bishops would once take into the priesthood better laymen and fewer (for of us they be made) all the matter were more than half mended.'[3] Similarly, John Colet, the celebrated Dean of St Paul's, gave considerable attention to the problems besetting the clergy. Speaking in 1512, he says that the laws restricting bishops in ordinations should be fully observed. There are laws, he says, 'that do warn you fathers that you put not over soon

[1] Dated Westminster 1510, see Hughes and J. W. Blench, *Preaching in the late fifteenth and sixteenth centuries*,(Oxford: Blackwell, 1964) p.75.

[2] Hughes, *Pastors and Visionaries*, p. 85.

[3] H. Maynard Smith, *Pre-Reformation England*, (Macmillan: London, 1938) p. 51.

Chapter Three

your hands on every man or admit into holy orders,' for the contrary practice is a source of evil, from which come many 'unlearned and evil priests'.[4]

The charges brought against the clergy by these distinguished critics and by others of less noble dispositions are manifold. Colet, for example, names greed in place of honour and dignity, carnal concupiscence, material greed and an overall worldliness, besides the comparatively minor complaints of abuses in episcopal visitations, in ecclesiastical courts, in tithes, offerings and mortuaries. Such criticisms are often used as evidence of both the depraved state of the clergy and also of a widespread anticlericalism, bitter and sarcastic in tone, which was a prelude to the Reformation.[5]

Moreover, men such as Colet, More and Fisher are often held to be exceptional, firstly for their perspicacity in pointing to the need for clerical reform; secondly, for having the courage to denounce their fellow clergy, even in the highest circles and thirdly, for having the drive and ability to instigate measures to effect reform.[6] On this basis they are heralded as distinct from their contemporaries, as something of 'forerunners' of the Reformation. Certainly they are rightly upheld for their concrete efforts at reform, but not on other counts. Closer examination of the period reveals that criticisms of the clergy, especially of the hierarchy, by their fellow clergy, secular and religious, was a constant feature of all preaching. Therefore, if we wish to appreciate the critical value of these comments by Colet, More, Fisher and others, we must be clear about the circumstances in which they were made.

A considerable amount of study has been completed on this topic. It demonstrates that the theme of clerical criticism by the clergy was a recurring phenomenon, not just in the late fifteenth and early sixteenth centuries but also reaching back into the early fifteenth and fourteenth centuries and beyond.[7] For example, speaking of the famous *Ship of Fools* and its German original *Narrenschiff,* Owst denies its reputation as a daring and original piece of work and claims:

---

[4] E.W. Hunt, *Dean Colet and his Theology*, (London: SPCK, 1956) p. 47. From Colet's sermon to Convocation.

[5] J. A. Williamson, *The Tudor Age* (London: Longman, 1964), p. 10, generalises about the state of the Church: 'Clerics who sought easy ways of making money, who roystered and drank and broke the vow of chastity, who exhibited no learning and did not work were sufficiently known to all… Abuses were so entrenched that little can be done.'

[6] Fisher's efforts at reform will be dealt with later.

[7] G.R. Owst, *Literature and Pulpit in Medieval England*, (Cambridge University Press: 1933) (henceforth designated as *Literature.*) G.R. Owst, *Preaching in Medieval England*, (Cambridge University Press: 1926) especially chs I and VI.

> *So completely is our Ship of Fools, from first to last, a compilation of*
> *the typical sermon matter of a century and a half of preaching, that*
> *it would be almost true to say that, apart from its metric form, there*
> *was nothing original about it except its woodcuts.*[8]

Further, the language of John Fisher, which we shall examine later, is
almost exactly reflected in the words of a predecessor, Thomas Brunton,
Bishop of Rochester in 1350, who inveighs forcefully against his fellow
bishops, calling them 'dumb dogs' and saying: 'Assuredly, if there
were not notable defects among incumbents, prelates and especially
confessors, so many abominable crimes and errors would not reign in
England.'[9] Again, William de Melton observed:

> *Some (priests) are engaged in ignoble and servile tasks, while others*
> *abandon themselves to tavern hunting, swilling and drunkenness.*
> *Some cannot get along without their wenches; others pursue their*
> *amusements in dice and gambling and other such trifling all day*
> *long.*[10]

And we find this to be very much an echo of a synodal sermon of the
Franciscan, Nicholas Philip, in the thirteenth century:

> *Where, I ask, will you find the many of the priests today? Think you*
> *mourning between porch and altar? Assuredly, I fear, in no wise, but*
> *rather playing lasciviously around the prostitute and brothel-house;*
> *nor by any means praying in the choir, but in truth wandering in the*
> *market place; nor in the sanctuary, the temple of God, but rather in*
> *the tavern and the ale-house.*[11]

Consequently, outspoken denunciations of clerical behaviour must be
seen as part of a long established pattern and tradition. The call for
reform had been continuous, but there is little evidence to suggest that at
the close of the fifteenth century there were any startlingly fresh grounds
for an outcry. So in assessing the importance of the evidence of sermons
and exhortations addressed to clerics, we must show caution, for here
are themes, patterns, styles of preaching and a whole range of subject
matter which are of long standing. These were well rehearsed and often
heard exhortations with which everyone would have been familiar.
Under such circumstances, then, attention to fact and accurate detail will
not have been foremost in the speaker's mind. His subject matter was

---

[8] Owst, *Literature*, p. 232.

[9] *Ibid.*, pp. 246-247.

[10] A. G. Dickens and D. Carr, *The Reformation in England* (London: Edward Arnold, 1967), p. 15.

[11] Owst, *Preaching*, p. 250.

readily accepted with approval from tradition; his task was to make his presentation effective and forceful. As Oberman says:

> *Since it is the preacher's purpose to convince his listeners of the multitude and gravity of sins committed, we should realise that the dark colouration of this presentation may have more pedagogical than historical value.*[12]

That preachers list and decry the faults of bishops and priests is not sufficient for us to state that thus it was; for otherwise, we must presume that the survival of the Church in England was something of a miracle, and the emergence of much sound spirituality and theology totally without correlation in the behaviour of the Church's ministers. Rather we must temper the evidence of sermon and exhortation with as many hard facts as are available to us.

Against the charge of avarice and exploitation by tithe and offering, then, we must remember the actual economic circumstances of many of the clergy. The £34 4s 2d of St Oswald's, Lythe, was an exceptional income, for research has shown that, taking the dioceses of Coventry and Lichfield as examples, the income of 87% of the livings was less than £20 a year: that of 79% was less than £10, while 10% had less than £5 a year.[13] Further calculation presents £16 a year as a working minimum for a parish with a curate and £10 a year for a one-man parish. Clearly then the majority of parish clergy were not spared the difficulties of an economic struggle, and since the tithes were a major source of the parish income, court records of numerous indictments for failure in payment of dues does not necessarily mean that the clergy were greedy and grasping.[14] Even if economic necessity did not force the insistence upon due payment, then wisdom should have done so,

> *for a lapsed right, in a medieval society, was often a lost or an expensively contested right and an interval of forebearance by one incumbent could mean a lifetime of bickering and litigation and hardship for his successor.*[15]

Complaints about the lack of strict supervision over those who entered clerical orders and of the consequent protection gained by them through their clerical status and in ecclesiastical Courts, must similarly be moderated, though not totally denied, by other considerations. In the

---

[12] H. A. Oberman, *Forerunners of the Reformation* (London: Lutterworth Press, 1967), p. 5.

[13] P. Heath, *Medieval Clerical Accounts*, (St Anthony Hall Publications, No. 26: 1964) p. 24.

[14] A. Tindal Hart, *The Curate's Lot*, (London: John Baker, 1970), p. 32, remarks, 'No wonder they left little behind when they died.'

[15] Heath, p.24.

diocese of Lincoln, where the figures of convicted clerics are most copious, Longland's register lists a total of 148 convictions. Divided over a period of twenty years which it embraces, and the eight counties involved, this makes a record of barely one a year in each shire-county,[16] and during the period 1495 to 1521 only sixty parishes out of 1,700 complained of misdemeanours by their chaplains.[17] The conclusion of Heath is:

> *Chronic and universal indiscipline among the clergy was not the result. There certainly was more clerical disorder than our society would deem appropriate, but its magnitude has been enlarged by careless reading of the sources and by neglect of the strains placed upon the clergy by their social status, and by celibacy. In fact recidivism was infrequent and the juridical machinery of the Church was as effective as any other law courts of the time.[18]*

While little statistical evidence is available on problems of sexual morality, clearly it was a major preoccupation of the Church legislators and law-givers,[19] and Heath maintains that only marriage, a solution that would not have been advocated by Colet or Fisher, would have solved the problem.

However, it is the matter of clerical learning and theology that is our major concern and in this field too we must exercise caution. We must not be carried away by the eloquence of Colet or by de Melton's 'ruined and useless clergy', nor by the comments of Erasmus, but we must apply to our evidence the same criteria of evaluation. Given the educational provision of the day, however, such men were surely correct in maintaining that without a basic willingness and a minimum ability in Latin, then the possibility of the clergy making progress in spirituality, in knowledge of the Scriptures and theology, and in preaching ability were slight. But, as academics, they were fairly unrealistic in their estimation of the capabilities and needs of priests working in parish circumstances.[20]

---

[16] Heath, *The English Parish Clergy at the Eve of the Reformation*, (London: Routledge & Kegan, Paul, 1969) p. 133. Heath concludes 'The hordes of incorrigible burglars and murderers which alarmed critics, inhabited their imagination rather than reality.'

[17] Tindal Hart, p. 34.

[18] Heath, *Medieval Clerical Accounts*, p. 188.

[19] *Ibid.*, p. 108.

[20] Erasmus, in a letter to Francis Deloin, written in 1517, says that his *Novum Instrumentum* and *Adnotationes* 'were compiled for the new recruits of the literary army, or for some dull and unlettered divines... It was upon the Cimmerian darkness of such people as these that we tried to let in a little light.' F.M. Nichols, *The Epistles of Erasmus* (London: Longmans Green & Co, 1901–18), Vol. II, Ep. 512, p. 489. P. S. Allen, *Opus Epistolarum*, Vol.II, Ep. 535, p. 480. As often happened, Erasmus attempts to flatter his correspondent, but shows a lack of awareness of the level of any intellectual achievements or capacity below his own.

Chapter Three

But if we do not accept their remarks simply at face value, what indications have we for judging the intellectual life of the local clergy at this time? Firstly, the pattern of grammar education in a collegiate or charity school was held as sufficient to have provided the large numbers of clergy who did not attend university with an overall ability in English and a minimum facility in Latin. Thus equipped: 'he (the priest) could complete his education from books such as had been written in the vernacular as well as in Latin from the early fourteenth century for the guidance of just such a priest.'[21] From this we can conclude that it was within the competence of the majority of the clergy to use for their own improvement the available books. Consequently, it comes within our task to examine the handbooks in order to come to a fuller assessment of the probable standard of their theological understanding.[22]

Further, we must recognise that the preaching of a parish priest can give us an immediate display of his theological ability, and fortunately evidence of such preaching survives. Therefore, a study of the preaching and of the parish handbooks of this period is the means we adopt for estimating the level of clerical learning and of parish teaching of the faith. The various appraisals of English preaching in this period available to us indicate first of all that regular preaching was indeed a feature of parish life at these times.[23] However, for the most part, these studies concentrate upon the style and method of preaching and not on the content. In fact, they point to the characteristics of its styles as the main weakness of this preaching, insisting:

> *A more serious criticism of even the best parochial sermons of that time is of their stale and hackneyed structure, their derivative and ossified mode of interpretations. The sermons, though functional and wider in scope than is often allowed, were uninspired and uninspiring.[24]*

---

[21] Heath, *Medieval Clerical Accounts,* pp. 85–6. He continues with a study of the books left in priests' wills in the Norwich diocese for 1500–50 as an indication of the extent of practical literacy. It shows that a minimum one quarter of the clergy were book-owning and of these over half were non-beneficed clergy, generally regarded as the most ignorant.

[22] Working from different sources, H.A. Oberman, *Forerunners of the Reformation* (London: Lutterworth Press, 1967), p. 7, concludes: 'A careful comparison between the learning of the parish priest at the beginning of the sixteenth century and his counterpart before 1400 shows that there is good reason to believe that he is by and large better trained.'

[23] P. Janelle, *L'Angleterre Catholique à la Veille du Schisme* (Paris, 1935), p. 21. Heath, *Medieval Clerical Accounts,* p. 93. J.W. Blench, *Preaching in England in the Late Fifteenth and Sixteenth Centuries* (Oxford: Blackwell, 1964), p. xiv. G. R. Owst, *The Destructorium Viciorum of Alexander Carpenter* (London: SPCK, 1952), p. 21, with the contemporary comment, '... now in many places there is greater abundance of preaching of the Word of God than was customary before our time.'

[24] Heath, *Medieval Clerical Accounts,* p. 103.

Moreover it is precisely style and method in preaching that are seen as binding together in a continuum the preaching not only of the centuries before the Reformation, but also that of many post-Reformation decades. Speaking of Hugh Latimer (1485-1555) Owst says:

> It is only complete ignorance of medieval preaching in England that has hitherto prevented editors and critics of his sermons from realising that they follow directly the style of homely vernacular discoursing employed in the pulpits of the fourteenth and fifteenth centuries. His racy anecdotes and snatches of reminiscence, his simple directness of speech, his use of popular proverbs, his outspoken denunciation of corrupt judges, unpreaching prelates, deceitful merchants and cloth workers or servants who defraud their masters, are all too precisely given in the medieval style to allow any doubt as to where the manner of speech was learned.[25]

The work of J.W. Blench, in my opinion, falls down on this point of continuity. His failure to grasp this continuity springs from his methodology which seeks for tidiness rather than accuracy, for he rigorously divides all sermons by their structure into 'Ancient' and 'Modern'; and overall by their periods: Catholic 1450-1547, Reformers 1547-1553, Marian 1553-1558, Elizabethan 1558-1603. He betrays surprise when they prove to be less tidy in reality, for speaking of themes of Elizabethan preachers he admits, '…other complaints are on yet older topics; it is indeed remarkable that the stock theme of medieval moral preaching should persist so strongly after dogmatic revolution.'[26]

Consequently, while it is evident that questions of style are not unrelated to an examination of the material being presented in sermons, in order to isolate the pre-Reformation from its neighbouring periods, our primary interest must lie not with matters of style, but with the theological content of the sermons. Wherever possible our task is to look beyond manners of speech, no matter how unaccustomed and at times distasteful they might be, in order to bring into focus the exact nature of what is being said, especially in terms of statements and instructions of faith. Moreover, since morality only indirectly reflects theological understanding, wherever possible we will concentrate upon theological statements and not moral exhortations. In some detail, then, we must

---

[25] Owst, *Literature*, p. 99. He stretches this continuity into the seventeenth century, maintaining of *Pilgrims Progress*: 'No one mirrors more clearly than he the mind and method of an English sermon-allegorist of the later Middle Ages and the influence of their message upon subsequent generations of Englishmen.' p. 109.

[26] Blench, *Preaching in England*, p. 309.

examine sermon and handbook material in a new light.[27] We are seeking
clarification about the level of popular theology, of the depth and fullness
of understanding about the tenets of faith to be found in the parishes.

In general, the authors of these handbooks and collected sermons
opened their works with an exhortation to the parish clergy to be
conscientious in striving to give good sermons, and not to be stifled by
pride, even old age, but to accept help and advice from others.[28] Despite
radical differences of approach their exposition of doctrinal matters
consistently followed a well-established outline of Christian doctrine and
morals. This had been laid down in 1281 by Archbishop John Pecham
(c1240-1292) in his decree *Ignorantia Sacerdotum,* which advocates
exposition about the articles of faith, the Ten Commandments, the
precepts of the gospel, the seven works of mercy, the seven mortal sins,
the seven principal virtues and the seven sacraments.[29] The influence
of this decree is to be seen throughout the subsequent centuries. Based
on this structural foundation, in a considerable variety of ways, the
various manuals and sermons attempted to provide their priest readers
with sufficient knowledge and material to enable them to carry out their
duty of educating their people in matters of faith. Varying degrees of
thoroughness and detail are to be found here, and so in order to achieve
a representative picture, I have chosen to examine in some detail a cross-
section of the most popular of these works.

The works chosen are these: firstly the *Exonatorium Curatorum,*
an elaboration of Pecham's instruction which is formal in tone and
concisely accurate in treatment. It was printed by Worde in 1515 and in
1520 and reprinted by Notary in 1519, by Pynson in 1520, Pepwell in
1530, Treveris in 1530 and Godfrey in 1532, such was its popularity.[30]
Then, by way of the application of this instruction in the realm of
theological handbooks, I take two contrasting works: The Doctrinal of
Sapience, a heavily medieval work translated from the French original
of 1388 and printed by Caxton in 1489;[31] and the above-mentioned
Manipulus Curatorum, notable for its strictly scholastic orientation and
terminology.[32] This work was first printed in Hamburg in 1481, then in

---

[27] The difference between collections of sermons and handbooks is difficult to draw because
the sermons presented in them were rarely intended to be used verbatim, but more as
suggestions and a guide. See, E. H. Weatherley, *Introduction to the Speculum Sacerdotale*, (Early
English Text Society, henceforth *EETS*: Original Series 200) p. xxxix.

[28] *Doctrinal of Sapience*. Ch. I, f.A iii-iv. Prologue of *Manipulus Curatorum* says the work is
intended for 'the instruction of learning priests.'

[29] D. Wilkins, *Concilia Magnae Britanniae*, (London: R. Gosling, 1737) Vol. II, pp. 54-57.

[30] *Exonatorium Curatorum* is henceforth designated EC.

[31] *Doctrinal of Sapience* is henceforth designated DS.

[32] *Manipulus Curatorum* is henceforth designated MC.

London in 1500 by Pynson, in 1502 by Worde and again by Pynson in 1508. It lays down the fundamentals of the Christian faith with precision and detachment and it is a far cry from the normal works of piety and exhortation such as won the patronage of Lady Margaret Beaufort, but must have done much to provide a stability of basic doctrine.

Of the more direct sermon material, we have the collection *Speculum Sacerdotale,* an early fifteenth century compilation of sermons very similar in structure and content to the famous *Festival* of John Myrc.[33] However, the style of the *Speculum Sacerdotale* is less ornate; narrative, exemplar and exhortation are used with moderation but are not as overpowering as in the Festival. To balance this I have chosen the *Quattuor Sermones,* which are wholly without exemplar, 'comprehensive, concise and lucid, indispensable as a summary of doctrine to parish priests.'[34] This work was commonly published together with the Festival and so did serve as a balance. It was published by Caxton in 1483 and 1491; by Worde in 1493, 1496 and 1499; by Pynson in 1493 and 1499, Ravynell in 1495 and by Notary in 1500, which makes it one of the frequently printed works of the period. Finally, I add the *Instructions for Parish Priests* by John Myrc, which is a translation of a little known work called *Pars Oculi* and represents the least academic and unpretentious level, being concerned mainly with the practicalities and legalities of running a parish.[35]

According to the instructions of Pecham, the articles of faith are the first subject for elaboration, and in all these works this is taken to mean an analysis of the creed. In a number of works we find the creed divided into twelve articles, and each attributable with the authorship of an apostle, a most unsatisfactory piece of popular lore.[36] However, apart from this considerable lack of historicity, the expositions of basic statements of faith are adequate. On Trinitarian theology, for example, the *Doctrinal of Sapience* shows commendable ability. On the Godhead of Christ it comments:

> *Here thou ought to believe and understand that he is the same as the Father in all things that appertain to the Word and is one and the same with Father, except that the person of the Father is other than the person of the Son.*

---

[33] *Speculum Sacerdotale* is henceforth designated SS.

[34] Heath, *Medieval Clerical Accounts*, p. 94.

[35] John Myrc, *Instructions for Parish Priests*, (Early English Text Society, Series 31) (henceforth IPP).

[36] DS, ch. 1, f.A iii. We find this repeated in a handbook of 1530.

And of the Holy Spirit it observes:

> *The Holy Ghost is the gift of the love of the Father and of the Son, from whom are all the means of grace, which is the one same God and one thing with the Father and the same Son, except that the person of him is other than that of the Father and the Son.*

The Doctrinal of Sapience here concludes:

> *And if because of simplicity thou hast believed or believed otherwise in any of the foresaid articles, then be attentive always to the belief held from the first as holy Church holds and believes.*[37]

Significantly, on this level of faith, the main threat to orthodoxy is seen as simplicity or ignorance.

However, much more revealing of their understanding of the essentials of faith are the series of questions to be put to a dying person. In a manuscript dated about 1470, attached to the 'Instructions for Parish Priests', we find seven questions to be asked at the time of death, and in the *Exonatorum Curatorum* five very similar questions.[38] The first question of both series is concerned with conformity to the Church: 'whether thou holdeth all that belongeth to Christian faith as Holy Church believes and teaches.' Then the major topic of all the preaching of this era appears, that is knowledge of sin, desire for forgiveness, readiness to forgive others and readiness to make amends. This occupies questions three to five in the *Exonatorum Curatorum* and questions two and six in the other work. The remaining question is more interesting, especially as it follows immediately upon the emphasis on contrition, confession and satisfaction, for it states:

> *Believest thou fully that Christ died for thee, that thou may never be saved but by the merits of Christ's passion, and then give thanks thereof to God with thine heart as much as thou mayest.*[39]

A similar emphasis of the salvific work of Christ, and on our total dependence upon that action is found in a Christmas Day sermon in the *Speculum Sacerdotale*. Christ comes at the will of the Father by the work of the Holy Spirit:

> *and in that flesh suffered unworthily a death for cleansing man's sin and call man unto the centre of heaven, the which man had lost by deceit of the devil that brought him to damnation. For from the time of Adam had sinned unto the time that the Saviour came, there was*

---

[37] DS, ch. 1, f A iii, f A iv.

[38] BL, MS Lansdowne 762, f 21. EETS. O Series 31, pp. 69-72

[39] EETS. O Series 31, p. 70.

> *great discord betwixt God and man, betwixt man and angels, betwixt man and man, betwixt spirit and flesh.*

God, however, humbled himself for he could have saved mankind in a different way, but since the fall came through a woman,

> *so God showed unto a woman, the blessed Mary the virgin, that she should conceive a child the which should repair redemption and heal mankind. And as all mankind was by a tree lost, so Christ by his death on a tree brought healing to mankind.*[40]

The Pauline character of this theology is plain for all to see, and it is an indication of the extent to which the primacy of the work of God and mankind's dependence on it were maintained during this period. Further examination will show this to be at the basis of many words and exhortations concerning penance, forgiveness and readiness of God to give us his mercy. This is a small item of support for the statement of H.A. Oberman who insisted the utter fallacy of the long-defended thesis that 'on the eve of the Reformation, St Augustine had been forgotten except for some isolated Augustinian lights in a Pelagian night, such as Gregory of Rimini and Thomas Bradwardine'. In fact he maintains that applying the standards of the Council of Trent, there is not one medieval theologian who was even a Pelagian, who taught that man can really earn his salvation without the aid of divine grace.[41]

An Easter sermon, and a survey of Easter sermons by Heath, shows that at Easter the main message of preaching was hope: 'by his resurrection he gave to us a certain hope of our rising again,'[42] so that we are called to rise spiritually with him to be with him in heaven. To the preacher this implies a rising from sin and a sharing in Communion: 'And know that he that must rise from sin must have three things; serious contrition of heart, confession of mouth and satisfaction of deed and work.'[43] This is a good example of the immediate application of the main tenets of faith to the life of the individual. Many aspects of the Resurrection are left untouched so that the more immediate application of forgiveness and Communion may be developed.[44]

Similarly, the role of the Church is minimally developed in this theology. Understanding of its foundation, nature, structure and its authority is simply taken for granted and the Church is presented as the

---

[40] SS, pp. 5-6.
[41] H. A. Oberman, *Forerunners of the Reformation* (London: Lutterworth Press, 1967), pp. 123–40.
[42] SS, p. 117. Heath, *Medieval Clerical Accounts*, pp. 96–103.
[43] SS, p.120.
[44] Heath, *Medieval Clerical Accounts*, pp. 96–103.W. O. Ross (ed.), *Middle English Sermons* (EETS, Original Series, 209), pp. 61–5.

means whereby the individual may attain salvation and sanctification. Conformity to the teaching of the Church guarantees adherence to the truth: 'So all should understand that those who depart from the unity of the faith may never be loosed from sin, nor enter into the bliss of heaven.'[45] Parents and godparents are instructed and encouraged to ensure the continuity of the faith by teaching children the Creed and the Our Father.[46] A font in Bradley, Lincoln, constructed about the year 1500 bears clear evidence of this in its inscription: 'Pater Noster, Ave Maria and Creed your child needs to learn.'[47] Thus topics which were later to become vital issues win but scant and passing attention.

The poverty of these contemporary sermons in crucial areas is readily illustrated. On the subject of the primacy of the Pope, for example, the only mention I can find is a sermon for the feast of St Peter and St Paul which deals mainly with the life and calling of Peter, concluding with a call to observe the feast with great devotion, 'that you may through his merits and prayers be forgiven of all your sins against God by the foresaid Saint Peter and God's Vicar on earth, to wit, the minister of holy Church.'[48] Similarly, while the place of good works receives considerable emphasis in practice, as seen in wills, we have only one explicit statement about the relationship between good works and faith. It occurs in a sermon for the feast of the Purification and the analogy used is that of a candle:

> *In this candle we may be informed that if we will be purified before God, we must have three things, to wit, true faith, good actions and right intent. For a candle that is in a house without the light is understood as faith without good works. For as a candle without its light is but deed, the light without the candle is not possible; so faith without good works and good works without faith is but deed. Now I call the wick that is within the wax with right intent. For Saint Gregory says, 'If you do a work in public, hold its intention in secret.'*[49]

Further, no estimation of the role and standing of Scripture and its relationship with Tradition and Church teaching is attempted in these documents. Some statements are made expressing the vital importance of Scripture, but since there was no urgent current challenge at that time, there is no real development of the issues involved. The *Quattuor*

---

[45] SS, F. Cr.
[46] SS, p. 114.
[47] IPP, p. 78.
[48] SS, p. 33.
[49] SS, p. 27.

Sermones upholds the unique position of the Scripture with normal Catholic understanding. The Scriptures are 'where we may find all things that is necessary and expedient to our soul's health, not to follow therein our natural will but to submit our will to the rules of faith after the understanding of the holy doctors.'[50] And in the *Doctrinale of Sapience* we have this interpretation of 'our daily bread' in the Lord's Prayer: 'the soul is fed with the bread of holy Scripture and the body of natural bread.' Its application is that it is the task of the priests to provide this bread, but they are often neglectful.[51]

The relationship between the Spirit of Christ and the Church, which is later at the heart of the writings of John Fisher and his contemporaries as an exclusive identification of the two, finds no worthy treatment in these writings. The role of the Holy Spirit for the individual is understood and presented well, but seldom in the context of the collective Church, and there is no movement to identify the presence of the Holy Spirit with the life of the Church.[52] The pattern of the theology is purely personal: the role of the Church is to teach the truth and to bring the sacraments to the individual; the presence of the Holy Spirit is as a formative influence in the lives of individuals, and aspects of the Church as a community in the Spirit are absent. The sermon for Pentecost from the *Speculum Sacerdotale* is typical of this. It develops the contrast between the old covenant by which Jews received the Law, and the covenant by which we are given the Spirit of Christ. The apostles received the Holy Spirit 'with the finger of God hallowing within them the spiritual understanding', the effect being 'they were made disciple by the grace of the Holy Ghost', and from being fearful and hidden were now bold and courageous. That call is also made to us: 'that we may be made worthy in that day to take the Holy Ghost to our sanctification and to be his temple.'[53]

Only in the understanding of the sacraments does the presence of the Holy Spirit become connected with the work of the Church. It is through the sacraments brought to us by the Church that we receive the Holy Spirit: 'We ought to know that each man takes the Holy Ghost in baptism and he stays as long with him as he remains in right belief and good works.'[54] Our sources go to considerable effort to give detailed accounts of the working of each sacrament, insisting upon the effective presence of the Spirit of Christ in the sacraments and maintaining that

[50] *Quattuor Sermones* (henceforth designated QS), f. D ii.
[51] DS, Cpt. Xi, f F v.
[52] IPP, line 484, p. 15 has the only statement directly concerned with the Church and the Spirit.
[53] SS, pp. 158-159.
[54] SS, p. 160.

the power of the sacraments is derived directly and exclusively from Christ:

> *The sacraments take their beginnings from the gracious well of the side of Our Lord Jesus Christ in his passion. At the death of our Lord there ran out of his side blood and water by the virtue of which passion the sacraments of holy church take first their strength and beginning.*[55]

It is this direct and immediate dependence upon the power of Christ that is the foundation of the *ex opere operato* teaching, so the *Manipulus Curatorum* can assert that the correct celebration of the sacrament is sufficient to confer grace from Christ.[56] Much misunderstanding of this doctrine is at large. In reviewing J. M. Todd's book *Reformation*, Clark criticises Todd for accepting a magical notion of *ex opere operato* doctrine as representative of late medieval theology. Clark comments that late medieval theology had not lost sight of the need for actual faith in the adult recipient of a sacrament and that the *ex opere operato* doctrine can be understood as a correct interpretation of St Paul's sacramental realism.[57] Similarly, the *Doctrinal of Sapience* can assure its readers that an evil priest does not invalidate the sacrament, but 'he damns himself right profoundly and resembles and is like the torch of wax which does good and gives light to others and wastes himself.'[58]

This objective working of the Spirit of Christ in the sacraments is supported also by the claim that Christ is the founder of all the sacraments:

> *All the sacraments were instituted by Christ and they belong to him who by right approved them. Now Christ whom we claim was the giver of the New Law initiated them, as is abundantly testified by the Apostle [Paul] in his letter to the Galatians, and Paul has it from Elijah who appeared with Our Lord [Matt. 17:3] as the law giver, so he himself will come and save us and be our Saviour – to him alone belongs the authority to institute the sacraments of the New Law.*[59]

However, such clarity of logic is not so easily upheld with direct scriptural evidence, and difficulties are encountered as the author tries to give immediate references for each sacrament. For extreme unction the *Manipulus Curatorum* presents St James as a promulgator and not a founder. For marriage it admits there is some doubt as to the scriptural

---

[55] QS, f A viii.

[56] MC, f v.

[57] See, F. Clark, *Semper Reformanda, Clergy Review*, Vol. LVII, No. 11, 904, p. 889.

[58] DS, Ch. Lxii, f H viii – I i.

[59] MC, f. 3.

foundation and insists that marriage is a sacrament under the aspect of a legally binding promise.[60] The bond of the humanity and divinity in Christ signifies the bond of marriage. It is when it offers texts to show that each of the six minor orders were instituted by Christ directly that the full weakness of this approach is shown.

Each of these works gives considerable attention to the individual sacraments, and four of these works go to some trouble to give precise definitions of the sacraments.[61] These definitions served to pinpoint the true nature of a sacrament, to guarantee a minimum understanding of its precise purpose in the Christian life, and often to present the legal requirements of the sacrament in question. The Instruction for Parish Priests concentrates on the practicalities, the form of baptism and urgency; the intricacies of marriage legalities; items of advice, such as to leave the forehead unwashed for eight days after confirmation; the relations enjoined by confirmation, and detailed instructions on how to visit the sick and administer communion to them.[62]

Baptism is defined as an external washing, with a set form of words which are a sign of an interior change that removes original sin, confers grace and aspires to eternal life.[63] Confirmation is:

> *A manner of anointing on the forehead by the hands of the bishop whereby the Holy Ghost gives strength against the feebleness of sin of our fore father with a marked impression of the soul whereby you shall know the faith and love of Christ.[64]*

This definition is given to marriage: 'It is man and woman legitimately conjoined into one individual life and held by custom – moreover man and woman mutually dependent, man and woman woven together.'[65] Extreme Unction 'avails much to forgiving sins. Often it allays the illness for it was established for the health of the soul and for the health of the body.'[66] And Holy Orders are defined as 'a sign to the end that and through which spiritual power is officially bestowed by ordination and laid down when one is ordained by proper authority.'[67]

These definitions and the accompanying development indicate that at least a minimum of Catholic doctrine was commonly on the lips of the preachers. Even if only a part of this clarity and soundness of thought

[60] MC, f. iv.
[61] These are QS, MC, DS and EC.
[62] IPP, 1. 87, f p. 3-4. 1. 180, p.6. 1. 664, p.20. 1. 173, p.6. 1. 1839-1912, p. 57-59.
[63] MC, F. xiii-xiiii.
[64] QS, F. A viii.
[65] MC, f. lviii.
[66] DS, Cpt. lxviii, f. I iii-vi.
[67] MC, f. xlviii.

was conveyed to the congregations, it would guarantee a reasonable basis of belief and piety. The major threat to firm doctrine, of course, was the mode of presentation, for the illustrations and stories used often lacked the precision of these statements, and could lead to waywardness.

Teaching on the Eucharist illustrates the point well. In the *Doctrinal of Sapience* there is an example of an illustration which is highly disruptive of sound doctrine. The author states that Christ is 'contained properly' in the Eucharist, and goes on to narrate the story of a woman whose doubts about the real presence were resolved when, attending a Mass celebrated by St Gregory, she saw the host turn into a finger, and then back to a host again.[68] Stories of this kind are plentiful, and we find them too in Fisher's own writings on the Eucharist. However, the influence of such stories must be estimated in the context of many statements of faith which are simple, direct and balanced. In the *Quattuor Sermones*, for example, the sacrament of the altar is 'the which is Christ's body, his flesh and blood in form of bread, the same that was born of the Virgin Mary and placed on the rood [cross], this is made through virtue of God's word and priests that have power'.[69] This receives elaboration in the *Manipulus Curatorum* and appreciation also: 'He has established a superlative sacrament of love that is of his precious body and of his precious blood. In which himself is all contained and to which he gives himself to us unto the end of the world.'[70] Not all then was narrative and exemplar, fantasy and myth.

The unsympathetic reviewer of the writings of this period is quick to point to a morbid preoccupation with sin as their dominant characteristic.[71] Closer reading reveals that this critical approach is distorted, though there was considerable material devoted to sin and repentance and these were indeed major facets of the spirituality of the age.[72]The distortion is about their tone and atmosphere. The underlying message is that God is always kind and forgiving; that forgiveness is always available; that no one need ever lose hope and that the way to greater perfection is open to us. It is certainly a message of hope and encouragement, not one of gloom and punishment.[73]

---

[68] DS, Cpt. lxi, f. H vii.

[69] QS, f. B iii.

[70] MC, f. xxviii cf IPP, i. 244 f. p.8.DS,Ch. Lx, f. H vi.

[71] Blench, *Preaching in England,* pp. 1–7, 232–3, 258.

[72] The outline of Pecham demanded considerable attention not only to the sacrament of penance, but also to the major virtues and vices. Of the 1,934 lines of IPP, 1,013 deal with these topics. One of the four *Quattuor Sermones* is devoted entirely to penance; the three of the MC are *de Sacramentis, de Penitentia, de Fide et Praeceptis,* and just less than half the chapters of DS deal with similar topics.

[73] The last words of advice to parish priests are: 'Be not too hard... But yes do mercy in God's dread. He is full of mercy, yes, be thou also, I pray.' IPP, 1. 1639-42, p. 51.

The movement of sinful man back to God by continual self-knowledge and repentance is central to the spiritual dynamism of this period, and it is notable that in these works, underlying the attention given to the sacrament of penance, considerable stress is placed on this movement as an individual religious experience. The sacrament of penance is described in many ways:

> *Confession is of so great virtue that it is as a second baptism, and as a fountain in which be washed and forgiven all sins whatsoever they be, and thy confession as Saint Bernard says destroys all sins and re-establishes all virtues.*[74]

The movement to repentance is reported in traditional terms:

> *Penance is a needful thing to the sinner that desires to recover health of his soul. And in doing penance there be three things to be considered: serious compunction of heart, confession of mouth and satisfaction by deed.*[75]

However, the experience is often more extensive than the canonical sacrament, for it is asserted that 'compunction of heart' is quite sufficient for forgiveness, 'In time of need and in point of death, if there be no priest ready or if the sick have no space or power to make confession', and more surprisingly, 'when thou entrust on the sea in so great peril thou may also by that confess thee to a layman, and have forgiveness,'[76] provided that if the person escapes, then a full sacramental confession is made.

The first requirement for sacramental forgiveness, compunction of heart or contrition, is set forth as:

> *A sorrow of the soul formed by grace which comes of fore-thinking of sin and dread of high doom; with a steadfast purpose to be confessed and to do satisfaction after the precept of the Church. It is also a conversion of heart from evil to good, from the devil to God and from vice to virtue.*[77]

And this account shows all the important aspects of contemporary theology: the contemplation of sin and punishment, the ecclesiological setting and the importance of a personal '*metanoia*' or change of heart.[78]

An argument from reason, for the necessity of sacraments, is among the more interesting accounts given for the position of the Church and

---

[74] DS, ch. lxxx, f. K vi.

[75] SS, ch. 22, p. 63. DS, ch, lxxix, f. K vi.

[76] SS, Ch. 22, p. 63. QS, f. C vi.

[77] QS, f. C iii and DS, ch, lxxix, f. k vi.

[78] MC, f. lxxviii.

the sacraments. It is found in *Manipulus Curatorum* and repeated in the *Quattuor Sermones*. After a wrong has been perpetrated between two parties, reconciliation is required. An arbiter must be able to touch both parties, and so for sin the sole mediator is Jesus Christ, who after his Ascension left this power of mediation with his apostles.[79] The *Quattuor Sermones* speaks of the '*mene*' (means) between God and man as being the ordained priest, and both accounts refer to the raising of Lazarus for their authority. His coming out of the tomb would have profited him little if he had not been loosed from his bonds. Christ raised him from the dead, which also happens in the hearts of sinners, but it is by confession to the priest, the work of loosening done by the apostles, that the sinner is finally set free.[80]

The balance between the mediation of the Church and the necessity of God's initiative is maintained, for the same Gospel incident is used by the *Speculum Sacerdotale* to indicate the absolute necessity of God's call as prior to all else, and the *Quattuor Sermones* takes great pains in showing that forgiveness is the work of God. Christ died, it declares, and gave us the Spirit 'giving understanding that sins are not forgiven through merits of man but through the goodness of the Holy Ghost.' Here there is 'no power but God' and 'no man doth away with sin but Christ alone'. So the exhortation is given, 'acknowledge your sin as soon as thou mayest and do thou due satisfaction after the wisdom of the Church and this is the most sure way.'[81] Even in the stricter sacramental context the dimensions of personal experience is given prime importance and accordingly no charge of mechanical sacramentalism can be fully maintained:

> *Contrition is to have sorrow at heart and great repentance of all his sins and to have steadfast purpose to keep and abstain him from all deadly sins. For who has intention to return him to deadly sin, his confession avails him nothing.*[82]

Similarly, with the actual confession of sin, 'the quality of it is nought to be considered but with that mind and what affection he does do it.'[83] In the assessment of a suitable penance it is noted, 'If he be sorry for his sin and full contrite as thou must know, weeping strongly and with true

---

[79] MC, f. lxxxi.QS, f. C v-vi.
[80] MC, f. lxxx.
[81] QQS, f. C v.
[82] DS, Ch. lxxix, f K vi.
[83] SS, p. 66.

sorrow; and ask for mercy reduce his penance then by much, for God himself forgives such.'[84]

The role of the Church and the minister, and the canonical structure of the sacrament, including the verbal confession, is clearly presented.[85] The people were instructed to ask if the priest did possess the correct faculties and were constantly reminded that they were bound to confess to their own priest except in certain definite circumstances. The *Manipulus Curatorum* is unambiguous about the context of confession and the *Quattuor Sermones* declares; 'The passion of Our Lord Jesus Christ is a great remedy against sin be it original or actual, the virtue whereof is expressed in the sacrament of Holy Church.'[86]The overall emphasis of the teaching contained in the sermons could not be described as encouraging an unthinking or permissive reliance on the working of the sacrament to the detriment of personal commitment in faith of the power of Christ and the constant need for spiritual renewal.

The forgiveness of sin is not won by man; the primacy of God is strictly maintained, and the Church has a mediative role only. Confession itself is profitable in a number of ways: it is pedagogic, showing us our sin, our peril and the need for humility. It gives glory to God, confounds the devil and gives us strength. The soul is washed with sorrow of contrition and 'by lowly confession of mouth thou must rub off the foul spots of sin that are rusted on the soul.' So we are urged, 'To hold out thy heart before the Lord God, as the prophet sayeth as water, not as oil, lest the fatness abide; or as milk, lest the whiteness appear, not as wine, lest the savour abide.' To come 'with hope of forgiveness, saying with David, I have sinned, I have done wrong.'[87]

This analogy of washing, which we find in the same setting in the work of Fisher, is used to introduce the third aspect of forgiveness, that is, satisfaction.

> *though the soul be soaked with bitter sorrow of thine heart and cleanly rubbed with confession, yet must it have many diverse rinsings after with satisfaction, till it be so cleanly purged here or in purgatory that it may cleanly appear after in the sight of Our Lord.*[88]

In this quotation satisfaction is understood as making amends for sin, and though this may be the expected understanding it is not, in fact, the more common in these works. Rather, satisfaction is presented 'after

[84] IPP, 1.1399, p. 43.
[85] IPP, 1.700f. p.22. SS, p. 66. DS, Ch. 1xxvii, f. K v-vi.
[86] MC, f. 1xxxi. QS, f. C v.
[87] QS, f. C vii.
[88] QS, f. C vii-viii.

diverse doctors as a putting away the cause of sin.' This curative purpose is manifest in the lists of penances commonly recommended, for the *Manipulus Curatorum*, in summary style, describes the three main roots of sin as 'avarice, *luxuria* and *superbia*' and indicates three aspects of satisfaction as directed against these weaknesses: almsgiving against avarice, fasting against bodily concupiscence and prayer against pride.[89]

Almsgiving is divided into three parts: first, of the heart as when with contrition we offer ourselves to God; second, of bodily treasure in money and support given to all who are in true need, whether they be good or bad, for we give 'that nature may be sustained and not the sin nourished'; third, of 'pity and compassion for the state of others', 'thus bodily or ghostly everybody may give alms.'[90]

Fasting is 'a wilful abstinence from meat and drink whereby the sin is washed and the flesh made low for desire of everlasting bliss, ghostly fasting is from deadly sin and temporal joy.' Prayer is 'a loving desire of thy soul to God with speech of mouth or gathering of words, to ask good of God with utterings of thy voice.'[91] These are the weapons to be used in the struggle against sin, and they are urged upon the penitent not as an exercise in self-depreciation, but as helps towards self-control and freedom of spirit.

Considerable advice is given to the priest to help him question the penitent when necessary and to give appropriate penances; and the duty of the priest to maintain the seal of confession is most forcibly declared.[92]

> *See now, therefore, how the soul may be reformed and brought again to God. Thy soul hath mind, reason and will: mind for it should rest in God, reason for thou should know God, and will to love God. But by sin the mind is made unstable, the reason blind and the will crooked.*

So by prayer we bring our mind back to God: by adhering to the faith of the Church and the knowledge available in the Scriptures, our reason will come to know God; and by confession and the virtue of penance we will bring our will to 'withstand vices and to abide and increase in virtue.'[93]

We have given so much attention to this subject because it is of paramount importance in the spirituality of the times. Personal

[89] QS, f. C. viii. MC, f. C ix. IPP, 1. 1399 ff. p. 43. SS, Ch. 23, p. 80. Also MC, f. C ix. QS, f. C viii. SS, Ch. 22, p. 73.
[90] QS, f. C viii. MC, f. C ix.
[91] QS, f. C viii. F. D i.
[92] IPP, 1. 805-1396, 1399-1650. Pp. 15-51. DS, Ch. xxviii, f. K vi.
[93] QS, f. D ii.

spirituality, the call for an active participation in the sacraments derived its dynamism from this call to continual reform and renewal, and the forward movement of the Church at large also operated on this basis. Patterns of reform in the years before the Reformation were centred on a personal return and conformity to the ideals and laws of Christ and his Church. This same manifesto was used by Fisher and Colet and throughout many of their writings the same appeals are made for the same reasons. Reform is not a matter of radical changes of structure or teaching, but rather an issue of personal lives being reformed in the pattern of already existing laws and teaching.

Throughout these sermons, then, the central theme of preaching and instruction was that a living faith in Christ that would bring people back again and again into the fold of the Church and her sacraments, where all that is necessary for salvation would be found. The Church is indeed the means of salvation for all. But in these sermons the understanding of the Church that is presented is seriously limited. Exposition of the exact nature of the Church, of her authority and right to teach, especially in relationship to Scripture and in the matter of papal primacy are left largely neglected. In fact at this level of understanding, so much emphasis has been given to the sacramental life of the Church that belief in the Church at times appears to be equal to belief in the sacraments.[94] It is not then surprising that an attack on the sacraments more than anything else provoked the major response from English Catholic apologists.

One product of the post-1530 period may act as an illustration of how little change was wrought in the parishes by upheavals in higher places. The call to reform continued in this same pattern just as much as the style of sermons and handbooks remained largely unaltered for some time. A handbook for house-holders was written by Richard Whytforde, who was known as 'the wretch of Sion'.[95] He was a fellow of Queen's College *c.* 1495 and was counted among the friends of Erasmus and More. He was still living in 1541 and is recorded as being a zealous opponent of the Reformation. His work follows the same model, consisting of an exposition of the Pater Noster, Ave Maria and the Creed, again attributed to the twelve apostles in the traditional manner, the commandments, the seven virtues and vices. The context is also largely

---

[94] DS, Ch. 1. F. Aiiii. 'The X article is such: I believe in holy Church Catholical… in this article then understand the vii sacraments of holy Church.'

[95] Richard Whyteforde, *A werke for householders or for them that have the gydynge or governaunce of any company,* (Wykyn de Worde: Ashmole Ms. of 1530. No. 1215).

traditional, an opening emphasis on the inevitability of death and the transitory nature of life, followed by a call to repentance and resolution. Whytforde shows considerable ability in didactics especially when he talks directly to the parents:

> *Teach them (your children) also to know the names of the five wits and to put the first finger of the right hand to the instruments of the same wits, that is to say unto the ear, the eye, the nose and the mouth and then to clap both hands together saying thus: hearing, seeing, smelling, tasting and touching. It shall also be well done to teach them the seven works of mercy, which you should (after your power) set forth in works as you teach them in voice.*[96]

And he is always ready with an appropriate story. He follows the general pattern of late medieval times, but he has a crispness of style and an easy familiarity which is quite enlivening.

When the topic is one of the sacraments or commandments his applications are instructive for all. The ninth commandment, for example, has three very practical consequences: 'that they hurt no person in name or fame by detraction, backbiting or scandal or by evil example of lying not yet that they curse or ban or wish evil to any person in heart.'[97] His work concludes with an interesting section made up of a catalogue of events in Christ's life, to be learned by heart and kept in mind: 'and lay up as it were treasure in a chest or coffer all such matters of the Gospel and that do appertain unto the acts of our Saviour.'[98] It opens with the Incarnation and continues right through the life of Christ, describing the Last Supper, for example, as:

> *When he returned again to the table did of bread and wine consecrate and make his own holy body and sacred blood and therewith did commune and communicate (houwsell) his apostles and gave them power to consecrate and make the same, whereby they were all made priests.*[99]

Whereas this form of catalogue is somewhat exceptional, for the most part the content is familiar, but when he talks of the Holy Spirit he introduces elements which are not at all in continuity with the previous decades, but which are usually a result of anti-Lutheran controversies. His understanding of the Church is based on the Holy Spirit, for He was sent to the Apostles 'whereby they were all fulfilled with grace and confirmed therein as the first Church of Christ and so hath continued

---

[96] Whytforde, Ashmole 1215, f. F (i).
[97] Thou shalt not bear false witness against thy neighbour. Whytforde, Ashmole 1215, f. F (i)
[98] Whytforde, Ashmole 1215, f. F iv.
[99] Whytforde, Ashmole 1215, f. G. ii.

and doth and shall continue in the Church unto the end of the world.'[100]

Apart from this, and a short repudiation of Lutheran ideas, the book demonstrates the continuity that exists from the fifteenth to the sixteenth centuries. Spirituality and the practice of piety have a persistence and durability which are left untouched when many other aspects of religious life begin to change, and the parish theology and practice of England are among the areas least touched by the arrival of the new learning, of Lutheran ideas and of eventual Reformation.

Setting out from attentiveness to contemporary criticism of the clergy, we are now more in a position to assess the strengths and weaknesses of the theological understanding to be found at the popular level in the parishes at the time. Certainly considerable weaknesses emerge. First of all, we have noted a lack of awareness and appreciation of the visible Church as other than the provider of the sacraments and the possessor of truth. The visible Church as the community of believers who helped and supported each other, an understanding of the sacraments as binding the community together in Christ and not merely personal devotions are neglected topics. Thoughts about the gift of corporate life as given by the Spirit of Christ, the relationship between the visible and invisible Church are absent. Even the consequences of the Resurrection, other than that of hope, are not emphasised, so there is little call to joy and celebration of the risen Christ. Further, on the level of the individual's life so strongly developed in some points, it is an imitation of Christ supported by grace that is propounded rather than an adoption, or incorporation into the life of Christ; neglect of St Paul as a source of spiritual rather than dogmatic theology is responsible for this. So, while much of Catholic doctrine was presented in clear statements, there is little to inject vigour or excitement into piety, and little to provide the strong meat of a profound spiritual progress: rather, there is evidence of a tradition being continued with little more than sincerity and thoroughness.

With the oncoming of the linguistic studies, there is little evidence in the wills and book lists of the parish clergy to suggest that they were moving with the times. In fact the findings of Heath suggest that from 1500 to 1550 the books we have been considering were still largely representative of parish reading.[101] For this later period, then, his conclusion is acceptable when he says that the clergy must not be charged with illiteracy, but rather with reading the wrong books. No

---

[100] Whytforde, Ashmole 1215, f. G. iii.

[101] Heath, *Medieval Clerical Accounts*, p. 88. He names books such as Myrc's Festival, *Legenda Aurea, Pupilla Oculi, Manipulus Curatum* as the most popular in this later period also.

sign betrays acquaintanceship with, or even awareness of, the dramatic advances of Biblical scholarship and interpretation which characterised this half century.[102]

For the earlier period, however, we have not found sufficient evidence to uphold criticisms of widespread ignorance and neglect among the clergy. If the consequences of the evidence available to us are reliable, then we must posit a popular level of understanding of faith that is not without commendable clarity and firmness, even if lacking in some respects. Further, we should accept the evidence of anticlerical feelings only with reservations, understanding it more as a negative wrangling over conflicting interests such as tithes and property rather than a more serious distrust and rejection of the clergy as ministers of the Gospel.

The same charge of ignorance about the New Learning, however, cannot be brought against John Fisher, for in his later life he was intensely involved with its study and advance. In his earlier years, whether he was actively engaged in parish work or not, he probably came under the influence of the parishes, both as a young boy in Beverley, and also as a student in Cambridge. Simply put, this was the spirit of the times in which he grew up, and there are many aspects of this spirit, as we have propounded it, which become visible in his later life. The sermons on the Penitential Psalms especially, echo closely many of the central themes of contemporary preaching, particularly those concerned with penance and forgiveness. The steadfast insistence in this teaching on the possibility of a renewed life in Christ because of the love and mercy of God; clear statements of faith in the presence and the nature of God; belief in the Church and her sacraments; application in the nature and practice of devotion to God; trust in the means of grace available to man, such statements are given clearly and unambiguously and applied with immediacy to everyday life. It is not a sophisticated theology, but it is permeated by sureness, by sensitivity to the human condition and by attentiveness to the love, mercy and hopefulness of the Christian Gospel.

Fisher shows kinship to this in his firm and unrelenting adherence to the basic statements of faith, an adherence which remained unaltered by his subsequent learning. The spirit of John Fisher was very much the spirit of the age, of the sermons and handbooks we have studied. His many years of contact with the New Learning had their effects, and contributed to his ability in theological debate, but throughout his life he shows a definite sympathy for the simple striving of the soul for

---

[102] Heath, *Medieval Clerical Accounts*, p. 89.

perfection after the traditional pattern as was taught and learned in the parishes.

We must now try and explore his years of higher theological study at Cambridge to see how they complemented these rudimentary formative influences. Having done this, we shall then be in a position to present the reactions of John Fisher to his inheritance, his response to ordinary Church life of diocese and parish and his response to the academic life of Cambridge when he eventually arrived in a position to act and react creatively.

University Life

John Fisher was a prolific writer. Once the course of his studies was completed and he was settled into his pastoral ministry, then increasing amounts of his time were given to writing. At first he wrote works of spirituality, but later circumstances led him to devote his time to theological work, all in the defence of the Catholic Church. Before examining and assessing this work in detail, it is essential that we are as informed as possible about the exact nature of the theological studies undertaken by John Fisher while he was at Cambridge. Here he received his formal training; yet we know little of the details of the study in which he was involved both as a student and a lecturer.

The poverty of our general knowledge of theological studies in the universities of England in the years prior to the Reformation is due first and foremost to a lack of evidence pertaining directly to that period. In part this is due to the style of studies carried out. The absence of printing facilities meant that books were not readily available for all, so that the main method of study was by word of mouth. As we have already mentioned, the reading aloud of texts was an important task and a vital means of communicating learning. In the course of these studies, therefore, most of the emphases and interpretations which would have characterised a particular place or period were given orally, noted down by students for their own use and only gradually, if at all, finding their way into text books in the form of further marginal or interlinear commentaries. The broad patterns of these studies and the books which formed their bases are known to us partially because they seem not to have changed much for many decades, but the more important detailed information about the precise quality of the theological interpretations given in lecture and debate is of its very nature difficult for us to determine.

This difficulty which arises from the method of work used is compounded by the fact that very few works proper to the Reformation period have survived in the University of Cambridge. The changes brought about in the course of the Reformation included an almost complete rejection and destruction of Catholic theological writings. This appears to have been rigorously carried out in Cambridge for today it is extremely difficult to find manuscripts and books of a theological nature belonging to this period. Consequently, the very books which could have carried the notes and comments containing theological thought of the day have been lost and the task of research into the precise nature of that thought is made all the more speculative.

Faced with this considerable lack of evidence there are but few steps which we can take to bring light to bear on this genuinely dark period. Given this lack of direct evidence, we are forced to use evidence which at best can be considered as only indirect, aware that conclusions must be accordingly all the more tentative. Despite the weakness of findings based on such evidence there seems to be no alternative but to accept and explore whatever is available, maintaining an awareness that it is far from satisfactory, that much remains to be done in this area of study, yet that with careful handling this evidence is capable of shedding some light on our darkness.

The evidence we shall use is the collection of library catalogues for the University and some College Libraries in Cambridge for the later decades of the fifteenth century. The weaknesses of this evidence are immediately obvious: knowledge of the works which filled the library shelves does not give us any direct or certain information about lectures and debates. In fact the exact relationship between library contents and patterns of teaching must be impossible to establish. We have to be content that there will be some connection, however tentative, between the books which are available and the studies undertaken by the students. Even today, a glance at a person's bookshelves gives some indication of the person's general areas of interest, and the comparative scarcity of written material in this period may imply a greater importance attached to the books available. On the other hand, of course, the labour involved in the production of a printed or written work could be taken as indicating a far greater divergence between the books on library shelves and the current interests as expressed in the spoken word. This is our dilemma.

Further complications arise when we examine the catalogues themselves: there is no guarantee of their completeness or accuracy; the content of the book is not always clear from its catalogue title or author; and finally some catalogues register only the first work of a volume which often contained more than one work in a single binding. These complications are lessened by the fact that very broad patterns of subject matter do emerge from the examination of these catalogues, and so the occasional unknown author, or unrecorded works, would not be too disturbing or invalidating. By examining these library catalogues then, we aim at establishing a picture of the books that were available to the student of theology in the time of John Fisher. Our supposition is that the books available were those that were in use and the pattern they showed was, to some extent, the pattern of the studies undertaken. So our conclusions are tentative, but without the rediscovery of some of this primary source material it is impossible to take any further steps at the moment.

The material available to us is this: a complete catalogue of the University Library from the year 1473, and a comparable catalogue from 1424; the catalogue of St Catherine's Hall Library for 1480; of Peterhouse Library for 1480; of Queens' College Library for 1472-1474, and, of less significance, of King's College Library for 1452.[1] Taken together with the fact of no known major additional influences in the late fifteenth century, the catalogues give us a comprehensive survey of the books known to be in public use in Cambridge around 1480. From this we can draw some conclusions as to the theological studies in progress at that time, although, bearing John Fisher in mind, it is unfortunate that there is no record of the Michaelhouse Library. As we have noted, Michaelhouse was incorporated with King's Hall in 1546 to form Trinity College, and even though each possessed a library nothing remains of them today.[2] The only relic we have is an entry in the Otryngham Book recording the generosity of Richard Holme, Warden of King's Hall, who in 1425 gave funds and a good endowment of theological books to Michaelhouse Library.[3] It seems likely, then, that as a Fellow of Michaelhouse, Fisher would have had a considerable theological library at hand; our total lack of knowledge about its contents means that the conclusions we draw from this survey depend somewhat on the assumption that the Michaelhouse library followed the general pattern.

The University Library Catalogue is the most important. This library was available to all graduate students, wearing academic dress, and to undergraduates when accompanied by a graduate, irrespective of their

[1] H. Bradshaw, Collected Papers (Cambridge University Press, 1889), p. 16f. St Catherine's: G. E. Corrie, 'A Catalogue of the Books which were given to the Library and Chapel of St Catherine's Hall, Cambridge, by Dr Woodlark, the Founder of the College', Cambridge Antiquarian Society Publications, Vol. I (1840), pp. 1–5. Peterhouse: M. R. James, A Descriptive Catalogue of the Manuscripts in the Library of Peterhouse (Cambridge University Press, 1899), pp. 1–25. Queens' College: W. C. Searle, 'Catalogue of the Library of Queens' College in 1472', Cambridge Antiquarian Society Publications, Vol. II (1864), pp. 165–93. Kings College: M. R. James, A Descriptive Catalogue of the Manuscripts other than Oriental in the Library of King's College, Cambridge (Cambridge University Press, 1895), pp. 69–83.
[2] R. Sinker, The Library of Trinity College, Cambridge, (Cambridge: Deighton, Bell & Co, 1891) p.1.
[3] Otryngham Book, p. 21. Also R. Willis and J.W. Clark, The Architectural History of the University of Cambridge, (Cambridge University Press, 1916) p. 399.

colleges.[4] Further, the survival of two catalogues, for 1424 and 1473, enable us to study the growth of the library. From a collection of 132 volumes in 1424, it developed to 330 by 1473. It was housed on three sides of a quadrangle, the books being kept in nineteen 'classes' or the traditional high book stalls with reading desks. Of the 1424 books, 69 were books on theology; but by 1473 this had risen to 193. However, the breakdown of these figures is more significant. To quote Bradshaw, the well-informed Cambridge Librarian:

> *Our historians are very fond of telling us that the libraries of the middle ages were choked with the writings of the schoolmen, that the Bible and earlier Fathers of the Church had been supplanted by Petrus Lombardus and his commentators. A glance at the arrangements of the University Library in 1473 will show us how false is this assumption, and a cursory examination of the history of most of our libraries will show that the great bulk of the scholastic writers were added to our collections by the benefactors of the seventeenth century when facts show that these subject matters were very deeply studied, though it is not always convenient for those writers to remember it who seek to depreciate as contemptible everything that was studied before the Reformation. The last four classes on each side of the room were devoted to Theology represented by the Bible text and leading commentators: St Augustine, St Jerome, the Glossa Ordinaria, Cardinal Hugo, Nicholas of Lyra and others. One class only next to the preceding, was set apart for Theologia Disputata, the Master of the Sentences and his expositors.[5]*

In terms of figures, in 1473 there were 27 books of *Theologia Disputata* (from 15 in 1424) compared with 166 books of Scripture and commentators (from 54 in 1424).

This is a definite and unquestionable emphasis on the study of Scripture, corresponding to the statutory requirements of students in theology and it finds some further confirmation in the College library catalogues. Study of, and commentary on, the texts of the Scriptures occupied a large part of the students' time and energy; and though the quality and the exact nature of this study will be examined later, we may assert with confidence that in academic circles the Bible was not a neglected work. Constant private reading of the text, the public reading in lectures, the studying and developing of commentaries on the Scriptural texts were major components in theological training. The later

---

[4] C. E. Sayle, *The Annals of Cambridge University Library*, (Cambridge University Press: 1916) p. 83.
[5] Bradshaw, *Collected Papers*, pp. 186-187.

works of John Fisher and his constant and thoughtful use of Scripture are evidence of this.

The library of St Catherine's Hall shows a similar bias in favour of Scriptural studies and it is perhaps of some moment that this library was adjacent to Michaelhouse, having been built on land held on lease from Michaelhouse. The Hall, founded in 1475, had a well-defined theological purpose: 'For the use of the Church, administration of the most holy Word of God, and for sacred theology.'[6] The Fellows of this college were allowed to graduate only in theology. This must have given the Hall considerable affinity with Michaelhouse, which had been founded along similar lines. The libraries of Peterhouse, Queens' College and King's College do not show such a clear predominance of Scriptural studies, but the proportion of Biblical and theological books is sufficient to support the general contention of high regard for and devotion to Scriptural studies.[7]

In assessing the contents of the *Theologia Disputata* section, one feature stands out quite prominently: the domination of St Thomas Aquinas. Most of the major medieval theologians are represented, including Augustine, Boethius, Lombard, Anselm, Alexander of Hales, Albert, Bonaventure, Hugh of St Victor and others; but Aquinas is outstanding. There are records of about fifty volumes of works by Aquinas, whereas the next most represented author, Augustine, records only twenty-six volumes. Scholasticism is represented by its most brilliant exponent. The overall pattern that emerges, then, is that the early high scholastic writers dominate the study of *Theologia Disputata*, to the comparative exclusion of Ockham, and to a lesser extent of Scotus and their followers.

References to the *Sentences* as an important representative work add further support to the contention of the preponderance of the early scholastic writers. There are in these libraries a total of sixteen copies of the *Sentences* by Peter Lombard, accompanied by eleven commentaries by Aquinas, four by Bonaventure, two by Albert the Great and six by Petrus Tarentasius (1225-1276), a Dominican who became Archbishop of Lyons, later Bishop of Ostia and ultimately Pope Innocent V. His theology is pre-Aquinas scholasticism, with a notable practical element and emphasis. In contrast to this there are only five

---

[6] Willis and Clark, *The Architectural History of the University of Cambridge*, Vol. I, p. lxvii.

[7] Statistics:

	Scripture	Disputata
Peterhouse	60	69
Queens'	50	67
King's	24	30

copies of Commentaries by Scotus, one by Ockham, one by Gregory of Rimini and one by Durandus of St Pourcain (d. 1332) who in fact anticipated the terminism of Ockham.[8] So, as with the Scriptural studies, the pattern of the statutory requirements, stressing the importance of the *Sentences*, is reflected in these book lists; about one third of all the books of strict theology are on the *Sentences*. Furthermore, this study seems to have emphasised the earlier authors, before the *Sentences* and its commentators came under the extreme influence of Ockham and his theories.

Works other than Commentaries on the *Sentences* show a similar pattern. There is a preponderance of Aristotelian-based academic theology; though a complementary theology, known as the 'Augustinian-Franciscan' line,[9] is also well represented with Richard and Hugh of St Victor (six volumes), Bonaventure (five volumes), Grossetete (six volumes), one volume by Wallensis, an Oxford Francisan of c. 1260, and Richard de Middleton, who was also an Oxford Franciscan (d. 1308).[10] Books written after this date are few and far between. There are only two copies of the *Quodlibeta* of Scotus, one copy of the *Defensorium* by Ockham, one collection of sermons by Robert Holcot (c.1300-1349)[11] and two copies of the *De Causa Dei* by Thomas Bradwardine (1290-1349).[12]After Bradwardine, the only Englishmen to emerge with original contributions to make were John Wycliff (1324-1384) and Reginald Pecock (c.1390-1460). In different ways both represented the right of individual judgement: Wycliff in conjunction with Scripture and Pecock by the use of reason. The fact that the only reference made to these works in the library lists is by way of refutation speaks for the efficiency of a campaign launched by Archbishop Thomas Arundel (1353-1414) in his *Constitutions*. Issued in 1408, these *Constitutions* banned the teachings and works of these authors, a ban that was most effectively carried out in Cambridge University.[13] So, in the libraries

[8] E.C. Thomas, *History of the Schoolmen,* (Williams & Norgate: London, 1941) pp. 260, 475.

[9] Searle, p. 188.

[10] Thomas, *op. cit.* p. 522.

[11] Robert Holcot was an English Dominican who followed Ockham's insistence on the importance of free-will, but also maintained that there was no correlation between human action and divine grace, for God was absolutely free. So the only indications that a person has of an unknowable God were the Scriptures and the Creeds.

[12] Thomas Bradwardine, for a short period the Archbishop of Canterbury, wrote against this contemporary form of Pelagianism, asserting the need for and effectiveness of God's grace in man. He is remarkable for his breadth of learning, much of which was acquired by using the splendid library of Richard of Bury, Bishop of Durham (1287-1345).

[13] *Statutes* of King's College, Cambridge, for 1457, 'Therefore we state … that whosoever would be a scholar… would not favour the damned and erroneous opinions of the heretic John Wycliff, Reginald Pecocke, nor any other heretic…' See also J. B. Mullinger, *The University of Cambridge from the Earliest Times to the Royal Injunction of 1535* (Cambridge University Press, 1873), p. 296.

we find works by Thomas Netter of Walden (c.1370-1430), a Carmelite friar who wrote considerable volumes against Wycliff, two copies of which are recorded, and works by Philip Repyngton (c1360-1424), cardinal bishop of Lincoln, who, after initially defending the opinions of Wycliff, did a *volte face* and attacked them most forcibly. There are three copies by him and one by William Wodeford who is remembered as a Franciscan friar chosen by the Synod of London about 1396 to answer Wycliff.[14]

The vigour of the purge established by Arundel is to be seen quite clearly in the absence of works considered to be unorthodox. Equally clearly, though, such a powerful insistence on strict orthodoxy contributed to the disappearance of much theological enterprise which seems to have occurred in England during the fifteenth century. Evidence of enthusiastic enquiry, of originality of thought and expression is conspicuously absent in this period.[15] However, too much blame must not be laid at the at the door of scholasticism, for the evidence of these library catalogues indicate quite firmly that it was the more rewarding and unified scholasticism of Aquinas and his contemporaries that seems to have received most attention, and not the labyrinthine complexities of the later scholastic writers. If imagination and inventiveness are largely absent from the works of Catholics in defence of their faith against contrary opinions of the early sixteenth century, clarity, precision and system are not.

The cautions recorded in the *Grace Books* A and B add a further dimension to our survey. The cautions were objects of value, deposited by a student as a pledge that he would complete his course. Often books were offered as security, and the surviving lists give us a picture of the books which were in possession of the students. The books may, however, have been given to the student as a gift, have been a family possession, and have been used at the University solely for credit purposes, and so may in no way reflect his interests. Be that as it may, these lists show a predictable pattern, for they are dominated by the Bible, the *Decretals* of Canon Law and Service or Liturgical Books. Among the theological books offered, Aquinas is again in the forefront, but there are a considerable number of works by Scotus in evidence too. From the lists of 1454-1485 there are twenty volumes of Aquinas, thirteen copies of the *Sentences* and eleven works by Scotus; made up

---

[14] T. Tanner, *Bibliotheca Britannia*. (London: G. Bowyer, 1748) p. 622.

[15] The research of R. Weiss suggests that the closing decades of this century did not witness any significant presence of humanist studies in Cambridge. *Humanism in England in the Fifteenth Century*, (Oxford: Blackwells, 1937) pp. 160-167.

of nine commentaries on the *Sentences*, and one *Quodlibeta* and one *Logicalia*. Similarly from 1488-1511, Aquinas is recorded thirteen times and Scotus six, with Lombard mentioned on nine occasions and Albert the Great on five.[16] The relative importance of Scotus in these lists must be used to complement the evidence of the libraries and indicates a more considerable attention to his work than is suggested by them. Certainly, as we have already observed, Erasmus mentions him as having been studied at Cambridge and, more impressively, so does Fisher. We must not be too definitive in drawing conclusions from the evidence of the libraries on this point. Lectures and interpretations of the *Sentences* may well have been more Scotist than the catalogues imply. Nevertheless, our general contention still stands: that the emphasis of theological study was first upon the Bible and secondly on Aquinas and the earlier scholastics.

These findings demand that we are critical of remarks which caricature the intellectual life of Cambridge before the advent of the New Learning. Mullinger writes of the 'traditional teachers' at the University:

> *[they] must expect, if teachers of the new schools once gained a footing at Cambridge, to have all those subtle distinctions, in which they had so long delighted, treated as the creatures of a perverted ingenuity – those latent meanings of Scripture which they once laboured to evolve, characterised as the unauthorised tamperings of the plain and literal sense – their great oracle (i.e. Scotus) disparaged...their own efforts at interpreting his thoughts as vain and nugatory...each of them in fine would be called upon to confess 'after a search thus painful and long that all his life he had been in the wrong.'[17]*

At least we must observe the lack of direct evidence in support of these comments and at most state that the evidence available leads to different conclusions.

Turning now to the scripture stalls in these libraries, we must attempt to assess the value of the books we find there, again remembering the limits and weaknesses of our method of study. Apart from the books of the Bible, three main works dominate the Scripture sections of the libraries: the 'Gloss', the works of Hugh of St Cher and the works of Nicholas of Lyra.[18] It is necessary that we look at these authors in some detail. The word 'author' can be used of the Gloss only in the loosest

---

[16] The statistics can be found in *Grace Book A*, pp. x-xvi. *Grace Book B*, pp. viii-xiii.

[17] Mullinger, *The University of Cambridge*, p. 432. He continues by quoting Petrarch: 'Behold these men who devote their whole lives to wrangling and to the cavillings of sophistry wearying themselves unceasingly with idle speculations...'

[18] Statistics: all catalogues – Gloss 65, Hugh 25, Lyra 20, Scripture 180.

possible way, for the title 'Gloss' is used to indicate a biblical text which has been annotated with interlinear and marginal notes progressively over what is generally an unknown period. The practice seems to have started at the monastery of Laon, where initially under St Anselm of Laon (c1050-1117), the *lectio divina* was complemented by a scribe writing into the text the more favoured interpretations.[19] Since the *lectio divina* derived its inspiration from St Augustine, its main intention was the immediate nourishment of the soul in search of God.[20] Consequently, the general quality of the early Gloss was a concern for the direct application of Scripture to personal spirituality: the spiritual sense of Scripture.

The practice of the Gloss found promotion at the hands of many, including Peter the Chanter, Robert of Bridlington and Peter Lombard. In fact the Biblical *Glossa Ordinaria*, which has parallels in Civil and Canon Law, came to represent the accumulated learning of the preceding centuries providing, as they did, a representative selection of extracts from the Fathers and other masters from the third to the early twelfth centuries. The constant process of rewriting and adding to the notes given with the Biblical text make it impossible to trace the origin of any Gloss or to know the exact nature of the large number of 'Gloss' simply presented as such in the library catalogues. Consequently it is hard to comment on the significance of such a large number of 'Gloss' to be found in these libraries. The quality of the work varies considerably and certainly textual and linguistic errors abound. However, the range of authors quoted is vast and we may assume that most of the valuable work of the preceding scholars was to be found there, even if it was overlain with quantities of material of little value.

Apart from the blanket and indeterminable representation achieved by the 'Gloss', the libraries also housed works which represent some of the best achievements of the work of scripture scholars throughout the preceding centuries. This is particularly true of the stream of study which concentrated on the literal meaning of the Scriptures, for in the works of Hugh of St Cher and later of Nicholas of Lyra the best of the systematic and careful study of the meaning of the Scriptures comes into the hands of the theological student in the pre-Reformation period.

---

[19] B. Smalley, *The Study of the Bible in the Middle Ages*, (Oxford: Blackwell, 1952) pp. 37-82.

[20] 'Whatever there is in the Word of God that cannot, when taken literally, be referred either to purity of life or soundness of doctrine, is to be classified as figurative.' Augustine, *De Doctrina Christiana III*, 10.14, *Patres Latini*, xxxiv, col. 71. Also H. A. Oberman, *Forerunners of the Reformation* (London: Lutterworth Press, 1967), p. 284.

Hugh of St Cher lived from 1200 till 1263.[21] He inherited from the previous century the development of Scriptural studies which had begun to formulate a clear methodology for students of Scripture. Andrew of St Victor, the chief spokesman for studies of the literal meaning of Scripture in the twelfth century, had turned to Jewish scholars and from them learned how to handle Old Testament texts. Consequently he won for all subsequent scripture scholars a freedom from the insistence on the spiritual interpretation of the Old Testament as its only justification.[22] This freedom was readily embraced by Hugh who, accepting that the literal interpretation was the only basis for all sound understanding of Scripture, gradually composed a commentary on the whole Bible which always started from the literal sense, though sometimes moved into spiritual application too. Hugh's commentary was not marginal or interlinear but continuous and it introduced to the students for whom it was available the developments which had taken place since the compilation of the Gloss. Not only did this work help to clarify the distinction between spiritual writings, spiritual commentary and theological disputation but he also brought to the forefront an awareness of the need for textual accuracy. Since the early twelfth century the growing insistence upon the literal meaning of Scripture had given rise to the issuing of *correctoria* or lists of corrections and alternative readings. He also organised the drawing up of Biblical concordances. Smalley concludes that 'this is only the best known example of a great movement of tabulating references to the Scriptures and Fathers which is still impressing students of medieval libraries.'[23]

Hugh of St Cher was very popular in the Scripture libraries in Cambridge. In fact St Catherine's Hall Library shows a distinct predominance of Hugh over both Nicholas of Lyra and the Gloss, and we must remember that this was the College established in 1475 for the promotion of the Word of God. Further, Hugh Damlet (d.1476), the learned Master of Pembroke Hall, bequeathed fifteen volumes of theological works to the various colleges and eight of these left to

---

[21] *New Catholic Encyclopaedia*. (New York: Hill. 1967) Vol. 7, p.193. Hugh was born at St Cher, near Vienne. He is known as Cardinal Hugh and he died in 1263. His chief work was *Postilla in Universa Biblia*.

[22] Smalley, *op. cit.*, pp. 112–95. Andrew learned to expound the literal text of the Old Testament from men such as Rabbi Solomon (1040–1105). For example, he gives a long exposition of Isaiah's 'Man of Sorrows' without ever once referring to Christ. He did not offer any systematic understanding of the connection between Old and New Testaments, nor between literal and spiritual meanings.

[23] Smalley, *op. cit.* p. 334.

Pembroke Hall were commentaries by Hugh of St Cher.[24] There are sufficient indications for us to be sure that there was in this period a continued regard for the genuine biblical ability of the thirteenth century which held the literal interpretation as the basis of all sound understanding of Scripture.

The best known and most highly regarded of the medieval Scripture scholars is Nicholas of Lyra. He has been regarded as a solitary light in the surrounding darkness but, as is often the case, the progress made through years of discussion, combined work and gradual clarification finds its fullest expression in the work of one outstanding exponent. To appreciate fully this one author, he must be held in his true context and not left in isolation. By the time Nicholas entered the arena of Scripture studies, eventually to stand alongside Hugh as the major influence in the Cambridge libraries, much had been done to prepare for his achievements and fame. Most importantly of all, Albert the Great and St Thomas Aquinas had tackled the theoretical problem of the exact relationship between the various interpretations of Scripture. The traditional distinction of interpretations received new clarity in Thomas' work and a guarantee that properly used they would not lead to confusion.[25] This, together with the emergence of a clear theological method based on the Aristotelian concept of a science, achieved independence for both exegete and theologian. The task of the theologian could now be distinguished from that of the scripture scholar and no longer was the bible looked upon as a divine encyclopaedia written in cipher, the elucidation of which was the theologian's main task. With the development of systematic theology, the concerted study of Scripture in its own right was enabled to make progress.

Nicholas of Lyra was able to rejoice in this clarity and freedom. Drawing heavily on the work and riches of the past,[26] he argued for the crucial importance of the literal sense of the Scriptures and drawing on European Jewish learning he attempted to give an up-to-date guide to the Hebrew text and Jewish tradition. His introduction to the *Postilla Litteralis super Biblia* reads:

---

[24] Emden, *Biographical Register*, p. 176.

[25] 'Since all the senses are founded on one – the literal – from which alone any argument can be drawn, and not from those intended in allegory.' Aquinas, *Summa Theologica* I, q. 1, art 10. Oberman, *Forerunners of the Reformation*, p. 285..

[26] Nicholas drew from works by Gregory, Bede, Jerome, the Victorines, Hugh of St Cher, Albert, Bonaventure as well as Jewish authors such as Rabbi Solomon, Rabby Moyses (Maimonedes), Rabbi Joseph ben Simon Kara and others. See 'Nicholas de Lyra' in *Histoire Litteraire de la France*. (Paris: 1927.) Tome XXXVI, p. 391.

> *It is to be known that the literal sense is largely darkened on account*
> *of the mode of explaining commonly used by others [the Scholastics],*
> *who, although they said much that was good, did not much touch the*
> *literal sense. So we propose to avoid such an approach, and with*
> *God's help insist upon the literal sense.* [27]

In the course of this development he came to a wider understanding
of the literal sense as the intention of the author, being strict in his
understanding of the Old Testament, except where he saw a direct and
immediate intention of the author to designate the person of Christ.
So, except for a small number of Psalms and certain passages from the
Prophets which entailed a double literal sense, all applications of the Old
Testament to the tenets of the Christian faith became clearly the task of
spiritual interpretation. [28]

Nicholas of Lyra also appears to have rejoiced in a second type of
freedom in his scriptural studies. Not only did he enjoy a clearly defined
method and area of enquiry, but he also appears to have considered
himself free to reject, if necessary, the findings of his illustrious
predecessors. Not only did he not feel constrained by his Jewish
sources, he did not feel bound by his Christian heritage either. He readily
disagreed with St Jerome when he feels he has grounds to do so and
throughout his works he shows a freedom of enquiry which was not
common. [29] The probable source of his freedom is significant, for he was
the first of all the medieval exegetes to express a confession of faith in
the interpretative authority of the Church, thus freeing himself from any
particular interpretation of the Fathers. He said:

> *I protest to assert nothing except in so far as it was clearly determined*
> *explicitly by the Holy Scriptures and the authority of the Church. All*
> *the rest should be stated by the Scholastics by way of exercise. That*
> *is why all that I say and will say, I submit to the correction of Holy*
> *Mother Church who possesses wisdom.* [30]

The circumstances of this confession are unknown, but it may have
contributed something towards the originality of Lyra's enquiries,
especially when employing his knowledge of Hebrew learning and
tradition. Following the clear paths marked out by Aquinas, his works
contain little in the way of theological development. Theological
statements abound but he refrained from developing them and limited

[27] Nicholas de Lyra, *op. cit.* p. 370.
[28] Oberman, *Forerunners of the Reformation*, p. 286.
[29] E.g. on Matthew 6:35. See SPICQ, p. 339.
[30] Prologue de Commend. Script. P. L. CXIII-31. Also SPICQ, pp. 338-339.

himself to textual commentary.[31] With this single mindedness of purpose he achieved simplicity of style, for he always kept himself close to the text and avoided elaborate expositions. On odd occasions, for example, with certain Psalms and on parts of the Synoptic Gospels when treating them for the third time, he allowed himself some spiritual interpretation, but soon returned to his close textual commentary.

Such a massive work as his had considerable repercussions. There is hardly a book list, either of library or private collection, dating from the end of the fifteenth century that does not include some works by Lyra. Even though the work of the scribes means that the later volumes are not always identical with the earlier manuscripts, the spirit of Lyra is dominant and formative of all subsequent additions.

Nicholas of Lyra, then, brings to a climax the work of medieval scripture scholars. Their work was one of a slow but steady progress in understanding the part to be played by the Scriptures in the medieval scholastic pattern of theology, and of gradually developing the ability to handle the Scriptures in the systematic way that theology demanded. Lyra brought together the knowledge and understanding that had been acquired over the centuries from a Christian and Jewish heritage and with these limited resources achieved a style of work notable for its thoroughness and discipline. While it is true that, in the light of later linguistic achievements and under the demands of a changing theological method, his achievements appeared as seriously inadequate, in their own context his handling of Old Testament texts is commendable and provided a systematic source for the dogmatic theologian.

The only works of a similar or later date than Nicholas of Lyra to be found in the libraries of Cambridge are two copies of a New Testament commentary by 'Notyngham', a Franciscan who died about 1330 and six copies of works by Robert Holcote (d. 1349).[32] As with dogmatic theology, then, the later fourteenth and fifteenth centuries added little to the shelves, the major contributions coming from the scholars of the twelfth, thirteenth and early fourteenth centuries. In fact, after Nicholas of Lyra there seems to have been a profound loss of impetus in scripture studies, almost as if he had taken that line of study as far as it could go with the limited resources then available. The lack of constructive theological activity at this time which has been noted must have left

[31] The copy of Lyra's *Postilla* in the Rylands Library, Manchester, printed in Basle in 1506, along with the *Glossa Ordinaria*, includes a *Repertorium Alphabeti* which is a list of the theological statements made in the course of the Commentary. See Vol. 7 and Vol 6 fol. 152. Lyra's purpose was never the proposing of theological statements.
[32] Tanner, *Bibliotheca Britannia*, p. 362.

Scripture studies without another possible incentive and so the gradual breakdown of the scholastic methodology left systematic study of the literal meaning of Scripture in isolation. Just as the emphasis in theology moved to what has been called the Augustinian approach, so too Scripture studies moved away from the literal meaning to developing the 'second literal sense', or the prophetic literal sense of the Old Testament. Eventually, with Jacques Lefevre d'Etaples (1460-1536), this prophetic literal sense was proclaimed to be the only valid sense of the Old Testament for Christian believers, and the scholarship of Lyra and his school became looked upon as fruitless and as murdering Christian spirituality.[33] This led to Erasmus' well known complaint about the monks who 'stick as long as they live to the letter and do not search for spiritual understanding' and to the complaint of the young Luther concerning the 'letter that kills' as explained by the 'Judaizers'.[34]

However, there is no evidence of these developments being represented in the Cambridge libraries which remained dominated by the Gloss, Hugh of St Cher and Nicholas of Lyra. Together these three represent the line of development which took place in Scripture studies, ending in a fundamental emphasis on the literal sense of the Scriptures which was to be expounded systematically and thoroughly. Presuming that this too was the emphasis of the Scriptural studies undertaken by theology students such as John Fisher, how can they best be evaluated?

On the positive side first of all, a study of the works of Lyra and Hugh of St Cher must have made considerable demands on the discipline of the student. A conscientious student would have gained from his studies a thorough knowledge of the Scriptural texts, an appreciation of the scholastic principles of the use of Scripture and a wide ranging familiarity with traditional lines of interpretation. He should have gained an ability to use the Scripture in a disciplined manner using material drawn from all parts of the Bible and making clear distinctions between the various levels of interpretation. Within the limits of this level of scholarship, the student should have been clear-headed in his use of Scripture and especially able to handle the details of Old Testament exegesis in the strictly traditional manner.

However, the limits of this level of scholarship must be seen to be serious, and the lack of any contemporary influence must have cast a shadow over the whole course of studies. This level of scholarship was

[33] Oberman, *op. cit.* pp.288-289.
[34] Erasmus, *Enchiridion Militis Christiani,* (Leiden: Omnia Opera. 1704.) Vol. V, col. 9. Also Oberman, *op. cit.* p. 290, p. 292.

limited first of all in the texts it used. There was an almost total reliance on the Vulgate of St Jerome, assisted only by the contribution of Hebrew texts deriving mainly from Jewish sources. Despite an awareness of the need for accurate texts and the textual work that was achieved, the findings of Renaissance scholarship highlighted the shortcomings of earlier resources. Further, the availability of textual resources meant that most attention was given to the Old Testament, for the Hebrew language and Rabbinical tradition could be learned from European Jews whereas a journey to Byzantium Sicily or Southern Italy was necessary to learn Greek. Consequently, the desire to deal attentively and systematically with the texts of Scripture in their literal sense found its greatest expression in tackling the problems of the Old Testament where the details of Jewish law and spirituality could be expounded.

The New Testament was less easy to handle in this literal manner and while spiritual use of the New Testament was plentiful,

> *One misses any concerted effort to break new ground and to open up sources of information... Moreover a substantial section of the New Testament, the Pauline Epistles, was resigned to the theologians. Dialectic, not scholarship, was the chosen instrument for expounding St Paul.*[35]

It was precisely this area of the scriptural sources which was dramatically opened by the compound factors of the Renaissance. New approaches in theology and newly acquired skills in Scriptural languages enabled scholars to extract far greater riches from New Testament texts, in contrast to which the traditional offerings of the Middle Ages were weak and wanting. It may well be precisely in the lack of any innovation or development in the decades preceding the Reformation that the greatest weakness of this study lay, for while its principles and its achievements were limited but valuable, when John Fisher and his contemporaries came to study these works they were old and must have been almost lifeless. Unless the particular manner in which these texts were used was such that brought them to life with the vitality of relevance to contemporary needs, it would seem that the best these Scripture studies could produce would be a disciplined and thorough appreciation of the literal use of Scripture in theological debates with emphasis on Old Testament texts, and a quite separate use of Scripture in a spiritual manner for the writings of devotion and piety. Fisher's own writings, as we shall see, display these characteristics.

---

[35] Smalley, *op. cit.* p. 363.

As we have already seen in the development of theology, it was predominantly the achievements of the twelfth, thirteenth and early fourteenth centuries that stocked the library shelves. If properly used, these books could be the basis for a sound and thorough theological training. The pedagogic influence on the student of concerted study of these sources would have been considerable, and, if we judge by these library catalogues alone, we should expect to find as a product of university education a man of the Thomistic theological school, skilled in dialectic and well versed in the literal interpretation of the Scriptures, especially the Old Testament. The absence of later works would indicate some exclusion of any major influence from Ockham, Nominalism or the resurgent Augustinian type of spiritual interpretation of Scripture. The absence of contemporary influences is a factor that is difficult to assess. For some it may have produced a lack of inventiveness or originality and an accepted dependence upon traditional methods and answers. In others, however, it may have produced a dissatisfaction with the past, giving rise to a desire for new ways and means, new explorations into their faith and its growth. The poverty of our evidence does not permit us to be more specific in these conclusions; indeed they may be more than speculative, indicating possible patterns of study and merely the most obvious of its formative factors.

A further absence inhibits our enquiry even more. The lack of any work of systematic theology from John Fisher's period makes it still more difficult to know the detailed influences of his training. His own theological writings, as we shall see, are either apologetic or devotional, and at no point does he undertake any systematic development or exposition about his understanding of his faith. We are left to glean from his defences the indications of his positive approaches to various topics; and a man on the defensive is rarely as expressive of himself and his thoughts as a man who is relaxed.

In conclusion then we must not be over depreciative of the theological education that John Fisher is likely to have received, nor of the theological activities of the University of Cambridge at that time. During the ten-year period of his theological development, Scriptural studies were the prime concern and in truly scholarly circles it must have been disciplined and worthwhile. The theological work seems to have been centred on the Sentences, as presented in the systematic treatment of the Aquinas tradition. The absence of any unorthodox material indicates that the whole pattern of studies was under the supervision of Church authority and, while there was plenty of scope for debate, the position of a magisterial Church went largely unquestioned and unexplained.

This consideration has not been an attempt to point to areas which, with hindsight, can be seen to have contributed to the course of the Reformation in England. Rather we have tried to outline and appreciate the educational circumstances and theological training encountered in the student days of John Fisher. Our study of parish life has brought to light a considerable emphasis on personal spirituality, entailing the proposal that the significance of the Church lay in the Sacraments. The strengths and weaknesses of parish preaching and theology have been scanned and now a similar examination of the University reveals a certain correspondence. The role played by the authority of the Church, unexplained in the parishes, is similarly neglected in the halls, while still continuing to exercise an oppressive influence. The serious limitations in the appreciation of the Church as a community, as formed by the Holy Spirit and as living in the hope of the risen Christ, which we found in the parishes now finds an echo in the Scripture scholars' inability to handle the New Testament texts and the consequent neglect of Pauline theology. Certainly, we can detect an evident monotony both in parish and university life, where the major characteristics are definable as being common to many preceding generations.

The effects of this environment on John Fisher we shall study in subsequent chapters. For now it is sufficient to conclude that we have learned that the life of this age, for all its limitations, demands that we treat with respectful caution comments such as those of Erasmus when he says:

> *It is notorious that hitherto there have been theologians who have altogether neglected the Scriptures and that too, not for the purpose of studying the Sentences, nor indeed with a view to any other single thing save only the dilemmas of the quaestiones.*[36]

Reformation or no, with libraries such as these this was not simply an era of intellectual darkness, of tortuous decaying scholasticism, of an absence of a valid appreciation of Scripture or of a disintegrating medieval spirituality. Yet, by their fruits you shall know them.

---

[36] Erasmus to Bullock, P. S. Allen, *Opus Epistolarum*, Vol. II, Ep. 456, p. 328. Nichols, *The Epistles of Erasmus*, Vol. II, Ep. 441, p. 324.

Reformer

enry VII wrote to his mother, Lady Margaret, in 1504 announcing his choice of John Fisher for the vacant See of Rochester:

> *I am well minded to promote Master Fisher, your confessor, to a bishopric; and I assure you, Madam, for none other cause but for the great and singular virtue that I know and see in him as well in cunning and natural wisdom and specially for his good and gracious living. And by the promotion of such a man I know well it should encourage many others to live virtuously and to take such ways as he doth.[1]*

He asked for Lady Margaret's advice and confessed his hope that at least this one appointment would make amends for his previous appointments which had been based on expediency rather than spiritual suitability. Fisher was consecrated at Lambeth by Archbishop William Warham on 25 November 1504, and installed by proxy in the cathedral at Rochester on 24 April 1505.

Rochester was the smallest diocese in England with revenues of only £300 a year. Nevertheless, as bishop, Fisher was placed in a position to take a significant and active part in the events of his day. As the Lady Margaret Reader in Divinity at Cambridge and even as Vice-Chancellor, he did not command the attention that became his as the learned friend of Lady Margaret and Bishop of Rochester. From that moment his activities appeared to have been carefully recorded and his writings readily appreciated and preserved.

The anonymous sixteenth-century biographer, eulogised his virtues as a pastoral bishop, describing his official visitations to the parishes and monasteries of his diocese:

> *exhorting them to obedience, chastity and true observations of their monastical vows, sequestering all such as he found unworthy to occupy that high function, he placed other fitter in their rooms; and all such as were accused of any crime, he put to their purgation not sparing the punishment of simony and heresy with other crimes and*

[1] E. E. Reynolds, *Roper and Harpsfield: Lives of Thomas More* (New York: Everyman's Library, 1963), pp. 24–5. C. H. Cooper, *Memoir of Margaret, Countess of Richmond and Derby* (Cambridge: Deighton, Bell & Co, 1874), pp. 95–6.

> *abuses. And by the way he omitted neither preachings to the people,*
> *nor confirmings of children, nor relieving of needy and indigent*
> *persons; so that by all means he observed a due comeliness in the*
> *house of God...Wheresoever he lay, either at Rochester or elsewhere,*
> *his order was to inquire where any poor sick folks lay near him...*
> *And where he saw any of them likely to die he would preach to them,*
> *teaching them the way to die, with such goodly persuasions, yet*
> *for the most part he never departed till the sick persons were well*
> *satisfied and contented with death. Many times it was his chance*
> *to come to such persons' houses as for want of chimneys were very*
> *smoky, and thereby so noisome that scant any man could abide in*
> *them. Nevertheless himself would there sit by the sick patient many*
> *times the space of three or four hours together in the smoke...And in*
> *some other poor houses where stairs were wanting, he would never*
> *disdain to climb up by a ladder for such good purpose.[2]*

Such a report, supported as it is by some of our evidence, gives a glimpse of the way Fisher tackled some of the pastoral problems of his time. We have described his upbringing and education; the heritage into which he entered in its pastoral and academic aspects. It is now time to examine the response of John Fisher to the circumstances of his life, the areas in which he chose to accept the past and those in which he pushed ahead with reform and new ways. In this he was symptomatic of the best of his age.

The Diocesan Registers of Rochester record that Fisher made official visitations throughout his diocese in the years 1505, 1508, 1511, 1514, 1517, 1520 and 1529, and though there is no detailed record of the events of each visitation, the enthusiasm and dedication displayed in such a consistent performance suggest that the picture portrayed by his biographer is not far from the actual truth.[3] Fisher possessed a genuine pastoral concern for his people. His life and writings display this, for his constant exhortations to perfection and his struggle with error and heresy are directed to the one aim of maintaining a good and sound religion in which the common person would find a way to salvation. His dedication to this task was total; even when offered promotion to richer Sees, as in 1514 when he was offered Lincoln and in 1515 when he was offered Ely, he refused saying that it was to Rochester he was bound and he would not change his poor old wife for the richest widow in England.[4]

---

[2] Van Ortroy, *Vie, Vol*. X, pp. 216–23.

[3] Diocese of Rochester, *Episcopal Register V*, (1492-1542) ff. 42, 49, 56, 71, 74, 102, 145.

[4] M. Macklem, *God Have Mercy*, (Oberon Press: Ottawa, 1967), p. 12. Lewis, *The Life*, Vol. I, pp. 15–16.

The Registers of Rochester, then, portray Fisher at work defending the religious life of his diocese against the disruptive influence of erroneous teaching. His dealings with various cases of heresy display not only the hallmarks of Fisher's characteristic thoroughness but also a deep compassion for those caught in error.[5] In the early part of his administration such people appeared to Fisher as ignorant and misled rather than malevolent. Interestingly, throughout Fisher's time at Rochester there is no record of anyone in the diocese being handed over to the secular authorities for punishment. This cannot have been due to any ideological problem on the part of Fisher, for in his writings he expressly supports the legality of such action.[6] But the practice is different from the theory, and Fisher's own appreciation of excommunication from the Church as a fate worse than death no doubt accounts for his reluctance to take any further measures. In 1521 as Chancellor of Cambridge, for example, Fisher was called upon to pronounce the sentence of excommunication against an unknown person who had defaced copies of the Papal Bull against Luther which had been posted at all the college gates. After having had no success in urging the culprit to confess, Fisher came to the point of reading the sentence,

> but after he had proceeded a space in the reading thereof, he stayed and began again to consider in his mind the great weight of his grievous sentence, which so much pierced his heart that even before them all he could not refrain from weepings.[7]

Such a horror of excommunication reveals much about Fisher's understanding of the Church and its role in the economy of salvation. It clarifies the deep motives of faith which inspired the continual drive of his theological writings against those opinions which he saw as destructive of the eternal salvation of his people. As a bishop, Fisher was committed to the service of his people. The rigour and discipline of his academic life found new application with his changed responsibilities. He spared no effort to meet the pastoral needs of his diocese, to provide the people with leadership and encouragement, and to protect them from error and confusion. In this he was an exemplary bishop and rightly held up for our admiration.

Besides work in the Diocese, the position of Bishop entailed many other responsibilities, and the Register records the great number of

---

[5] The details of these cases can be found recorded in the biographies: Reynolds, *op. cit.* pp.61–6; M. Macklem, *God Have Mercy*, (Oberon Press: Ottawa, 1967) pp. 13–15.

[6] John Fisher, *Confutatio*, article XXIII: *Excommunicationes esse poenas externas dumtaxit*.

[7] Van Ortroy, *Vie*, Vol. X, p. 233.

journeys to London made by Bishop Fisher. (These journeys irritated Fisher as they caused him to be absent from his diocese and to be unable to attend to his diocesan duties.)[8] He was summoned to Convocations in 1510, 1512 and 1515. At the Convocation of 1512 Dean Colet made his famous speech denouncing the abuses of the clergy and calling for reform. Bishop Fisher surely listened to him with great sympathy, for both men had already expressed similar concerns on a number of previous occasions. In fact, considerable affinity existed between the programme of these reformers and it is unfortunate that there is no further evidence of contact between them.

John Colet, son of a prosperous London business man, born in 1466 first presented his ideas for Church reform in his commentaries on the letters of St Paul, which he gave as lectures in Oxford, beginning in 1496 with the letter to the Romans.[9] In these lectures Colet brought to the task of scriptural interpretation an intellectual approach not previously employed in England. From 1492 until 1496, while Fisher was studying traditional material in Cambridge, Colet was in France and Italy, most probably in the company of the champions of the new humanist learning: Marsiglio Ficino (1433-1499), Giovanni Pico della Mirandola (1463-1494) and others.[10] Here, instructed in the tradition of men such as Lorenzo Valla (1407-1457), who had attacked as spurious the *Donation of Constantine* on linguistic grounds, Colet acquired considerable ability in the grammatical method of the Italian humanists. Accordingly, he was able to bring their concern for language and textual structure into the field of scriptural studies.

His concern was to expound the direct meaning of the letters which St Paul had intended originally to communicate to his readers; in his own words, 'All St Paul's sayings must be cautiously examined before any opinion touching his meaning could be given.'[11] So a large part of Colet's work was spent in expounding Paul's figures of speech and to do this he had recourse to images of his own choosing: light to explain the presence of grace in man, fire to explain the power of Christ and the platonic understanding of the universe to explain the structure and working of man's faculties.[12] This platonic or neo-platonic influence was also brought from Italy by Colet and it drew him nearer to the

[8] Reynolds, *op. cit.* p. 56ff.

[9] J. H. Lupton, *The Life of Dean Colet*, (London: George Bell & Sons, 1909.)

[10] F. Seebohm, *The Oxford Reformers*, (London: Longmans, Green & Co. 1887.)

[11] P.A. Duhamel, *The Oxford Letters of John Colet*, *Journal of the History of Ideas*, Vol. XIV. 1953, p. 504.

[12] Duhamel, *op. cit.* p. 502.

sources which had inspired the early Church Fathers.[13] Throughout his exegeses, Colet's choice of image and form is of this tone and he makes no references to the work of the Middle-Ages.[14]

These lectures of Colet have been heralded as 'the turning point in the slow change from Medieval to Renaissance'.[15] However, we must be clear about the correct grounds for such a proclamation. It was not his concern for the literal meaning of the text which set Colet apart from the preceding tradition, since we have seen such evidence suggesting that the literal sense of Scripture was still the predominant concern in the theological studies of the University. Rather the uniqueness of Colet's work was two-fold. First, as we have seen, he was able to bring new abilities to his task: his platonic philosophy and his contact with the early Fathers along with his linguistic and textual proficiency. Even though he knew no Greek, these skills enabled him to achieve new depths in the literal interpretation of the New Testament.[16]

Secondly, Colet is distinguished by the way he used literal interpretation. Up to this time, the literal interpretation of most Scripture, and especially of St Paul, had been used only in a strictly theological context, while the spiritual life of the age was drawn from the spiritual interpretations of the Old Testament, particularly the Psalms and from the Gospel narratives.[17] But Colet applied his literal interpretation of St Paul to the spiritual life of his audience, and so broke new ground. So, for example, whereas Lyra used Romans 5.12 to present basic notions of original sin, original justice, the infinite merit of Christ, the justification by faith of all people alike, and the figure of Christ as the second Adam, Colet uses it to remind his listeners of the horror of sin and of the abiding power of God which is capable of restoring them to a whole and a happy life.[18] He constantly expounds practical 'canons of living' which arise from St Paul's letters descending to many specific points, such as the correct conduct of married life, avoidance of litigations and the importance of women wearing hats in church, but always according to the literal interpretations.

---

[13] Duhamel, *op. cit.* p. 499.

[14] J. Colet, *Treatise on the Seven Sacraments*, ed. J. H. Lupton (London: 1867, reprinted Farnborough: Gregg International Publishers, 1966), p. 44. The year 1488 saw the Paris publication of the works of Dionysius in Latin by Ambrosius, Lupton, p. 41f.

[15] P.R. Adams, *The Better Part of Valour: More, Erasmus, Colet and Vives,* (Seattle: University of Washington Press, 1962) p. 21.

[16] E.W. Hunt, *Dean Colet and his Theology* (London: SPCK, 1956), p. 88.

[17] Lyra in *Glossa Ordinaria*, (Basel,1506-1508) Vol. 6, fol. 12-13.

[18] Duhamel, *op. cit.* p. 502. *Commentary on Romans* in J.H. Lupton, *op. cit. pp.* 141-2

A vivid example of the refreshing impact of this feature of Colet's work is found in one of his letters to Richard Kidderminster. Colet describes a visit he received from a priest who had attended his Oxford lectures. Confessing his great love for the writings of St Paul, the visitor begged Colet to:

> Draw forth something for me now…In this way I may have something both to commit to memory as a result of our sitting here talking together and may also be able, when reading St Paul myself, to catch from you some method of marking and noting down what most deserves to be noted down.

Colet obliged and expounded for him the first chapter of the letter to the Romans, and therein claimed support for his contention that in every part of the Epistles,

> There was a marvellous fertility both of matter and knowledge; so that if a man did but note and carefully consider them, he might, if he chose, draw from almost every word of the Apostle thoughts to be admired and marked.[19]

In this opening up of the theological wealth of the New Testament letters in terms of individual spirituality, Colet does herald a new age. In providing the method for 'marking and noting down what most deserves to be noted down', he presented to the men of his times a whole new source for spiritual growth, a source which we have seen to be lacking. Here Colet began a work which was readily welcomed by many of his contemporaries and which bore fine fruit.

In many other aspects Colet is a more traditional figure, not least in his call for reform throughout the Church.[20] This appeal for reformation is built into his commentaries on the Letters to the Romans and the Corinthians, but its most concerted presentation is in the 1512 Convocation Speech. He first appeals to bishops and priests, for just as the clergy follow the bad example of the Pope, so the laity follows the bad example of the clergy.

> Priests and bishops are the light of the world… if priests and bishops that should be as lights, roam in the dark way of the world, how dark then shall the secular people be? Wherefore Saint Paul said chiefly

---

[19] P.A. Duhamel, *op. cit.* p. 502. J.H. Lupton, *op. cit.* pp. 91-92

[20] For example, Lupton observes that Colet's theological positions on questions such as justification (*Romans,* in *Life of Dean Colet,* pp. 245–8), free will (Romans, in ibid., p. 38), Papal authority (*Two Treatises on the Hierarchies of Dionysius,* in ibid., p. 264), and the Eucharistic presence (*Ennaratio in Epistolam Sancti Pauli ad Corinthios,* in *ibid.,* p. 235) and the Mass as Sacrifice (*Corinthians,* in ibid., p. 242) are orthodox.

> *unto priests and bishops: 'Be ye not conformable to this world but be ye reformed.'[21]*

Having analysed in some detail the causes and manifestations of clerical corruption, he is adamant about his remedy:

> *The clergy and spiritual part once reformed in the Church, then may we with just order proceed to the Reformation of the lay parts; the which truly will be very easy to do, if we first be reformed.[22]*

To achieve this reformation he says there is no need for new laws or institutions, but a real conformity to present laws: 'There are no trespasses but that there be laws against them in the body of Canon Law'.[23] So he launches his great appeal:

> *First let those laws be recited which admonish you, fathers, not to lay your hands on any or admit them to Holy Orders rashly...let the laws be recited which direct that ecclesiastical benefits should be conferred on the worthy...Let the laws be recited which command the personal residence of curates at the churches...concerning your just and canonical election...concerning the residence of bishops in their diocese...[24]*

This confidence in the Church and the desire for law and order has the profound basis that it is the Holy Spirit who is at the heart of the Church, the *causa efficiens* which 'predisposes an object to the proper form'. In these terms the Church is 'informed' by the Holy Spirit.[25] In fact, the Holy Spirit is

> *everywhere, throughout the whole Church, filling and penetrating it in every part by his life-giving power: that he may bind together and consolidate in himself the naturally frail and fleeting members and that things in the Church may be established, governed and moved by the steady upholding of the Spirit.[26]*

So too, the laws of the Church should reflect this influence and, if they are observed, they are sufficient for the good order of the Church:

> *As there is one God, who is our Father, one Christ, who is our Master, one faith, one baptism, one church; so ought there to be one law and principle of living; even the divine canonical law, wherein is contained the rule of Christian life... As for the municipal laws of*

---

[21] Lupton, *op. cit.* p.294. Hunt, *op. cit.* p.22.

[22] *Ibid.* p.302. *Ibid,* p.46.

[23] *Ibid.* p.300. *Ibid,* p.47.

[24] *Ibid.* p.300.

[25] Corinthians, in Lupton, *Life of Dean Colet,* p. 257. Hunt, *Dean Colet and his Theology*, p. 7.

[26] J. Colet, *The Composition of Christ's Mystical Body,* ed. J. H. Lupton (London, 1876), pp. 38–9. Hunt, *Dean Colet and his Theology*, p. 71.

this realm, composed as it is of the absurd decisions of wrangling men, it is scouted and exploded in the Church of God, by virtue of the law of Faith and Love.[27]

Such an appreciation of the Church, such a concern for its good order, such a high expectation from a dutifully observed Canon Law, shows profound similarity with the thoughts and words of John Fisher. Not only does Fisher appeal for a reformation of the clergy in a similar fashion and for a similar motive, but his theological basis for doing so is essentially the same. It was not until six years later that we hear of Fisher's own thoughts on these matters, given in similar circumstances.

Soon after receiving the appointment of cardinal *a latere*, Wolsey called a Synod for an undefined purpose, though the sixteenth century biographer, Van Ortroy, offers his opinion that it was 'to notify to the world his great authority and to be seen sitting in his pontifical seat'.[28] Fisher addressed the assembled clergy in a speech reconstructed by the biographer. He spoke out against the 'ambition and incontinence' of the clergy, condemning the enormous expense wasted on the

wearing of costly apparel, indecent and superfluous raiment, delicate fare and other worldly vanities... For what should we exhort our flocks to eschew and shun worldly ambition, when we ourselves, that be bishops, do wholely set our minds to the same things we forbid in them? What example of Christ our Saviour do we imitate, who first exercised doing and after fell to teaching? If we teach according to our doing, how absurd may our doctrine be accounted? If we teach one thing and do another, our labour in teaching shall never benefit our flock, half so much as our examples in doings shall hurt them.

His bold appeal for reform by the leaders of the Church is then reported:

for he affirmed this kind of disorder to proceed through the example of the head and thereupon reproved his [Wolsey's] pomp putting him in mind that it stood better with the modesty of such pastor as he was, to eschew all worldly vanity, especially in this perilous time, and by humility to make himself conformable and like the image of God.[29]

Fisher had previously expressed similar ideas on reformation, but to a less significant audience, in his Sermons on the *Penitential Psalms.* Preaching on Psalm 102, he asks for prayers for the Church: 'But we take heed and call to mind how many vices reign now a days in Christ's

---

[27] *Corinthians,* in Lupton, *Life of Dean Colet,* pp. 144-157.

[28] Van Ortroy, *Vie,* Vol. X, p. 255.

[29] *Ibid.,* pp. 255-259.

Church, as well as in the clergy as in the common people.'[30] Only repentance and reformation among the clergy would give the necessary foundation for total renewal and a good Church structure.

> *All fear of God, also the contempt of God cometh and is grounded of the clergy, for if the clergy be well and rightfully ordered giving good example to other of virtuous living, without doubt the people by that shall have more fear of almighty God.*

It is on Christ the cornerstone that we must build and not, as was being done, on the patterns of the Old Law. The glory of the Church 'standeth not in silk, copes of divers colours and craftily embroidered, neither in plate of gold or silver nor any other works of ornament'. These, says Fisher, are the foreshadowing in the Old Law of the things to come: 'The thing that was signified in the Old Law by gold is cleanness of conscience, and by precious stones virtues of souls.' He continues, 'In that time were no chalices of gold, but then were many golden priests, now be many chalices of gold and almost no golden priests.'[31] So he concludes with a prayer that God would send holy ministers to his Church that like a ship in stormy weather she may not be driven backwards, but move toward God, and by drawing all people to herself, bring them to the eternal pleasures of heaven.[32] A more detailed exposition of Fisher's theology will show that he had the same source of confidence and hope for the Church as John Colet. It is the Spirit of Christ who animates the Church and is, therefore, the guarantee of her progress.

The manifest similarities between Colet and Fisher which have emerged in this matter of ecclesiastical reform can be seen to include also the remedies proposed by both men. Having pointed to clerical inadequacies as the source of the trouble, both men looked to the promotion of greater learning and piety as the cure. While Fisher concentrated on later education, Colet's reform programme started with the youth. To this end, together with the reorganisation of St Paul's cathedral, he founded St Paul's School.[33]

Though not intended directly for clerical students, the school was designed as a centre for Christian humanist learning, for the promotion of

---

[30] 'Treatyse concerning the fruyfulsayynges of David the king and prophets in the seven penytencyall psalms. Devyded in seven sermons', printed by Wykyn de Worde in 1509 under the patronage of Lady Margaret. Available in Early English Text Society, ed. J. E. B. Mayor, Extra Series XXVII, pp. 1–267, (henceforth referred to as *PS. 102).*

[31] *PS.* 102, pp. 179, 180, 181. This is probably a quotation from Savanarola, Advent Sermon XXIII. See P. Villari, *Life and Times of Giordano Savanarola,* (London: 1896) p. 184. How this came to Fisher's knowledge is not at all clear; possibly by means of Colet.

[32] *PS.* 102, p.198.

[33] Hunt, *op. cit.* p. 50ff.

those studies which had contributed so much to Colet's own spirituality. The teaching of good Latin was to be emphasised above all else; the Latin of 'Tully and Salust and Virgil and Terence' which was the Latin of 'Saint Jerome and Saint Ambrose and Saint Augustine and many holy doctors learned in their times'. Through these studies Colet intended 'to increase knowledge and worshipping of God and our Lord Christ Jesus and good Christian life and manners in all children.'[34]

Fisher's contribution to this reformation programme centred on the University at Cambridge and consisted initially in a campaign for improved standards of preaching. As Vice-Chancellor, in 1502 he obtained a Papal Bull granting the University the privilege of appointing

> *twelve doctors, masters or graduates who shall be in priests orders, to preach throughout the whole Kingdom of England, Scotland and Ireland under the common seal of the University without any other license from a bishop.*[35]

Two years later, as Chancellor, he was instrumental in directing the enthusiasm of Lady Margaret into founding a Preachership in the University, to complement her Readership in Divinity which had finally been established in 1503. On October 30, 1504, the Preacher foundation was established by which a Fellow of the University, a Doctor or Bachelor in Theology, holding no other benefice, was to be appointed by the Vice-Chancellor and Masters of the Colleges to give twelve yearly sermons in London and the surrounding villages.[36]

What were Fisher's hopes in this drive for better learning? What was the style and standard of preaching at which he was aiming? The only indication of an answer available to us is Fisher's own preaching, which he would undoubtedly deny to be exemplary. Yet the sixteenth century biography leaves us these comments:

> *He was also a very diligent preacher and notablest in all this realm, both in his time and before or since, as well as for his excellent learning as also for edifying [his] audience and moving the affections of his hearers to cleave to God and goodness, to embrace virtue and to flee sin.*[37]

---

[34] Lupton, *op. cit.* pp. 279–80. Hunt, *op. cit.* pp. 2–17.

[35] Reynolds, *op. cit.* p. 17.

[36] C. H. Cooper, *Annals of Cambridge* (Cambridge, Warwick & Co, 1842), Vol. I, pp. 272–3. The places were these: in London at St Paul's Cross or St Margaret's, Westminster; at Ware and Cheshunt in Hertfordshire, St James Deeping; Bourn, Boston and Swineshead in Lincolnshire; and at Bassinbourn, Orwell and Babraham in Cambridgeshire.

[37] Van Ortroy, *Vie*; *op. cit.* Vol. XII, pp. 269–70.

Significantly, the largest corpus of his non-polemical writings which have been preserved are his Sermons on the Penitential Psalms given in 1504 and printed 1509. So if we are going to attempt to appreciate the aims of Fisher's preaching reforms through his own works, then these sermons on the Psalms must form the basis of our study.

From the outset one point is clear. The choice of subject matter for these sermons is the first of many of their features which show them to be radically similar to the general style of contemporary spiritual writing, examples of which we have already examined. Closer examination and comparison will reveal the detailed similarities, but the choice of the Psalms is significant in itself. They were popular ground for the spiritual writers of the age and concentrated on the *Penitential Psalms* and gave precise opportunities for the development of one of the most popular medieval themes, that of repentance for sin.

In the course of these sermons Fisher comments on the Psalms line by line, following the text as closely as possible. His commentary is wholly spiritual and he applies the Psalms, phrase by phrase, to the life of the sinner as he strives for repentance. Only once does he draw attention to the literal meaning or context and that is at the very beginning of the very first sermon, on Psalm 6 when, attributing the Psalm to David, he observes: 'Now you understand who made this psalm, what occasion caused him to write it and what profit he gave by the same.'[38] Thereafter his analysis and application of each Psalm is directly to the theme of repentance and forgiveness.[39] So many characteristics similar to the devotional literature of the period become manifest: exclusive concern for the doctrine of contrition, confession and satisfaction, emphasis on the mercy and kindness of God and hope offered to all, emphasis on the sacraments of the Church as the means to salvation and a very typical abhorrence of sensual excesses.

Contrition, confession and satisfaction are defined in contemporary ways:

> *Contrition is none other but an inward sorrow of the mind set in the private place of the heart which needs must go before confession made by mouth for truly confession without contrition had before profiteth very little or nothing.*[40]

Satisfaction is portrayed in terms of almsgiving, fasting and prayer and the whole process of forgiveness is understood in terms of the sacrament.

[38] *PS*, 6, p.7.
[39] The structure of each Psalm is given e.g. *PS*, 32 pp. 27-28.
[40] *PS*, 130, p. 211 ff.

> *The great authority to forgive sin is left amongst us in the Church*
> *of Christ and the same power given to priests that they by that*
> *authority may absolve every true penitent and forgive all their sins*
> *which is authorised by the words written in Christ's law 'whosoever*
> *sins you remit, they are remitted'.*[41]

God calls us constantly to repent and be forgiven, 'shall we not give credence to almighty God', for even if we waver in our promises God does not.[42] This message of hope is the motivation behind all his attention to sin, for:

> *without which [hope] everything that we do is of no value, for let us*
> *never so much wail and sorrow our sins, confess them to never so*
> *many priests and last study to purge them by as much satisfaction as*
> *we can, all these profit nothing without hope.*[43]

The example of the forgiveness received by the great sinners of the past is offered as testimony that God does provide the forgiveness that we need.[44]

In this search for forgiveness, humility and sincerity, acknowledging our sins are required on our part, but it is the Church who assures us that the promises of God will reach us, for 'the Church of God may in no ways beguile in these things that longeth to our faith and to the undoubtfull health of our souls.'[45] The persons of the Holy Spirit and of Christ are in the Church and consequently the sacraments of the Church are more than empty signs. They have a 'private and hidden virtue given unto them by the merit of the passion of Jesus Christ', and the receiver of the sacrament is 'sprinkled with the drips of the same most holy blood whose virtue pierces to the soul and maketh it clean from all sin.'[46] It is quite evident that at this first popular level of writing, Fisher's theology of the Church is close to that of the 'parish theologian'. The spiritual value of the Church lies in her as a provider of the sacraments; by these means can the sinner come into contact with Christ, receive forgiveness and be brought to salvation.

Contemporary spirituality clearly played a major role in the writing of these sermons and it is difficult to trace any influences of the academic

---

[41] *PS*, 130, p .220.
[42] *Ibid.*, p. 222.
[43] *PS*, 38, p.81.
[44] *PS*, 6, p. 17. & 38, p. 8, *et al.*
[45] *PS*, 51, p.108.
[46] *Ibid.*, p. 110.

world of John Fisher.[47] The analogy of the sprinkled blood is continued with the statement that the hyssop of Psalm 51 is a foreshadowing of the sacraments; for the hyssop, which is a hot sweet herb, is a figure of Christ as the loving victim offered to God. This rather striking analogy is found in the *Glossa Ordinaria*, but on the whole there is little correlation of interpretation between the Gloss and Fisher's work.[48] In his commentaries, Lyra gives a consistently literal interpretation of the Psalms, with only the occasional remark that *moraliter* an application to the sinner can be made. On these occasions, a similarity with Fisher becomes apparent as, for example, when commenting on vv. 13 and 21 of Psalm 102, Fisher offers his interpretation of 'Sinai', 'Zion' and 'Jerusalem' as: 'Sinai' indicating the Jews under the Old Law; 'Zion' the Christian people in the time of grace and 'Jerusalem' as 'the blessed people in time of glory'. Lyra had commented that 'the sinner, who is in the Church will be named in Sion and listed in Jerusalem', but he developed it no further.[49] Fisher's interpretation of the three birds of Psalm 102 (the pelican, night raven and sparrow) to signify contrition, confession and satisfaction, while in keeping with the tenor of the times, is not found in any of the earlier commentaries.[50]

What is more, in these sermons Fisher makes no attempt to base doctrinal exposition on a literal study only, since his efforts are directed at devotion and not dogmatic speculation. He outlines his principle of interpretation when dealing with Psalm 51. The *spiritum rectum* (upright spirit), *spiritum sanctum* (holy spirit) and *spiritum principalem* (free spirit)in verses 10 to 12 he interprets as three presentations of the Holy Spirit, similar to the 'dove', 'breath' and 'fire' of the New Testament. He explains that where the author's meaning is uncertain, it is lawful to apply any interpretation as long as it is not contrary to other places in Scripture: 'But for as much as it is lawful for every clerk in any such doubts to show their minds not contradicting other places of Scripture I shall in few words declare (it seems to me) what he means.'[51] Again and again he returns to the theme of the forgiveness of sin, even by the most diverse routes as, for example, when he is giving an outline theology of Mary. He presents Mary as the 'morning light' which, although it comes before the sun and announces its rising, is in fact caused by the sun.

---

[47] Other images and analogies used by Fisher are found in contemporary writings: penance described as a triple process of washing (PS 51, p. 98) and as being similar to sprinkling with hyssop (PS 51, p.110).

[48] *Glossa Ordinaria*, (Basel: 1506-1508) Vol. III, on Psalm 50. Vulgate, fol. 181.

[49] *Ibid.,* fol. 236.

[50] *PS*, 102, p.151.

[51] *PS*, 50, pp.115-118.

Mary is therefore a great help for sinners as they seek to dispel from their hearts the darkness of sin.

In this context of simplicity of spirit, only occasionally do we have glimpses of any academic method. Again when speaking of Mary and of the relationship between night and day, Fisher remarks 'this order agrees both to nature, scripture and reason', which was the pattern of much academic theology. A Thomistic influence emerges when he observes 'understanding must be guided by the will, and the will must be ruled by reason, for the will is the middle part between understanding and reason.'[52]

The general pattern of these sermons, then, shows that they have been formed under the influence of contemporary traditional spiritual writings. The elements of theme, treatment, style and language reflect closely the pastorally orientated sermons and handbooks of the age which we have already examined. The continual application of the Psalms to one major theme, which is the conversion from sin, shows Fisher's reliance in these works at least upon the basic truths of religious experience which comes much more from the initial influences of his life in childhood and parish, than from the time of his prolonged study.

However, the fruits of these years of academic study are shown most noticeably in these sermons by Fisher's command of the Scriptural and Patristic sources. In the course of these sermons, excluding the continual reference to the text of the Psalms themselves, he gives some 160 quotations from Scripture; of which 40 are from the Old Testament, 60 from the Gospels and 60 from other New Testament writings. He occasionally uses whole biblical incidents or gospel parables as illustrations.[53] St Augustine is quoted ten times, St Jerome four times, John Chrysostom three times and Anselm, William of Auvergne, Aquinas, Origen, Cicero, Plato, Ovid and Demosthenes once or twice each. Compared to the intensive systematic quoting of authorities to be found in his apologetical works this is an insignificant collection, but it illustrates how readily Fisher was able to use these sources. But such knowledge and scholarship is lightly carried; he keeps his work simple and his concern deeply pastoral.

The funeral sermons for King Henry VII and Lady Margaret Beaufort which were given in May and July 1509 provide additional

---

[52] *PS*, 38, pp. 46, 48 and 62-63.

[53] For example, the Good Shepherd image is used in *PS*, 102, p. 141. The Prodigal Son in *PS*, 142, p. 232, and the story of Jonah in *PS*, 130, p.200.

material of a traditional style and content.[54] At Henry's funeral he spoke fearlessly about the luxury and worldliness of Henry's life in order to give emphasis to his main point that Henry was an example to us all since he died confessing his sins, asking God for pardon with great hope in his heart. Further,

> the cause of this hope was the true belief that he had in God, in his Church and in the sacraments thereof, which he received all with marvellous devotion, namely the sacrament of penance, the sacrament of the altar and the sacrament of anointing.[55]

Learning from his example, all were exhorted to pray for the King for, despite his piety, no one could be certain of salvation without special revelation. With due humility, however, comfort can be gained from the knowledge of God's great mercy.[56]

This same assertion is repeated at the Lady Margaret's funeral, where Fisher spent much more time recounting her virtuous life, and the great reasons there were for lamenting her death. Even here absolute certainty of salvation cannot be had and reliance must be placed upon the promises of Christ, in which she had full faith: 'Every person that putteth their full trust in Christ Jesus, albeit they be dead in their body, yet shall they nevertheless have life that never shall end.'[57] This distinctive late medieval flavour is found in all Fisher's remaining spiritual writings. From 1520 we have two sermons for the Feast of All Saints. The first of these centres on Matthew 5.20, 'unless your rightwise life be more abundant than was the living of the Scribes and Pharisees you shall not enter the Kingdom of Heaven', and using a vivid description of the Field of Cloth of Gold emphasises the transitory nature of earthly joy, its inadequacies when compared to the joy of heaven and the need for forgiveness through contrition, confession and satisfaction.[58]

The *De Necessitate Orandi* of 1521 is similarly of the traditional concern for the growth of the individual's relationship with God.[59] An undated sermon for Good Friday is notable for its long and strained analogy between the crucified Christ and a manuscript book and, together with the analogy in Psalm 51 of man's dependence on God compared to a man suspended by a slender cord over a deep pit, forms

[54] These are edited by J. E. B. Mayor and published in the same volume of the EETS as the Sermons on the Psalms, Extra Series no. XXVII, pp. 268–310.

[55] Henry Sermon, *ibid.,* p. 273.

[56] *Ibid.,* pp. 277, 281

[57] Margaret Sermon, *ibid.* pp. 291-308.

[58] This sermon was printed by W. Rastell in 1532. It is substantially reported by Reynolds, *Roper and Harpsfield: Lives of Thomas More*, pp. 80–5.

[59] E. Surtz, *The Works and Days of John Fisher* (Massachusetts: Harvard Univ. Press, 1967) p. 291.

the climax of Fisher's use of analogies.[60] Two spiritual works written while awaiting death in the Tower treat similar themes. The *Spiritual Consolation* is based upon a meditation on death, and the *Ways to Perfect Religion* was written 'to the health of your souls and the furtherance of it in holy religion'.[61] Both works were written for Elizabeth White, a half-sister to John Fisher, and they both express the same preoccupation with traditional religious belief and practice.

In conclusion then, the writings of John Fisher, which are not concerned with the defence of the Church, show great affinity to the traditional preaching and spirituality of the age. Repentance for sin, hope and trust in the mercy of God, humility, sincerity and recourse to the sacraments of the Church were his enduring themes. The knowledge and scholarship of Fisher are here displayed, but they are totally in the service of these simple traditional beliefs. In these works Fisher is relaxed and not concerned about controversy; he was writing for the love of his subject, and the spirituality and piety shown to be his love were shared by the majority of his contemporaries and predecessors.

We may conclude speculatively but not irresponsibly that Fisher's encouragement of renewed preaching was aimed at sermons and writings such as these. In urging better preaching we have nothing to suggest that Fisher was in search of something new. Rather, the traditional Catholic doctrine and piety were to be preached with greater fervour and with greater learning. Fisher's strength lay here, in his knowledge of the Scriptures and the Latin Fathers, and his drive for better preaching was directed at increasing the command over these sources by the preacher of the day. Much of his subsequent effort, therefore, was aimed at promoting greater learning.

In 1505 and 1506 Fisher was involved with the reformation and reshaping of God's House into Christ's College.[62] This process was largely the work of Lady Margaret, but came under the guidance of Fisher and John Syclyng, Master of God's House, who was possibly a close acquaintance of Fisher. New Statutes were drawn up and, while it is impossible to know their exact contributions, Fisher and Syclyng must have borne the lion's share of this work. The Statutes which they

---

[60] John Fisher, *Treatyse concerning the fruitful sayinges of Davyd the kynge and prophete in the seven penytencyall psalms. Devyded in seven sermons.* Copies are held in the Bodleian Library of Oxford, the Rylands Library of Manchester and the J.E.B. Mayor (1825-1910) collection donated to St John's, Cambridge. Available in the E.E.T.S. Extra Series. XXVII, pp. 1-267.

[61] Mayor, p. 364.

[62] Reynolds, *op. cit.* M. Macklem. *God Have Mercy.* (Oberon Press: Ottawa. 1967) , pp. 18–19. A. H. Lloyd, *The Early History of Christ's College* (Cambridge University Press, 1934), ch. XVI, p. 280ff.

produced were formal according to the model of the existing God's House Statutes; and many aspects of these new Statutes, such as the provision for college lectures and for the study of the poets and orators of antiquity, that were sometimes heralded as innovations were taken from the former Statutes. In fact, the only novel clause added at this time was a single clause forbidding any master or fellow to ask for a papal dispensation to over-ride the Statutes agreed by the Founder.

The year 1510 saw Fisher involved again in the life of Christ's College. In that year he came to the College as the official Visitor, whose task it was to examine the life of the College and to draw up a report making any necessary suggestions. His report has been preserved, and displays in detail some of his concerns as an educationalist.[63] In his report, Fisher first reminds Peter Thompson, Master of Christ's College, of his obligations: 'We commend that you apply diligently the injunctions written above, equally in conformity with your sworn promise made some time ago', and gives him the following instructions: Latin is to be used at all times, except where specified in the Statutes; half yearly accounts are to be rendered to the company of Fellows; a total inventory is to be submitted within eight days; three chests and a common chest are to be established and a close record of all transactions involving College treasures must be maintained. Further, the gates must be closed every night; Fellows showing negligence in chapel attendance must be fined and no dogs were to be kept in the College. All students were to take the oath of admission, and scholars were to fulfil their required residency, and students' dress was to conform to the Statutes. Finally, 'the Statutes should be read annually, according to the wishes of our founder, and that true copies of them should be affixed with a chain of iron to the stalls inside the chapel.' Three quarters of these instructions were reinforcing the original Statutes which may indicate that a certain laxity had entered the life of the College. The provisions did not escape Fisher's attentiveness to detail. Those concerning the establishment of chests, the restrictions placed on the Master by making him accountable to the Fellows and the forbidding of dogs were Fisher's own contribution, the instructions against the autonomy of the Master possibly arising from his experience at Michaelhouse.

The joint evidence of the original statutes and the Visitor's report furnish us with clear indications of Fisher's attitude to education. Both documents show his insistence on good administration and disciplined

---

[63] Taken from the Founder Chest of St John's College by Baker in his *Cambridge Manuscripts*, Vol. 8, f. 92-3.

student life. These appear to be his primary concern and later evidence confirms this impression. Only when a stable institution has been established would Fisher turn to matters of the curriculum and of innovation.

Lady Margaret had died in 1509, and her papers left provision for the founding of a further College in Cambridge and it fell to Fisher and the other executors of her will to realise her wishes.[64] The story of the struggle to bring St John's College to birth has been well narrated and one comment of Fisher's is sufficient to create the right impression: 'Forsooth it was sore laborious and painful unto me that many times I was right sorry that ever I took that business upon me.'[65] Even though the final transactions were not completed until as late as 1522, the College was formally opened in July 1516 and Robert Shorton was designated to be its first Master. His capable management undoubtedly saved Fisher much time and anxiety and, as recognition of his ability, Wolsey later appointed him as the first Master of his new College in Oxford.[66]

The Statutes were drawn up by Fisher in 1516, 1524 and 1530; more than any other single item they give precise detail of his ideas on education and learning, since in forming them he was given complete autonomy. His first concern, as with Christ's College, was for the good administration of the College. Accordingly provision was laid down for the governing of the College to be in the hands of the Master who, on important issues, acted with the advice of the senior Fellows. Two bursars were responsible for finance and two deans for discipline; provision was made for a steward, a manciple (one who buys provisions), cooks, a servant for the Master, a porter, a barber and a laundress. The College was to run as efficiently as possible with a minimum of interruptions to the study. The purpose of the College was clearly expressed, 'The worship of God, uprightness of life and the strengthening of the Christian faith'[67], and the pattern of life laid down was aimed at inculcating the discipline and dedication of scholarship. Fellows and scholars were to rise at dawn and the gates were to be locked at dusk. They were not to leave the College save for lectures and instructions and then always in company. No woman was allowed to enter the College except to nurse the sick and, even though fellowship was open to a small number of

---

[64] E. Miller, *Portrait of a College* (Cambridge University Press, 1961), pp. 1–15. B. Mullinger, *The University of Cambridge from the Earliest Times to the Royal Injunction of 1535* (Cambridge University Press, 1873), pp. 61–71. Reynolds, *op. cit.* pp. 49–55. M. Macklem. *God Have Mercy*. (Oberon Press: Ottawa, 1967) pp. 27–34.

[65] Reynolds, *op. cit.* p. 50.

[66] J.E. Paul, *Catherine of Aragon and Her Friends*, (London: Burns, Oates, 1966) p. 90.

[67] *Dei cultus, morum probitas et Christianae fidei corroboratio.*

medical students as well as the clergy, marriage and fellowship were incompatible. Daily Mass, morning and evening prayer and daily Bible reading in the hall were considered as important as lectures, and scholars were to be fined or even whipped for absenteeism.[68]

It was specifically laid down that poor candidates for places as scholars should be given preference over richer, and over half the students were to come from the northern counties, although not more than two were allowed from the same county at any given time. The provision of accommodation meant that most Fellows shared a room with one or two scholars, but this too was given a disciplinary and educational dimension, for Fisher ordered that:

> *the elder should advise their younger chamber-mates, giving them*
> *good encouragement and show them good example, instruct them in*
> *discipline, draw their attention to repeated trespasses and misdoings*
> *and, if necessary, report them…to the master, president or deacons.*[69]

The members of St John's College grew from an original small number of scholars to 35 in 1518 and to 52 in 1519, when the complement of the Lady Margaret foundation was established at 28 Fellows and 22 scholars. By 1545, private foundations added 16 Fellows and 36 scholars, giving a total residence of 152.

For Fisher, efficient administration and strict discipline were the criteria of a good educational establishment. Drawing on his long experience in the University, Fisher did all in his power to ensure that study and prayer were diligently maintained. The distribution of scholars' places indicates the final pastoral orientation of the College; one quarter of the Fellows were continually to be engaged in preaching in English to the people, and there was an underlying assumption that all would depart, sooner or later, into full-time active ministry. E. Miller has observed 'All in all, the college in its beginnings was not only in the main a school of theology; it was a school of practical theology.'[70]

With this close-knit and well administered community established, Fisher also laid down the academic curriculum to be observed. The fundamental education was to be in mathematics, logic and philosophy and it was to be carried out by lectures in the College, reflecting the system of Christ's College. The study of theology which came after qualification in the Arts followed the normal pattern that we have studied: with twice weekly disputations that, with explicit instructions

[68] Miller, *op. cit* pp. 8-11.
[69] *Ibid.* pp. 7-8.
[70] *Ibid.,*

from Fisher, were to start from the writings of Scotus. So far, all was in conformity with traditional medieval patterns, both in life-style and in studies.

In some fields, however, Fisher was pioneering. He ordered that the College was to have a Greek lecturer to teach grammar and literature daily, and Hebrew was to be included in the theology course. In fact, the 1516 Statutes read: 'Let them use no other language than Latin, Greek or Hebrew as long as they are within the precincts of the College, except in their rooms.' The 1524 Statutes lamented the lack of ability in languages, especially in relation to New Testament studies and they reinforce the study of literature, both Latin and Greek. The 1530 Statutes added Chaldaic and Arabic as languages wholly worthy of theologians to study. By 1530, therefore, St John's College had established its reputation as a centre for new linguistic learning, especially in Greek; Robert Pember, John Redman and the famous John Cheke had already been there as lecturers in Greek.[71]

Such advances into the realm of the New Learning may seem somewhat alien to John Fisher who has appeared to be thoroughly traditional in his spirituality, preaching and educational reforms. How do these two factors find reconciliation? What exactly is the real need for reconciliation, or where do the new linguistic studies, as demonstrated in practice by Colet, conflict with traditional ideals? Richard Croke was installed as Greek lecturer at St John's in 1519 and a report of his inaugural address gives us a clear account of Fisher's mind at the time:

> *What then is the message of my Lord of Rochester? Why he exhorts them to apply themselves with all diligence to the study of Greek literature...The exhortation of one who had never urged them to aught but what was most profitable, might alone suffice; but it has been especially enjoined upon the speaker to explain in detail the advantage of Greek literature...The utility of Greek in connection with the trivium and quadrivium having been thus vindicated, he [Croke] passes on to theology. He begs in the first place that they will not consider him to be, like many men of his school, a foe to theological learning. He loves Mayronius, he admires Erigen, he esteems Aquinas and the subtlety of Scotus he actually embraces; he only desiderates that culture which imparts brilliancy to the rest. Let them only add to the study of these authors the cultivation of Greek and Latin literature and learn to speak in such a fashion that their diction may recall the city and youth of Rome... For his own part, he had no wish to see the disputations of the schools abolished but he did not like to see men growing old in them: for subtleties like these*

---

[71] Surtz, *Works and Days*, p. 137. Miller, *Portrait of a College*, p. 12.

110

> *were harmful not to those who studied them for a time but for those who were continually engaged in them. When the mind was thus exclusively concentrated on extremely minute distinctions its powers were wasted and impaired and the student was diverted from more useful learning, from the Pauline epistles, from the Evangelists, from the whole Bible; and these had a paramount claim on the theologian whose true function it was to guide the minds of men as to draw them away from things of earth and fix them on those above.*[72]

Certainly the establishment of Greek learning in England was only slowly achieved, but it received every encouragement from Fisher.[73] As is here revealed, Fisher saw the findings of the New Learning as capable of making a significant and essential contribution to biblical studies and not at all in conflict with much traditional theology. R. Weiss concluded that such a utilitarian conception of the humanities included

> *its compromise and subordination to medieval culture rather than antagonism with it... Indeed it may be stated that the English learning at the end of the Reformation included the best characteristics of humanism and scholasticism.*[74]

Further J.H. McConica has commented:

> *Without leaving the broad tradition of medieval Christendom these people dreamed of a simplification of doctrine and reform of practice, especially through an infusion of humanist views into the aridities of the late fifteenth century controversy. Among such sponsors of this movement were Colet, More and Fisher in England.*[75]

Fisher consequently did all in his power to incorporate the new studies into the syllabus of St John's College. This was not a revolutionary innovation in its conception, for Fisher set out to bring the New Learning into the service of the old faith, hoping that exegesis and scriptural interpretation would thereby be enlightened. The crisis of authority which came about in the following years with its essential basis in the New Learning cannot have been foreseen by Fisher. His reaction to conflict once it was joined is evidence of that.

It is a measure of his confidence that linguistic studies were for the fruitful service of the Catholic Church that he went to pains not only to ensure that others were adequately equipped, but also to become

---

[72] Mullinger, *The University of Cambridge,* pp. 529–37. In a note he says that 'this very rare little volume' was found in the library of Prof. J. E. B. Mayor.

[73] A. Tilley, *Greek Studies in England in the Early Sixteenth Century, English Historical Review,* LIII. (1938) pp. 221-239 & 438-456.

[74] Weiss, R. *Humanism in England in the Fifteenth Century* (Oxford: Blackwell, 1937), p. 182.

[75] J. H. McConica, *English Humanists and Reformation Politics* (Oxford: Clarendon Press, 1965), p. 2.

proficient in Greek himself. While Fisher was host to Erasmus at the house in Rochester in August, 1516, and despite Erasmus' reluctance to stay, Fisher began then to study the Greek of the *Novum Instrumentum*.[76] Soon after this, both Erasmus and More were trying to persuade Hugh Latimer (1485-1555) to continue the tutoring of John Fisher in Greek. They met with no success, but in spite of this Fisher made progress.[77] Writing to Erasmus a year later about the *Novum Instrumentum*, Fisher says:

> *The New Testament translated by you for the common benefit of all cannot give offense to any wise person; when you have not only cleared up innumerable passages by your erudition but have also supplied a very complete commentary of the whole work; so that it may now be better read and understood by everyone than it would before. But I very much fear the printer has been often napping; for in practising the reading of St Paul according to the rules you laid down, I have myself often found that Greek expressions and often entire sentences are omitted. I have you to thank that I am to some extent able to guess where the Greek does not quite correspond with the Latin. I only wish I had been permitted to have you for a few months as a teacher.*[78]

Later that year, Erasmus sent Fisher a pre-publication copy of Theodore of Gaza's book of Greek grammar, translated and annotated by Erasmus, with the comment that 'the version is sufficiently explicit and you must not be put out by some mistakes made by the boy who has copied it'.[79] From his work it appears that Fisher acquired at least a working knowledge of the language.

About this time, 1516 and 1517, Fisher also gave some time to learning Hebrew with the help of Robert Wakefield. He used *De Arte Caballistica* by Johannes Reuchlin (1455-1522) as his text book.[80] This also had been sent to him by Erasmus and was the beginning of a lasting friendship between Fisher and the author. He makes minimal use of the Hebrew text in his writings and we may surmise that his efforts here were less successful than those at the Greek language.[81]

[76] P. S. Allen, *Opus Epistolarum*, Vol. V, Ep. 1489, p. 536. Colet also began to learn Greek at this time. Allen, Vol. II, Ep. 471, p. 351.

[77] P. S. Allen, *Opus Epistolarum*, Vol. II, Ep. 468, p.347; Ep. 520, p. 438; Ep. 540, p. 485. Nichols, *The Epistles of Erasmus*, Vol. III, Ep. 734, pp. 236–40.

[78] Nichols, *The Epistles of Erasmus*, Vol. II, Ep. 568, pp. 569–71. Allen, *Opus Epistolarum*, Vol. II, Ep. 592, p. 598.

[79] Nichols, Vol. III, Ep. 625, p. 41. Allen, Vol. III, Ep. 563, p. 75.

[80] Surtz, *op. cit.* pp. 144–8.

[81] Allen, *Opus Epistolarum*, Vol. III, Ep. 653, p. 75; Vol. II, Ep. 324, pp. 49–50. Nichols, *The Epistles of Erasmus*, Vol. II, Ep. 446, p. 373. Also Reynolds, *Roper and Harpsfield: Lives of Thomas More*, p. 47.

The friendship between John Fisher and Erasmus clearly centred upon the linguistic studies of the New Testament. Fisher invited Erasmus to Cambridge in 1511 to promote Greek learning, and the gradual emergence of the first and subsequent editions of the *Novum Instrumentum* were the occasions for more contact between them. Fisher not only encouraged Erasmus in his work, but also acted as a mediator between Erasmus and his English critics, especially Edward Lee, later Archbishop of York.[82] So great was Erasmus' appreciation of Fisher's contribution that he originally intended to dedicate the work to him, but characteristically decided that a dedication to Pope Leo X was more expedient.[83] For the most part contact between Fisher and Erasmus was maintained by letter, for their last meeting appears to have been in April, 1517, at least Fisher's letters retain their original warm affection to the end.[84] One moment of particular association occurred in 1512 when Fisher invited Erasmus to accompany him personally to attend the Fifth Lateran Council. A summons to Parliament made the journey impossible, but who can fail to speculate what the mutual effect of such a prolonged companionship might have been?[85]

Fisher also urged Erasmus to support him in his campaign for better preaching, but it was only after Fisher's death that the *Ecclesiastes* of Erasmus, started at the instigation of the bishop, was eventually finished. The aim of this work certainly would have met with Fisher's approval, for Erasmus maintains that preaching and teaching are the primary work of the priest and he can be prepared to do it well.[86] Other points made by Erasmus too would have had the full support of Fisher: that a preacher must live a good moral life, for preaching without the support of practice is empty; that he must be educated in the knowledge of Scripture and classical literature, and be able to use rhetorical devices with due proportion. Thus Erasmus urges the use of an *exordium*, or opening piece containing a striking figure; a technique that had often been employed by Fisher, and the use of Scripture in its literal and allegorical interpretation.[87]

[82] Macklem, *God Have Mercy*, p. 33. Reynolds, *op. cit.* pp. 38–48. Allen. Vol. IV. Ep. 1068, p. 191.

[83] Allen, *Opus Epistolarum*, Vol. IV, Ep. 413, p. 244. Nichols, *The Epistles of Erasmus*, Vol.II, Ep. 400, p. 269.

[84] Reynolds, *op. cit.* p. 45.

[85] Allen, *Opus Epistolarum*, Vol. I, Ep. 252, p. 498. Nichols, *The Epistles of Erasmus*, Vol II, Ep. 242, p. 58.

[86] R.H. Bainton, *Erasmus of Christendom*, (London: Collins. 1970.) p. 323.

[87] Erasmus, *Ecclesiastes I; Ecclesiastes II*, xxx, pp. 215–17; *Ecclesiastes III*. J.W. Blench, *Preaching in England in the Late Fifteenth and Sixteenth Centuries* (Oxford: Blackwell, 1964), pp. 28, 120, 212. Also C. Bene, *Erasme et S. Augustin* (Geneva, 1969), pp. 383, 400.

We must be cautious in drawing too strong an inference from this similarity between Erasmus and John Fisher, for the *Ecclesiastes* is not representative of most of Erasmus' writings. It has been described as the work 'of a mind fatigued which no longer sharply reacts upon the needs of the times' and it does not truly reflect the spirit of the *philosophia Christi* which was the hallmark of the Erasmian movement. This *philosophia Christi* consists in: 'the centrality of Christ found through the Bible, especially the Gospels, without reference to the dogmatic definitions of scholasticism or to many of the popular forms of piety which had developed in Catholicism.'[88] This definition is clearly unsuited to Fisher's spirituality, but it accurately details the main elements of the movement in which Erasmus immersed himself. It was this which drew him to look for peace and tranquillity rather than the cut and thrust of theological debate.

However, it was not any deep desire for a close knowledge of Christ that distinguishes Erasmus and Fisher, but rather the manner of that search. For Erasmus that search led to a new style of spirituality: as well as to other consequences of which he was never absolutely certain. For Erasmus, traditional piety had to be replaced by the simple profundity of the Scriptures, by a return to the origins. He was truly the 'biblical humanist' and the spirituality of the *Enchiridion* offered a stern and practical guide to living in the world, well suited to the needs of the non-cleric. In contrast, the traditional Catholic piety and doctrine of John Fisher were not structured first of all on the needs of the person who was immersed in the world and conscious of its goodness. The traditional presentation of the love and forgiveness of God drew men away from the world almost by way of compensation, and was monastic in essence. It tended to hold marriage and any form of lay life as a compromise and inferior.[89] This abhorrence of and dislike for the world lay at the root of the failure of the Medieval Church to provide a spirituality suitable for the committed layman. Fisher's search for 'piety of heart and mind', 'personal conviction' and 'loving kindness', despite being revitalised by his learning, was essentially traditional and did not meet those needs in the way that Erasmus' work did.

Secondly, differences emerge between Fisher and Erasmus in the latter's anti-dogmatic instinct.

---

[88] B. Hall, 'Erasmus: Biblical Scholar and Reformer', in T. A. Dorey (ed.), Erasmus (London: Routledge and Kegan Paul, 1970), p. 81.
[89] McConica, *English Humanists and Reformation Politics*, p. 22.

> *The essential theme of the philosophia Christi was marked by the anti-scholastic, anti-dogmatic and anti-speculative habit of mind and by a marked distrust of it, if not positive rejection of, much of the theology of the schools, whether Thomist, Scotist or Occamist.*[90]

This mistrust of theology resulted in Erasmus avoiding dogmatic conflicts, for he saw such employment as a turning away from the simplicity of Christ's teaching in the Scriptures. This alone was his goal, and the peace and tranquillity required to achieve it was to be preserved at almost any cost.

For John Fisher, on the other hand, life was different. He understood the connection between revealed truth and dogma, and because of this he saw the need to defend the dogmatic teaching of the Catholic Church. By upbringing and training Fisher was a man of the Church. As a bishop every other desire was subordinate to his duty to serve the Church and he often explained that it was his responsibility as a bishop to defend the teaching of the Church publicly with all his ability. This leaves us with a suspicion that had such a responsibility not been his, then very much like Erasmus, he would have chosen to maintain the peace and tranquillity in which to follow his profound instincts, leaving dogmatic fields to those who wished to occupy them. That, however, is conjecture. The facts are that Fisher was a bishop and that from 1519 he was deeply involved in theological controversy.

Fisher's work as promoter of the humanist New Learning did not stop. He continued to promote Greek studies and New Testament learning in Cambridge, especially at St John's. Yet even here we have a final indication that these interests of Fisher were thoroughly subordinate to the service of his deep-seated Catholicism with its accompanying dogmatic concerns. In the 1530 Statutes of St John's, Fisher makes an interesting alteration. He prescribes that if the study of Hebrew is being found to be unprofitable, then a Fellow may change to a more profitable one; for example, the theology of Duns Scotus.[91] While this may be indicative of Fisher's own experience with Hebrew studies, it is also significant that, as the heat of controversy rises, Fisher returns to emphasise traditional theological values.

Throughout his working life, Fisher was a reformer. He attentively observed the needs of the times and strove to meet them as best he could. His efforts for a renewal of preaching in the parishes came as a response to the pastoral needs of the people and the remedies that he put forward

---

[90] Hall, 'Erasmus', p. 108.

[91] Mayor, *Statutes*, pp. 250-2, 344-5.

centred on training preachers in the necessary skills. At Cambridge, he stood at the heart of a movement to renew the study of theology. He tried to ensure that the progress being made in the disciplines necessary for theological enquiry and expertise was available to the students of his day, and that it was brought into the service of the Catholic Church.

But the reform proposed by John Fisher knew strict boundaries. His dedication to truth and knowledge was formed first and foremost by his belief that they were to be served only within the context of the Catholic Church. As his academic theology will show, separation from the Church means a departure from the truth. So in times of crisis he stands quite firmly in the position of a man of the Church and not in that of a dedicated biblical humanist. This same loyalty to the Church permeates his spirituality. The needs of the people, and therefore the task of the preacher, find their solution in the tried and proved spirituality of the medieval Church. His own preaching shows all the characteristics of his immediate predecessors and in urging the clergy to attain a higher standard of preaching, and he seems to have had nothing else in mind but the acquisition of greater learning. In short, Fisher was able to see many of the contemporary needs of the Church. But in answering them he drew as much of the past as on the present and could never be described as truly radical.

However, in 1519, the time of crisis presented itself and Fisher's life turned to the defence of Catholic teaching. No longer did he feel able to devote himself to moderate academic reform and pastoral formation alone. A battle was being engaged, and Fisher had no doubts about what was required of him. Even though his writings lack the sweep and systematic approach of non-apologetical work, we must now try and trace out what appear to be the main elements and themes of his theology. Within these, particular influences are hard to trace. By the age of fifty, the effects of the formative years have long been subsumed into more personal opinions and convictions, and it is largely impossible to pinpoint them. In general terms, then, we now attempt to place John Fisher in the mainstream of Catholic theology and have some appreciation of his position, not so much in relation to his opponents, but rather in relation to other contemporary Catholic theologians.

Theologian

In 1525 John Fisher issued an invitation to any Lutheran to come and talk openly with him:

> ...to bare the bottom of his mind and he shall hear mine again, if it so please him and I trust in our Lord that finally we shall agree, that either he shall make me a Lutheran or else I shall induce him to be a Catholic and to follow the doctrine of Christ's Church.[1]

We do not know if any accepted this invitation, but it is a clear expression of the confidence and sense of purpose with which John Fisher had taken up the challenge of Lutheran theology.

In 1519, Bishop Poucher of Paris sent John Fisher a copy of the work *De Maria Magdalene et triduo Christi disceptatio*, written some two years earlier by Jacques Lefèvre d'Étaples.[2] Fisher had already read the work, but then he was asked to re-examine it and to write a refutation. Fisher agreed to do so and produced a lengthy refutation because he saw that if the book was allowed to stand unchallenged:

> ...how many books amended, what scruples it would occasion to many; how many handles it would give to scepticism, and what a cause it would be of men entertaining an ill suspicion of our common mother the Church who for many ages taught otherwise.[3]

Concern to defend the past life and teaching of the Church was both the motive and the method of Fisher's response.[4] No less was he concerned to defend the trusting faith in the Church of people with lesser intelligence and perception, and to ensure that future generations were not assailed by false and confusing teaching. It was for these motives that he continually wrote and published in the years from 1519 to 1527, defending the traditions and teaching of the Church hoping as much to

---

[1] Preface to the sermon of 11 February 1525, on Quinquagesima Sunday, as printed by T. Berthelet, f.A iv, (henceforth referred to as *Quinqua).*

[2] *De Maria Magdalene et triduo Christi disceptatio* (Paris: Ex officina Henrici Stephani, 1517).

[3] J. Lewis, *The Life of Dr John Fisher, Bishop of Rochester in the Reign of Henry VIII*, 2 Vols, (Joseph Lilley: London, 1855) Vol. I p. 78, (henceforth cited as Lewis, *The Life*).

[4] *De Unica Magdalena libri tres*, (henceforth referred to as *Magdalene)* published in 1518 and again in 1519, *Opera, quae hactenus inueniri potuerunt omnia, Würzburg*, 1597, (henceforth cited *Opera)*. In the work, the authority of a long catena of Fathers is listed to oppose Lefèvre d'Étaples' teaching.

defend the innocent bystander as to persuade to the truth those who had erred.[5]

The Preface to the Sermon of *Quinquegesima Sunday*, written in the quiet of his study, reveals much of his mind and intention in these matters. Energetic work against heresy, he explains, is his bounden duty and he would be guilty and deserving of great punishment if he were negligent:

> *Know therefore when so little diligence is done about the ministering of this true doctrine, it is necessary that all those who have charge of the flock of Christ, endeavour themselves to gainsay these pernicious heresies.*

So he 'puts forth this sermon to be read which for the great noise of the people within the church of Paul's when it is said might not be heard.'[6] He offers to talk with any Lutheran, then, affirming his loyalty to and confidence in the Catholic Church: its past, its present and its future.

The following exposition of the central themes of Fisher's theological writings will reveal that the very topics which we have seen neglected for the most part in the popular writings of the previous decade then became the central issues.[7] Again and again Fisher relies upon his understanding of the Church as the basis for his arguments. Previously presented only in terms of the individual's needs, in terms of the sacraments and personal piety, now it is the nature of the Church in itself, her right to teach definitively, the relationship between her teaching and the Scriptures and the use to which both of these may be put that become the pivots on which his theology hinges. Fisher is prompt to rebuke any man who casts doubt on the divine nature and authority of the Church and he does so by consistently reaffirming his view of one's duty to respect and obey the Church and her teaching.

There is little in Fisher's earlier writings about the Church. In his commentary on Psalm 101: 14f (Vulgate), he sees the Church built of the living stones of its members, upon the living foundations of the Apostles, after the image of St Paul in the letter to the Ephesians 2:20. He repeats the theme attacking Luther's claims, *Assertionis Lutheranae Confutatio*.[8] The Church is the community of believers in Christ, the

---

[5] In the preface of his work against Luther, *Assertionis Lutheranae Confutatio* (Antwerp: M. Hillenius, 1522) f. 2, *Opera*, 273, Fisher proposes to defend weaker souls.

[6] *Quinqua*, f.A iii–iv.

[7] Surtz, *Works and Days* provides the relevant publications by Fisher in this chapter.

[8] *Assertionis Lutheranae Confutatio*, Published on January 2, 1523, in Antwerp. Hereafter referred to as *Assertio*.

Mystical Body of Christ; for the Church is born of Christ and lives by and in him.[9]

In order to describe the Church further, Fisher makes use of the traditional hallmarks of the Church: unity, holiness, Catholicity and Apostolicity.[10] But of these it is the mark of unity which is most important to him and brings us closer to the heart of his ecclesiology, for this is a unity which binds together not only present day members of the Church but stretches back through time.

> *The succession of Christ's Church…has continued and shall continue till the world's end, even like the flood that passes continually. The waters go and pass but yet the flood continues and retains still the name of the flood: so the succession of Christ's Church ever continues and is called the Church Catholic.[11]*

Such a unity might be thought amazing until one considers its sources.[12] It is the Holy Spirit which forms and maintains the unity of the Church, for this was the promise of Christ to be with and guide the Church for ever. Fisher understood there was a total identity between the presence of the Holy Spirit and the Church, which is always and unquestionably the Catholic Church of Rome.[13]

This is expressed most succinctly in the *Assertio*:

> *This is why the Holy Spirit was sent for him to remain perpetually in the Church, so that whenever errors of any kind would appear, he would remain and make her more certain. And the Holy Spirit was for that purpose sent by the Father and the Son, Christ himself attests, so that he would remain with us eternally to teach the Church in all things essential to the faith whatever pertained. Hence, it is because of that that the perpetual presence of the Holy Spirit is the column support of the Church. So by the truth of the Spirit so solidly supported, it could not if in error survive too long.[14]*

The presence of the Holy Spirit in the Church, guaranteed by the promise of Christ, is the central point of John Fisher's theology. Because of this guidance of the Holy Spirit in the Church, then the truth of Christ is to be found in the teaching put forward by the Church. This pattern of thought was by no means original to John Fisher, although his presentation of

---

[9] *De veritate Corporis et Sanguinis Christi in Eucharistia adversus Iohannem Oecolampadium.* Published in February 1527, in Cologne, (henceforth referred to as *Corpus Christi*), 4th Proemium, *Opera*, 1134. & 4.25 *Opera*, 1068.

[10] Sermon I, Mayor, p. 343 (see Ch. 5 n60 above).

[11] *Quinqua*, f. Bii.

[12] *Assertio*, Septima Veritas, f. 10. *Opera*, 289.

[13] Sermon I, Mayor, p. 313.

[14] *Assertio*, Quinta Veritas, f. 9. *Opera*, 286-287, Also John 14:26.

it was marked by a deep certainty of faith and a wide ranging use of all aspects of traditional church teaching.

But such a firm belief in the working presence of the Holy Spirit in the Church demands further precision. Fisher rhetorically poses the questions: by whom does the Spirit speak? By whom does he teach us the truth? And he replies, 'By whom else but by the Fathers and Doctors of the Church'. Emphasising first of all the Fathers and the early Doctors, the *Sexta Veritas* of the *Assertio* states:

> *The Holy Spirit until now has been used through the tongues of the orthodox Fathers who taught the extirpation of heresies and full instruction in dubious matters. He has used them till now, and he uses them for all time.*[15]

The signs that were shown at the baptisms of Basil and Eubolius, for example, are held as clear indications of them being possessed by the Spirit of Christ, and so the *Septima Veritas* applies this axiom with this result.

> *Whoever does not receive the orthodox Fathers despises the teaching of the Holy Spirit, and it is clear that he does not possess that Holy Spirit.*[16]

He repeats the theme of St Paul in Ephesians 4 of the manifold gifts given to the Church, and maintains that some are appointed to teach, to maintain true doctrine while others have the right of believing and giving assent, but do not have the right of dissenting from their legitimate teachers.[17] Thus he rigorously upholds the functional distinction between the teaching and the learning Church, along with the distinction of clergy and laity. This was a distinction founded by Christ, intended for all the time of the Church militant. It is not to be negated or reduced, but rather it remains the duty of the Church in time rigorously to maintain that tradition. He points to the constancy with which we read in the New Testament of the people being spoken of under the figures of a vineyard, a field, a building or a flock, whereas those chosen for special ministry are called vine-dressers, husbandmen, builders and shepherds. Such a difference is quite reasonable, for the men thus set apart bear responsibility for the multitude. The various dangers of faith; the ease with which people fall into sin and error, and their sluggishness

---

[15] *Assertio, Sexta Veritas*, f. 9 .*Opera*, 287.

[16] *Assertio, Septima Veritas*, f. 10. *Opera*, 289.

[17] *Assertionum, Sexta Veritas*, f. 10. *Opera, 288. Defensio Catholica adversus Lutheri, Babylonicam Captivitatem, Defensio*, June 1525. Cologne, henceforth known as Defensio, 11, 3. *Opera*, 235

to do good, all contribute to creating the need for special guides and teachers.[18]

Not everyone is given all the gifts of the Spirit, and the presence of the Spirit is so imperceptible to the individual that it is only in the unity of the Church, with the correct ordering of these gifts, can we hope to come to the truth.[19] Due regard then must be given to the teaching Church, to those who have responsibility of teaching and correcting, and especially to the early Fathers who were most capable and most assisted in their task by the force of the Spirit.[20]

While the teaching of the Fathers and Doctors is for this reason to be reverenced, the assembled Church is even more assured of the guidance of the same Spirit:

> *Wherefore it is not to be doubted but in such holy bishops [Basil, Ambrose etc.] and doctors of the Church the Holy Ghost doth speak. But much rather in Councils when many of them were assembled together.[21]*

The difficulties caused when we encounter the errors of individual Fathers and the inconsistencies between them are resolved by reference to the teaching of the General Councils, for the guidance of the Holy Spirit is most certainly to be found in the group of assembled Fathers and Doctors. Yet even here a problem emerges, for occasionally councils are in contradiction with each other and can possibly make mistakes.[22] Fisher admits this difficulty:

> *And the Councils also, although some one of the last Councils which peradventure was not guarded in that meekness and charity that was expedient though one of them (which thing I will not affirm) in some article were permitted to go amiss.[23]*

And he seems to propose that the meekness and the charity of the gathering, the harmony and sincere simplicity of souls, are the marks by which we recognise the working of the Holy Spirit, together with the presence and agreement of the Pope unless discord is through his very palpable fault.[24]

---

[18] *Sacri Sacerdotii Defensio contra Lutherum*, June 1525, Cologne. Translated by P.E. Hallett. *The Defence of the Priesthood*, (London: Burns and Oates, 1935). Henceforth known as *Priesthood*. 2. 10, *Opera*, 1247, 2.11, *Opera*, 1247, 2. 4, *Opera*, 1244.

[19] *Priesthood*. 3, 15-21, *Opera*, 1279-83.

[20] *Defensio*, 3.1, *Opera*, 131-132.

[21] Sermon I, Mayor, p. 335. Also in *Assertio, Octava Veritas*, f. 11. *Opera*, 290.

[22] The Fathers may have erred, as did the prophets e.g. Nathan (2 Kings 7) and indeed Peter (Matth. 16) so that we may remember they are men. *Assertio*, f. 11.

[23] Sermon I. Mayor, p. 338.

[24] *Assertio, Octava Veritas*, f. 11. *Opera*, 91-92. And Art. xxix; *Opera*, 595.

Fisher is content to affirm in general terms that the Holy Spirit will guide the Councils of the Church and sees no need to give further clarification of the criteria by which the exact importance of a conciliar statement is to be assessed.[25] Certainly the Church is not at liberty to produce statements of faith of her own invention, for she must always allow herself to be guided by the Holy Spirit. He quotes Scotus on this point, saying 'according to which the Church has no power, whenever it rules for itself, either truth or error takes place' and insists that, nevertheless, assisted by the Spirit of Truth, the Church now pronounces to be of the substance of the faith that which was already implicitly contained there.[26] However, it is quite clear that there is a need within the structures of the Church for a definite and concrete means of discerning the true working of the Spirit from the mere product of men. That Councils be held in meekness and charity is an unsatisfactory criterion; that they be held in the presence and with the agreement of the Pope is more concrete and clear-cut. History attests that the Pope stands at the crisis point of debate on the authority of the Church.

Fisher does not hesitate to present the Pope as the ultimate indication of where truth is placed. He readily refers Councils to the Pope, betraying none of the hesitancy of St Thomas More in this matter.[27] For him the person of the Pope puts the final seal on the question of authority and removes all right to demur. Accordingly, Fisher gives great attention to the task of establishing the primacy of Peter and the consequent authority of the Pope, and he gives his fullest support to Papal authority especially when it is exercised in conjunction with the whole Church. 'The authority of the sovereign pontiff is great, but it is greater still if the custom of the Roman See is added to it, and greatest if the consent of the whole Church accrues to it.'[28] The passages of Fisher's works in defence of Roman primacy were to become the most widely acclaimed of all his writings and they undoubtedly made an important contribution to popular writings on a topic that had been so conspicuous by its absence.

The second part of the first instruction of the Sermon of 1521 presents Fisher's main argument in defence of the Papacy. It consists in an appeal to Scriptural evidence supported with strong backing from early Church writers. This sets the pattern which finds repetition and expansion in Fisher's later writings. In this sermon Fisher sets out to demonstrate

---

[25] *Assertio, articuli* xxviii and xxix, *Defensio*, 3. 10-18.

[26] Scotus, in *Assertio* , art. xxvii, f. 154. *Opera*, 583. And art. xxviii, f. 157-160.

[27] Thomas More advised Henry to play down the importance of Papal power in his *Assertio septem sacramentorum adversus Martinum Lutherum*. Later More declared that he changed his mind on the position of the Pope. R.W. Chambers, *Thomas More*. (London: 1935) pp. 193-194.

[28] Surtz, *Works and Days*, p.71.

that the 'Head of the universal Church is the pope'.[29] He commences by presenting the figures of Moses and Aaron as foreshadowing in the Old Law the figures of Christ and Peter in their roles as leaders of God's people: 'Governance was twain heads appointed one under another, Moses and Aaron without doubt they must be the shadow of Christ and his vicar Saint Peter.' He elaborates the analogy and defends it against the objection that there cannot be two heads of the Church by saying that, according to St Paul, a woman has more than one head.

> *See there be three heads unto a woman; God, Christ and her husband, and yet beside these she has a head of her own. How much rather our mother holy Church which is the spouse of Christ has a head of her own, that is to say, the pope. And yet nevertheless Christ Jesus her husband is her head and almighty God is her head also.*

Of the New Testament passages he uses, he makes special mention of Matthew 17:24-27 when Peter paid the temple tax shekel for Christ and himself which, says Fisher, shows him to be the head under Christ.

He then adds the testimony of the Fathers quoting Augustine, Ambrose, Gregory, Jerome, Cyprian, Chrysostom and Origen and concludes: 'If all these so many testimonies both of Greek and Latin shall not counter appeal against one brother [frère Luther], what reason is this?' Article xxv of the *Assertio* presents Fisher's positive arguments on the same point in a more disciplined manner. He starts by presenting ten gospel passages to show the primacy of Peter, follows them with ten incidents from the life of the early Church showing how Peter's position evolved in practice and then gives quotations from seven Latin Fathers and eight Greek Fathers, mentioning six others by name.

The Gospel Passages are these:

1. *Matthew 16:18. Christ changes Peter's name which is always the sign of conferring authority.*

2. *In the lists of the Apostles in Mark 3:16 and Luke 6:14, Peter is named first.*

3. *Peter's confession of faith in Matthew 16:17.*

4. *In Matthew 16:19 the keys are given to Peter and reference is made to the interpretation of Origen that here the Vulgate has 'of heaven' (caelorum), whereas the rest of the Apostles receive authority 'in heaven' (in caelo), see also Matthew 28:18.*

5. *Matthew 17:24 Peter pays the temple tax.*

---

[29] Sermon I, Mayor, pp. 315-321. Contains most of this material quoted.

6. *Luke 22:32 Christ prays for Peter's faith and is commanded to strengthen his brothers.*

7. *In Mark 16:7 as the resurrection is announced, Peter is mentioned particularly by name.*

8. *Fisher refers to the emphasis given in John 20:3-6 to the fact that Peter was shown deference and entered the tomb first.*

9. *Special pastoral responsibilities are conferred on Peter by Jesus in John 21:15-17.*

10. *Fisher maintains that Christ's instruction 'Follow me' in John 20:19 is addressed to Peter and indicates a special pre-eminence given to him.*

From these Gospel passages, which receive no special attention with regard to textual accuracy, authenticity or detailed exegesis, he concludes:

> *We affirm that Christ willed Peter to enjoy greater authority than all the rest and constituted him his vicar on earth and committed to him the care and administration of the whole Church. (f. 129)*

These findings are given support from the events in the life of the early Church by which, under the guidance of the Holy Spirit, she established her patterns of organisation and growth. Fisher adduces incidents in corroboration of Peter's primacy,

1. *The role played by Peter in choosing the successor to Judas in Acts 1:15-26.*

2. *In the early preaching and administration of the Church recorded in Acts chapters 2 and 5.*

3. *In the miracles worked by the Apostles in Acts chapters 3 and 5 where only Peter is mentioned by name.*

4. *In his mission to Samaria in Acts chapter 8:14.*

5. *In receiving the Gentiles into the community in Acts chapters 11 and 15:7.*

6. *Finally, in Galatians 1:18, the fact that Paul goes to Jerusalem to visit Peter specially.*

These items complete Fisher's use of the Scriptures in this section, although later on in the article he returns to the theme of his sermon and presents the same similarities between Moses and Christ on the one hand, and Aaron and Peter on the other.

Having completed his appeal to the Scriptures, Fisher next claims that his contention is supported by the universal opinion of the Church throughout the ages. Then he proceeds to give quotations from the Fathers, for the most part with apposite references: from Hilary's *De Trinitate*; Ambrose; Leo's Book III *De Pontifice*; Gregory's *Epistola* xxxii; Cyprian's *Tractatus* iii *De Simplicitate Praeletorum*; Augustine's *Sermo* cxxiv and Jerome's *Commentaria super Galatos*. He further makes mention of Bede, Bernard, Rabanus, Remi, Hugh and Richard. Turning to the Greeks who, he puts it, do not have the grace of Rome, yet recognise the super-eminent position of Peter, he cites the commentary on the Gospels of Matthew and John by Chrysostom; Eusebius' *Libro secundo Ecclesiasticae Historiae*, cap xiv; Cyril, Origen's *Super initium Evangelii Ioannis;* Athanasius; Theophilus' *Super Lucam*; Basil's *Libro secundo adversus Eunomius* and Dionysius. Finally he refers to the Council of Florence, attended by Greeks and Armenians alike, and quotes: 'We define that the Apostolic See and the Roman Pontiff holds the primacy over the whole and St Peter was the principal of the Apostles and they are his successors' (f. 134).

This is the widely embracing net cast by Fisher to collect as much of the evidence proving that Luther, in denying Papal authority, was breaking with the authentic Christian tradition and was thereby in error. It is a clear example of Fisher's thoroughness and attentiveness to detail that he should comb both the Scriptures and the early writers for the least traces of support for his case.

However, Fisher is adamant that not only is it right that the authority of the Pope should be recognised, but it was also reasonable and expedient. Such an authority is necessary to settle controversies of faith, to call general Councils and suppress all error and heresy, especially when there is a lack of agreement among bishops. 'For there must be in the Church superiority and authority to command. And if such authority be granted to any, most of all it is proper for it to belong to the Supreme Pontiff.'[30] It was then central to Fisher's intention of defending Catholicism that the Papacy should retain its position, for he saw it essentially in a defensive role, the practical working out of Christ's promise to conserve the Church from error.

We must not imagine that Fisher overlooked the less edifying implications of such a primacy, namely corruption and the misuse of power. We have already seen how he spoke out against clerical abuses and corruption, nor did he exonerate the Papacy itself on these counts.

---

[30] *Priesthood*. 3.24, *Opera* 1286. Also Surtz, *op. cit.* p. 369. From the *Responsum ad libellum impressum Londini 1530*, as translated by N. Harpsfield in his *The Pretended Divorce*, Book I, pp. 116-119, in which a similar argument is applied to the King's divorce.

However, he maintained that such abuses do not provide a reason for rejecting the Papacy, but writing against Ulrich Velenus, he turned the familiar arguments completely on their heads. He pointed out first of all that whereas all the Churches founded by the other Apostles had disappeared, the Church of Rome had survived. He outlined the evils then present in Rome and added:

> *The enemy may object this to us, but that confirms our purpose. All of the other Apostles' Sees are occupied already by the infidels, this one alone [St Peter's] is maintained in the Christian camp, although it would have deserved like the others to be deleted for its abominable crimes, it deserved not to survive. Since we cannot think otherwise, none other than its being the truest and that Christ is its truthful guide who, though it is wounded by so many and so great injuries and injustices, nevertheless keeps the promises even when it is weakened. The faith announced by Peter was never absent in Rome and to this day did not defect; and the true succession which began with Peter remains permanent, whose foundation will be constituted by the firm rock foundation established by Christ.[31]*

Fisher, like Luther, was not primarily concerned with abuses, nor would he be put off by them. His concern was dogmatic faith, and that would survive no matter how it is veiled.

So he maintains that true religion, the good earth of the parable of the sower, is only to be found in union with Rome:

> *This multitude, this succession is the very Church of Christ against the which the gates of hell shall never prevail...thus then you see which is the good earth: I say the multitude of Christian people, which hitherto by a continual succession was derived from the See of Peter.[32]*

The true Christian faith is to be found in the keeping of the Church. 'Thus then by a certain continuous succession of prelates, who succeed each other, hence the truth of the Christian faith has reached our times.' That for Fisher simply was the beginning and end of the matter.[33]

This exposition of how the Holy Spirit makes known the truth in the Church contains the essential structure of Fisher's theological thought. Fisher answers the challenges to Catholic doctrine according to this structure of relationships between the Church, the Holy Spirit

---

[31] John Fisher, *Convulsio calumniarum Ulrichi Veleni Minhoniensis, quibus Petrum nunquam Romae fuisse cavillatur* (1522). Surtz, *Works and Days*, p. 75.

[32] *Quinqua*, f. Fi.

[33] *Corpus Christi*. 5.38. *Opera*, 1224.

and statements of doctrine. Adherence to the Church is seen by him as the sole guarantee of possession of the truth, for the Spirit of Christ, the source of truth for mankind, is at work in the Church; past, present and future, and in the Church alone. The truth of this position is made clear by the basic unity of the teaching upheld by the Church, a unity to be seen when the consensus of Church teaching is displayed. Such overall unity is sufficient to counteract more particular conflicts of opinion which can be found, and leaves no doubt as to the detailed doctrines of the Church: doctrines which because of their status as long held teaching of the Church are to be regarded as the truth, the fruit of the Holy Spirit's work among people.

The arguments for the authority of the Pope add the final touches to Fisher's faith in the Church, for this authority is the ultimate and concrete touchstone by which we may be sure of the authenticity of any particular doctrinal statement. Any discrepancies or dilemmas within the proclaimed teaching of the Church are to be resolved by this ever present criterion of truth, the personalising of Christ's promise to guide his Church into all truth. The authority of the Papacy is never seen in isolation from the more basic sources of Christian truth, but it is proposed as the last and most immediate means by which men, through the gift of God, may be sure of their adherence to the saving truth of God.

Fisher's vision of the whole economy of revelation is consistent with this theology of the Church. He turns to the Trinitarian analogy to resolve unity in diversity, for he describes the various stages of revelation in terms of the persons of the Trinity: the Father works through the Elders and Prophets of the Old Law; the Son is present through the witness rendered by the Apostles and the Holy Spirit is formative of the life and teaching of the Church, at work especially through the Fathers, Doctors, the Councils and the Pope.[34]

The consequences of this ecclesiology are both simple and all embracing. Such an outright identity between the work of the Holy Spirit and the teaching of the Church gives a clear criterion in Fisher's mind by which to judge the orthodoxy of a given opinion. If conformity with a consensus of Catholic teaching can be proved, then the opinion can be held justifiably. Conversely, if such conformity is lacking, then the opinion is heretical and to be shunned at all costs. The Spirit has always been with the Church; therefore, the consensus of the past teaching of the Church is authoritative and can legitimately be appealed to as a criterion of truth.

---

[34] Sermon I, Mayor, pp. 332-335.

Anyone who opposes the Church and her teaching, wilfully and maliciously, was seen by Fisher as a great danger to society. He was always ready to decry such an individual in the strongest terms:

> *For heresy is a perilous weed, it is the seed of the devil, the inspiration of wicked spirits, the corruption of our hearts, the blinding of our sight, the quenching of our faith, the destruction of all good fruit and finally the murder of our souls...whosoever affirms contrary to the traditions and doctrine of the Church though he for his life be worthy to be believed, though he fast never so much, though he keep his virginity, though he works miracles, though he prophesies of things to come, for all this take him but a wolf intending corruption among the flock of Christ.[35]*

His view of Luther, too, is unambiguous. Luther's teaching he asserts is 'nor yet partner of the spirit of life because it is repugnant and divided from the whole body of the doctrine of the Church,'[36] In this way Luther is guilty of making the promised gift of the Holy Spirit to the Church appear unfulfilled.

> *O most miserable heretic who denies and despises all the Fathers that ever were before us; for in denying thou must needs affirm...that our Saviour Christ Jesus nothing regarded his promise all this long time. I say who may think that ever he that did so much for us would break his promise unto us. If he has not broken his promise, then hath he been with his Church all this long time of fifteen hundred years...and his most Holy Spirit also hath been all this time present in the Church.[37]*

The essence of John Fisher's apologetical writings, therefore, is to show that the propositions of the Protestants stand in opposition to the accepted statements of the faith of the Church. Although this method is essentially similar to the long practised procedure of identifying current errors with former heresies already condemned, Fisher brings to this work the comparatively rare talents of memory, attentiveness to minute details and a comprehensive grasp of traditional doctrine.

The whole of his first Sermon of 1521 is designed to show that because Luther opposed certain teachings and customs of the Church then he is necessarily possessed by the spirit of error:

> *...for he cutteth away the traditions of the Apostles and refuseth the general Councils and condemns the doctrine of the holy Fathers and doctors of the Church...and labours to subvert all the ordinances*

---

[35] *Quinqua*, f. A iv, *Assertio*, f. 2, (*Opera*, 273.)

[36] *Quinqua*, f. E ii.

[37] *Quinqua*, f. D ii and iii.

> *of the Church and namely the seven sacraments and taketh away the freedom of man's will and affirmeth that all things falleth by necessity contrary to all the doctrine of Christ's Church. We may be sure therefore that he hath some other wretched spirit, some spirit of error and not the spirit of truth.*[38]

The second Sermon of 1525, directed to the same end, centres round the differences between truth and error, between the Church and Luther, sight and blindness, light and darkness, right way and wrong way, wheat and weeds, harmonious song and discordant Babel, good soil and stony soil, hundred fold fruit and sterility.

When the opposition between Fisher and Luther becomes more academic and more concerned with precise issues, the same principles are employed by Fisher. In his defence of the priesthood, for example, Fisher simply amasses evidence from the tradition of the Church as proof of the error of Luther's opinions, claiming a classical justification for doing so in the opening chapter of the work. There he turns to Tertullian and his book *De Praescriptione* and reports how Tertullian always used the 'prescriptive right of long accepted truth' in his controversies with heretics. Fisher proposes to use the same method himself, for it is well suited to his purpose, for once he has presented the evidence of the ages, 'So if Luther cannot produce anything proper of this kind openly, it is clear for any impartial judge that we have a prescribed tradition against his lie and the novel comments made by Luther.'[39] Consequently, Fisher feels at liberty to construct his argument not from the statements of Scripture, but from the body of Christian writings since the second century. The weight of such consensus is sufficient to prove wrong any who stand opposed to it. Further, this same consensus, under the guidance of the Councils and the Pope, is the ground on which Fisher holds himself free to disagree when necessary with any one author on particular points.[40]

When writing in defence of Catholic teaching on the Eucharist, Fisher again turns to this well-tried method of arguing, but this time with more subtlety and scholarship. The occasion of this work was the realisation that the Protestants were not in agreement among themselves in their understanding of the presence of Christ in the Eucharist. Fisher seizes upon this lack of unity as a sure sign of the falsehood of their teachings, for once conformity with the Church is lost then further disintegration into manifold error is inevitable. Fisher ruthlessly hammers in the wedge

---

[38] Sermon I, Mayor, p. 336.

[39] *Priesthood*, 1.1, *Opera*, 1233.

[40] *Magdalene*, 1.3, *Opera*, 1407. Surtz, *op. cit.* p. 101.

between Oecolampadius and the Lutherans, showing that Luther was more 'Catholic' than his opponent, but both positions were irreconcilable with the truth.[41]

In the Preface of Chapter IV of *Corpus Christi* he gives a survey of the writings of the preceding fifteen hundred years, claiming a unanimous opinion of orthodox teachers against Oecolampadius who must, therefore, be in the wrong. It is significant that he achieves a new degree of literary discipline in this presentation for, unlike his earlier works, he shows a genuine appreciation of the demands of literary criteria, surely a result of his extended interest in the fields of the humanist New Learning.[42] Early works, against Clichtove and in defence of the priesthood, had been uncritical in their long lists of quotations; but against Oecolampadius he divides the time into five *trecanarii*, or periods of three hundred years, and presents opinions from the writers of each period, working back to Apostolic times.[43] Book V of the *Corpus Christi* again employs this method in support of a Eucharistic interpretation of John 6. He ends his survey with three conclusions: first, that all these writers believed in the Real Presence of Jesus Christ in the Eucharist; second, that those orthodox writers not mentioned because of the loss of their works never taught contrary to the Real Presence and third, that every person who does not believe in the Real Presence is separated from the Church and the legitimate means of salvation.[44]

For John Fisher, this is the touchstone of living faith. The Church, in her commonly accepted writings and her precise dogmatic statements, is instrumental in bringing truth into the grasp of each person. But clearly abstract truth alone is not the full interest of the believer, for the understanding and acceptance of that truth demands a sharing in the life of the Church. It is by personal faith that one is joined to the Church and becomes a member of the Body which is enlivened by the Spirit of Truth. Only by a full personal acceptance of the truths of faith, as expressed by the Church, can an individual participate in that saving truth. A mere physical joining with the company of the Church is not enough, 'if he come not also with the feet of his soul and fully assents unto the Church, he cannot have this true faith' and 'the faith of the

[41] *Corpus Christi, Opera,* 866, 1184 and 861. Also, W. Kohler, *Zwingli and Luther,* (Leipzig: 1924) maintains that this work of Fisher led to the clarification of terms such as 'transubstantiation', 'transmutation' and 'consubstantiation.'
[42] Surtz, *op. cit.* pp. 340-345.
[43] Ibid, p. 102. *Priesthood,* 1. 1-2, Lewis, Vol. 1. pp. 280-287,The *trecanarii* were: 1500-1200, 1200-900, 900-600, 600-300, 300 and before.
[44] *Corpus Christi, Opera,* 998.

Church, which by thine assent is made by faith, doth make thee safe.'[45]

The contemporary spiritual writings of the age, which we have examined, showed us that the faith by which a person is saved is trust in the saving power of Christ; but the concrete expressions of that power are the means of salvation offered to the individual by the Church. The Church, her teaching and sacraments are an essential part of the faith that saves, not in contradiction to the person of Jesus Christ, but as the necessary means by which Christ is to be found and the primacy of God's grace is carefully preserved. For Fisher the same holds true. The funeral sermons of Henry and Margaret display the same understanding of the nature of faith, for the hope of their salvation rested in the evidence of their faith in Christ and the Church; and in the practice of that faith, notably the reception of the sacraments. For Henry he said, 'the cause of this hope was the true belief that he had in God, in his Church and in the sacraments thereof, which he received all with marvellous devotion.'[46]In his academic writings, Fisher develops the same traditional teaching a little further. In his major work against Luther, the *Assertio*, he rejects Luther's teaching about faith on two points. First of all, Fisher somewhat misguidedly insists that Luther's 'faith alone' (*solafideism*) emphasis is in direct exclusion of the importance of good works, and consequently claims that faith is only consummated in action. Secondly, Fisher observes that the faith which is necessary for the reception of the sacraments is not constitutive of the sacraments given, for they receive their power from the Church as promised by Christ. The sacraments, in fact, are part of the object and movement of faith and do not depend on the faith of the individual for their validity.[47] In the work on the Eucharist he takes this a step further by saying that rather than being constituted by a person's faith, the sacraments support and nourish faith and that without them true faith would disappear. In fact, he continues, without the sacraments and their reception, no one can be certain that he has a living and formed faith, except through a special revelation, which is not given to many. In other words, for Fisher, individual faith arises within and is dependent upon the Church. Faith is a personal experience, but it flows to the person through the Church. The promises of eternal life for those who follow Christ were addressed to those who possess a living faith, and faith lives only in the context and life of the Church.[48]

---

[45] *Quinqua*, f. C i.

[46] John Fisher, *This Sermon was complied and sayd the body beynge present of Kynge Henry VII* (May 1509), p. 273. Copies in the Bodleian and the Rylands libraries.

[47] *Assertio*, art. 1, f. 15.

[48] Corpus Christi, *Proemium* 5, (*Opera*, 1134.)

Such a central position given to the Church in the coming together of the individual and Christ in a salvific faith is one of the key differences between Fisher and his Protestant opponents. For Fisher it was a truth beyond doubt, a truth which permeated his upbringing and his writing, both spiritual and academic. For Luther, on the other hand, the discovery and an experience of faith independent of the life and practices of the Church was a critical moment. Sometimes this is described as Luther's rediscovery of the essentially historical core of Christian faith; the rediscovery of the fact that the salvation of God came to mankind in Christ in certain historical events. From those moments, in which the course of history was changed, all human hope rests in an immediate contact with Christ who, once for all in those events, worked the forgiving and remaking of mankind.[49] Luther saw that there were various ways of distracting from this truth, of escaping from the historical singularity of Christ and so of distorting man's faith. One such escape mechanism was mysticism: God is accessible at all times to the waiting heart. A second was moralism: salvation by good behaviour here and now. A third was institutionalism: the revelation of God at a point in the past is continued in the present through an institution, the Church, which hands on to man that saving revelation.

In Luther's eyes, Fisher fell into this third category. The faith was distorted by the Church and, further, this distortion was no more clearly seen than in the use of Scripture. It was by the means of Scripture, the record of these unique events, that the saving relationship between the individual and Christ became possible. Together with the Holy Spirit, this presented to everyone all that was necessary for salvation. Moreover, this combination of Scripture and Spirit contained the criterion by which one could judge the truthfulness of all things, including the life of the Church. The outward Word, interpreted by the Spirit in each individual, enables a man to assess all things; it sets him above all institutions and moralities and yet imprisons him, a willing captive to the Word of God. The reception of the Holy Spirit by the individual is prepared for by a profound study of the Scriptures, by reading, meditation and contemplation and then, the individual knows not when, the Spirit would enlighten the mind.[50]

However, the apparent simplicity of this opposition between Luther and Fisher is misleading. For his part, Luther had to struggle with the

---

[49] R.H. Bainton, *Studies in the Reformation*, (London: Hodder and Stoughton, 1964) pp. 107-108.
[50] *Ibid*, pp. 4-11.

problems of Scriptural interpretation, the relationship between the various meanings of Scripture and the clear lack of total consistency throughout the Scriptures. Fisher, on the other hand, saw these problems in a different light. For him, Luther's refusal to accept the authoritative role of the Church was the central reason for falling into error, for Fisher's first principle, arising directly from his ecclesiology, was that all Scriptural interpretation must be done in harmony with the Church. It is the hallmark of all heresy that individuals insist on their own private interpretation of Scripture and refuse the guidance of the Church: 'Every one of these heretics grounded his heresy upon Scripture and many of them were men of full wits, of deep learning, of mighty reason and of pretended virtue.'[51]

Consequently, Fisher steadfastly refused to allow Luther the right to appeal to Scripture alone. From the beginning of any dialogue, he was constantly adamant that the due position of post-apostolic teaching must be recognised and accepted. We can be reasonably certain that from his own intense linguistic interests that Fisher understood something of the hopes contained in Luther's emphasis on Scripture, but his steadfast adherence to the right of the Church to authoritative interpretation eventually ruled out any fruit that could have arisen from this understanding. Fisher never gave an inch on this point, insisting always on full recognition of the role of post-apostolic writing. That there was no dialogue between Fisher and his opponents, that there was no fruitful contact between their writings is certainly partially a result of this fact.

Yet at no stage did Fisher, or the mainstream of orthodox Catholicism, suggest that the Scriptures could be ignored as a source of Christian revelation. It would be very wrong to suggest that Fisher had a slight or diminished regard for Scripture. His early writings alone are evidence against this for they were focused upon the revealed Word of God, and his great esteem for Scripture is often expressed:

> *The very bread of the Word of God maketh reason lady and ruler of the flesh to be held in bondage and as servant. The Word of God causeth all goodness in the soul, it maketh it moist and ready to spring in good works.*[52]

In these writings he gives the Scriptures his full attention and does not hesitate to use Scripture in all the traditional manners of interpretation.

[51] Sermon 1, Mayor, p. 341.
[52] PS 102, f. 149.

Chapter Six

Even in the cut and thrust of theological debate, where Fisher clearly prefers to take his stand on something he considers to be more reliable, his esteem for the Scriptures is not diminished nor is his intention lacking. It is the Holy Spirit who is the author of the Scriptures and although they are made up of many books, 'they make but one book and one body of Scripture, and have in them but one spirit and life; that is to say the Spirit of Christ Jesus.'[53] But underlying Fisher's extensive appeal to Scriptural evidence, are many issues involved in their use that need to be clarified.

For the most part, Fisher limited his use of Scripture in his theological works to the literal interpretation, as befits a man trained in the ways of Albert, Aquinas and Lyra. He himself repeats their insistence that only the literal meaning can contribute to dogma and that parables and allegory should never be used.[54] In fact he does so discipline himself for the most part. Articles in the *Assertio* on particular points use Scriptural references literally; the defence of the priesthood and the Preface and Book One of the *Corpus Christi* consist almost entirely of properly constructed scriptural arguments.[55]

At times, however, Fisher wavers from this standard and occasionally uses a spiritual interpretation in a theological argument. It is important to mention, however, that for the most part this occurs in the two sermons against Luther, and there can be no doubt that Fisher's approach in these works was substantially different to that used in the academic writings.[56] Perhaps he felt justified here in presenting the more colourful and less profound arguments based on an expanded application of Scripture. The *Quinquagesima* Sermon is built round two Gospel stories, the first of which is that of the blind man in Luke 18:35-43. Here the crowd is made to represent the people of God, of the Old and New Covenants, and the blind man is seen as the heretic. The state of the heretic and the path back to the truth are elaborated in this comparison. The second story uses the parable of the sower. He states:

> *All is spiritual that is meant here: the heavens, the influence, the sower, the seed, the earth, the fruit; all is spiritual and we must conceive all this spiritually. And therefore our Saviour said 'those*

---

[53] In an unprinted divorce tract – Cambridge University Library, MS 1315 – Fisher says, 'the Holy Spirit who inspired the Scriptures could not be ignorant of the future'. See Surtz, p. 116. *Quinqa*, f. E.

[54] *Corpus Christi*, 4.5, *Opera*, col. 1014.

[55] *Priesthood*, 3. 16-21, *Opera*, 1279-1283.

[56] He comments in the Preface to the Quinquagesima Sermon of 1525 that it is written 'to be spoken until a multitude of the people which were not brought up in the subtle disputations of the school...'

> who have ears to hear; hear': who that hath the inward ears of
> spiritual hearing and spiritual conceiving, he is worthy to hear and
> conceive this parable.[57]

In the sermon of 1521 he uses an argument from the positions of Moses
and Aaron in defence of Petrine supremacy. The argument develops the
relationship between Moses and Aaron, between them and God and
them and the people, and applies the findings directly to Peter and his
successors. He develops the comparison thus: Moses and Aaron are both
priests; Moses was intermediary between God and Aaron as was Christ
to Peter, praying for him. Aaron was intermediary between Moses and
the people as was Peter between Christ and his brethren.[58]Even given
the homiletic context, these are unsatisfactory arguments in defence of a
dogmatic position, but they are the more disturbing when they reappear,
though in a minor way, in Article XXV of the *Assertio*. Similarly, despite
his own principle, Fisher uses the parable of the rich man and Lazarus as
confirmation of the doctrine of purgatory.[59]

This type of lapse on Fisher's part is an indication of his deep
enthusiasm for and determination to defend Catholic doctrine; it leads
him to include all available arguments, even the loosely based richness
of the spiritual interpretation of Scripture. But it also indicates the
instinctive flair he has for the spiritual method of this age, the ease with
which he slips into a thoroughly medieval manner and the difficulty
he found in curbing this inclination, either for the sake of the stricter
demands of academic discipline or, as we have seen, for the sake of the
New Learning.

Fisher prefaces the analogies taken from the Old Testament with
statements concerning the relationship of the Old and New Testaments.
In the sermon of 1521 he likens the relationship of the New and the
Old to that between a tree and its shadow: 'Everything that is in the
tree hath somewhat answering unto it in the shadow. And contrary
wise every part of the shadow hath something answering unto it in
the tree.'[60] In the *Assertio* he makes the same statement, saying that all
things of the Old Law are nothing than certain figures of the New Law,
and this is repeated again in terms of shadow and prefigurement in the
Quinquagesima sermon.[61] The fact that this differs not at all from his
approach to similar problems in the sermons on the Penitential Psalms, a

[57] *Corpus Christi*, 4.5, *Opera*, 1015.

[58] *Sermon* I, Mayor, pp.316-317.

[59] *Assertio*, art., xxxv, f. 144-146., art., xxxvii, *Opera*, f. 221-228.

[60] *Sermon* I, Mayor, p. 315.

[61] *Assertio*, art., xxv, f. 144. *Quinqua*, f. B i-ii.

purely spiritual work, shows how unsatisfactory a method it is for strict doctrinal argument.

A further principle of interpretation often found in the hands of Fisher is that of the internal unity of the Scriptures. This principle of the analogy of faith demands that all Scripture is interpreted according to the themes of the whole corpus of Scripture. The setting of one part of Scripture in opposition to another is a sign of erroneous interpretation.

> *The analogy of faith is silently used as a unifying or integrating principle, as which it also functions in the development of dogma and declarations of the Magisterium, to obviate the tensions and possible one-sidedness which the mysterious character of the faith gives rise to.*[62]

As a biblical notion this was used by Augustine and Jerome and arose from the teaching of charismatic gifts for conformity with faith, as ordered by Paul in I Corinthians 12:10.

The validity of this principle is attested by the work of the Holy Spirit who, as the author of all the Scriptures, guarantees its unity. The Word of God is the pure seed:

> *Though there be many words and many truths in it, many specialities, many parables, many similitudes, many commandments, many counsels, many threats, many promises, many persuasions, yet for as much as it hath no falsehood nor untruth, none error, no wicked doctrine interfered therewith, but is all of one grain, of one growth, for all cometh from above.*[63]

Fisher consequently takes effort to maintain that basic unity, especially on texts from Paul and James concerning justification by faith and the Eucharistic narratives of Luke and Mark.[64] His accusation of Luther follows, for he maintains that:

> *Luther by his intricate expositions maketh one part of Scripture to be repugnant against another as he confesses himself that he cannot frame his other expositions with the Epistle of Saint James and with the Gospel of Luke.*[65]

Luther is accused of misapplying this principle by attempting to interpret all Scripture according to the solitary principle that 'the just shall live by faith'. In so doing Luther is said to have substituted not so

---

[62] *Sacramentum Mundi*, (London: Burns & Oates, 1968.) Vol.1, p.25.

[63] *Quinqua*, f. D, iv.

[64] *Sermon* I, Mayor, p. 328.

[65] *Quinqua*, f. E, ii.

much a book for the Pope, but rather a dogma for both Pope and book.[66] This is following the same pattern as his argument from prescription. Because of the consistency of teaching of the work of the Holy Spirit in Scripture and in the Church, consistency of teaching is a guaranteed fact and anything contrary to established teaching or interpretation is not satisfactory. Fisher brings these two sides of Church teaching together by comparing them to a melody and its descant:

> *In like manner it is of the Scriptures of God and of the doctrine of the Church: there be many singers and some sing plainsong and some sing descant; Saint Matthew, Saint Mark, Saint Luke, Saint John, Saint Peter, Saint Paul, Saint James, Saint Jude sing the plainsong. Then there be a great number of the doctors which descant upon this plainsong; but for because there is no discord, no repugnancy, no contradiction among them at least at any point concerning the substance of our faith, all their voices make but one song and one harmony.[67]*

Luther had introduced discord and consequently his doctrine is 'not one with the doctrine of the Church, nor hath not it the spirit of life.'[68] The interpretation of any particular text, then, must be consistent with the themes and findings of the whole body of Scripture; inconsistency is error.

Fisher also admits criteria of interpretation of a more literary nature, although they play a minor role. Appreciation of the differences of style and intention of the Gospel writers is necessary and allowance must be made for their individuality.[69] At other times he makes allowance for the historical circumstances of the author in a different way. For example, the Apostles avoided using the word 'priest' for a simple reason; 'It is because the old priesthood was still in place and sacrifices [of the Old Law] were offered daily.' He concludes that even if in the Scriptures the term 'priest' is not used, there is so much stated about their office that it is sheer foolishness to attack it.[70]

Similarly, he demands that attention be given to the whole context of a quotation and he reacts strongly against the use of quotation out of context.[71] Both with the Scriptures and the Fathers, Fisher shows an increasing awareness of the importance of textual and contextual accuracy, and his later works show more attention to this point. This

[66] G. Tavard, *Holy Writ or Holy Church*, (London: 1959).
[67] *Quinqua*, f. D iv – E i.
[68] *Quinqua*, f. E ii.
[69] *Confutatio*, f. 11-12.
[70] *Priesthood*, 1.19, *Opera*, 1240 and 3. 25, *Opera*, 1287-1289.
[71] *Priesthood*, 3.24, *Opera*, 1286.

is the influence of the methods and principles of the New Learning which he did so much to promote. We have already noted his linguistic achievements and, although there is considerable evidence that he used Erasmus' New Testament for example, we may again question the depth of this influence, for none of the resulting textual accuracy makes any significant contribution to his dogmatic positions or conclusions.[72]

The ambiguity of Fisher's attitude to the findings of the New Learning as applied to the use of Scripture in apologetic debate is further illustrated by his stance towards the Latin Vulgate. At one moment he cedes great authority to the original texts, but then he seems to withdraw it for the sake of his ecclesiology:

> *We think therefore that none of the versions (codices) ought to be rejected unless where there is error through the fault of the copyist. For the Latin version which has been accepted throughout the Church is to be considered of no less authority than either the Hebrew or the Greek. For the Greek version (I am speaking of the Septuagint) has proceeded from the Holy Spirit just as the Hebrew. But deference must be paid also to the Latin version, which in the course of so many years has now been approved throughout the Church, no less deference than either of the other two, because Christ who can neither deceive nor be deceived promised to give to the Church the Spirit who would lead it into all truth.[73]*

The position and role of the Church is again indispensible so that, as always, Scripture itself does not stand alone.

But when all is said and done, what does the Bible say? While all may claim that its essentials are clear, there is no unanimity as to what these essentials might be. An ultimate appeal to Scripture itself, for Fisher and the Catholic tradition, was considered to be a most ill-equipped method of settling controversy.[74] Accordingly, Fisher demands that Oecolampadius must

> *Lay aside the swelling arrogance of his mind, since he is above measure puffed up with the sense of his own abilities and attributes much more than his own wit than to the unanimous judgement of the most holy Fathers which have gone before us.[75]*

Guided by the Holy Spirit, the role of the Church is to interpret the Scripture for she, the community, was the first recipient of the Scriptures.

---

[72] Surtz, *Works and Days*. pp. 148-152.

[73] Surtz, *op. cit.* p. 153, from the *De Causan Matrimonii*, f. 8 (Alcala : 1530).

[74] *Assertio, Quarta Veritas*, f. 8. *Opera*, 285-286.

[75] Lewis, *The Life*, Vol. 1, p. 307.

To this end he is fond of quoting the saying of Augustine: 'I truly would not believe the gospel if the authority of the Church did not move me to do so',[76] insisting on the interpretative right of the Church in face of the Protestant challenge in favour of individual autonomy in matters of interpretation.[77] Fisher looks to the Church, not only for an authoritative interpretation of Scripture, but also for the authoritative teaching of dogma. How then does he relate the roles of Scripture and tradition as a means of coming to the knowledge of God? Do they form a mutually complementary source, or two independent sources of revealed truth about God and our salvation?

Unfortunately, Fisher does not see the question in such abstract terms and we are left to glean his answer from the many scattered statements relevant to this topic. Not surprisingly, then, we are left without a definitive position and in fact we find that Fisher appears to vary his stance according to the emphasis of any particular issue. For the most part, however, he appears to be adamant that tradition forms an independent source of revealed truth, and that many things are to be held in faith which are not to be found in the Scriptures. In 1521, quoting John 15:27, he observes:

> *Their witness then must be allowed of every true Christian man. Of these words and of others above rehearsed it shall appear that more testimony must be admitted for sufficient authority than only that that is written in the Bible.*[78]

Always we find the promised presence of the Holy Spirit in the Church to be the justification. This axiom naturally provides a ready argument for topics such as infant baptism, and many liturgical observations such as kneeling to pray, the sign of the cross, and women covering their heads amongst others.[79] The inadequacy of the written Scripture in these particulars is maintained both because of the unwritten Apostolic traditions, for which he quotes 2 Thessalonians 2:15 and John 21:25, and because of the guidance of the Church in her teaching by the Holy Spirit.

However, Fisher does not stand simply at the extremity of a double source relationship of Scripture and tradition, which often involved a greater emphasis on tradition, but he qualified this position somewhat in other statements. Writing in the *Assertio*, he states that he has no

---

[76] Surtz, *op. cit.* p. 128.
[77] *Assertio, Tertia Veritas* f. 6. *Defensio*, 10, 7. Upholds the collective opinion of the Fathers as the authoritative interpretation of Scripture.
[78] Sermon 1, Mayor, pp. 331 & 334.
[79] *Assertio, Nona Veritas*, f. 12. *Opera*, 293.

doubts that the Apostolic traditions could all be founded in the contents of Scripture.[80] While he says that Luther goes too far in expecting to find everything fully set forth in Scripture, at this point Fisher is maintaining at least the implicit material sufficiency of Scripture in matters of dogma. It is only when the evidence of Scripture is unclear, or in question, that he insists that one must turn to the traditional teaching of the Church, and this because the work of the Spirit guarantees the unity of Catholic teaching and the contents of Scripture. While certain matters of ecclesiastical custom and behaviour rely upon the authority of well-established traditions, essential matters of Christian dogma rest upon the content of Scripture. Certainly, Fisher never maintains that tradition is to be held above Scripture, and he is never reluctant to take up an argument from a point of Scripture. However, in the heat of the conflict Fisher invariably turns away from Scripture to the authority of the Church and her teaching.

His only formulation of an exact critical relationship between Scripture and tradition is somewhat minimal and here, more than anywhere else, do we regret the lack of positive theological exposition by Fisher to replace the entirely defensive apologetic slant of his theological writings. What he does present in fact is a negative norm:

> *The Scriptures then are not to be understood in the perverse way in which Luther understands them, as if nothing whatever is to be allowed beyond what they contain, nor anything added to them, for many things besides the Scriptures have been handed down from the Apostles by tradition, and many things added wisely by their successors. But rather we are to understand that nothing can be accepted which is contrary to the Scriptures nor must anything be added which in any manner conflicts with them.[81]*

Such a negative and therefore incomplete statement leaves us with a gap in his theology at a most crucial and difficult point. However, we must use all the material which is available to us before coming to a conclusion, and Fisher's statements concerning the formative influence and importance of tradition must be balanced with the facts of his great work for the furthering of Scriptural study. When the conflict is joined, Fisher is not at all averse to arguing from Scripture, as his training and study had equipped him to do, but he always demands that from first to last the teaching authority of the Church, including the right to the definitive interpretation of Scripture be acknowledged and respected.

---

[80] *Assertio*, Nona Veritas, f. 12, *Opera*, 293.

[81] *Assertio*, Proemium f, 5.

The conclusion to the *Veritates* of the *Assertio* reads:

> *Such are the armaments of Christians which we wield against the enemies of the Church. You cannot reject any of them if you wish to be called Christian. It will suffice for us to appeal to the public customs of the Church or a tradition that goes back to the Apostles; or the General Councils of the Church Fathers, or some approved interpreter. With these where there is lack of Scripture you are to be assailed. Indeed it is not licit to constantly produce Scriptures as appears to be obvious as we have observed, nor should we believe their interpretation to be true except it agrees with the orthodox Fathers and the Church in which we believe and in which we have no doubt that the Holy Spirit resides as the pillar and basis of truth.*[82]

These are the weapons to which Fisher turns to defend Catholic teaching. Indeed he did not hesitate to appeal to all of them, for in defending any particular point of teaching he applied every possible argument. This, in fact, betrays one of the more prominent weaknesses in Fisher's theological work. Whether he was appealing to Scripture, to the Fathers or to the teaching of the Church, he displays a significant lack of discrimination in the material he uses. Indeed, we might ask if he did ever really exercise a critical choice of material; for it seems that in his enthusiasm every possible reference, no matter how slender, was summoned by him as evidence. In doing so Fisher overfills his hand with too much dubious material.

We have appreciated Fisher's work in the promotion of the New Learning. His initiatives at Cambridge leave no doubt as to his sympathy for and commitment to linguistic studies. But we have also noted the limit of that commitment both in the context of university reform and here in his theological writings. Two factors governed his attitude to the use of linguistic achievements in Scriptural matters. First of all there was his fundamental commitment to Church authority in the interpretation of Scripture; and secondly, there was his recognition of the role to be played by traditional theological method in bringing the evidence of Scripture into theological discussion. Consequently, of the Scholastic method Fisher says: 'Take away the dialectics and you immediately take away the power either of demonstrating the false or establishing the truth.'[83] He feels free then to employ Scholastic support, criticising their theology only for its lack of good Latin style and its ignorance of Greek and Hebrew.[84]

---

[82] *Assertio*, f. 14, *Opera*, 296.

[83] *Assertio*, art xxxvii, f. 221-228. Surtz, *Works and Days*, pp. 155-179.

[84] For Fisher's use of Scotus see L. Siekaniec, Cardinal Fisher and Duns Scotus, Franciscan Studies (New York: 1941) Vol. 1, pp. 45-48.

While on the one hand Fisher's support for Renaissance achievements gives him the appearance of standing somewhat apart from the more traditional of his contemporaries; on the other hand the limitations of this support, the occasional slackness in his use of the Scriptures, the firm reliance on traditional methodology and the extensive reference to traditional material, both patristic and medieval, serve to demonstrate that the essential Fisher was a learned and erudite spokesman for all that was best of the medieval Church.

A further facet of his indiscriminate use of sources is seen in the absence of a systematic understanding of the relative importance of the various parts of Church teaching, articles of faith, liturgical customs and practices of piety. Fisher seems to lack a clearly defined method for distinguishing between the various levels of Church statements, and while some of the differences are matters of common sense, no satisfactory criterion is offered in serious theological debate. Fisher's failure to define an exact relationship between Scripture and tradition can be seen as accounting for this. At times he is tempted to give all aspects of Church teaching, traditions and customs a near definitive role, yet at other times he clearly recognises that some relationship with Scripture is essential. His appeal to the argument of St Augustine that the Church received the Scripture states the priority that dominates his thinking. But nowhere does he answer the Protestant contrary assertion that priority belongs to the Scriptures, for the Church was born out of the Gospel. A precise elaboration of the middle ground between these positions is required here on both sides, but the assumption of entrenched positions which occurred soon after the initial impact has made this the long and painful work of centuries.

The basic structure of Fisher's work is clear to us. It is a structure that knits together Scriptures, Spirit and Church in a close exclusive unity. Fisher attacks Luther for his lack of a similar cohesion. But within this structure and because of it, Fisher's work suffers from a surfeit of material. He was able to move quickly to the heart of a problem, but once the struggle was engaged he was content only when he had brought every possible argument into the fray. In doing so he spared no thought for the final length of his work; and the reader, while admiring the breadth of his knowledge, must often have been dismayed by its sheer bulk. Even Erasmus objected that his arguments against Lefèvre were disproportionately vast and this reliance upon quantity rather than quality served to blunt the cutting edge of so many of his arguments.

Theologian

While his firmness of stance and clarity of thought are beyond doubt, his works display nothing of that adaptability or agility of mind which could have given his qualities a thrust and incisiveness which contributes so much to theological debate.

The Gathering of Friends

J ohn Fisher was among the first to take up the pen against Luther. In the years that followed, a great number of Catholic apologists entered the debate, with greater or lesser perception and learning. We have seen Fisher drawing heavily upon the medieval and traditional sources of Catholic theology throughout the length and breadth of his writings. We have observed the close-knit structure of ecclesiology that was the basis of his thought. Now we must attempt to place this work of Fisher in the context of his contemporaries. Was Fisher in any way remarkable for his use of these sources and methods? Was this traditional approach also employed by his fellow Catholic authors? Did they also insist on the total identity of the Holy Spirit and the Church, denying the possibility of truth in any who opposed Church tradition? Was this perhaps the only method employed by Catholics at this stage of the Catholic – Protestant debate? In other words, what was the relationship between Fisher and the contemporary Catholic writers?

The work of John Fisher enjoyed a moderate popularity in European circles. In Germany Fisher was held in high esteem by Johann Cochlaeus (1479-1552), Johann Maier of Eck (1486-1543), Herborn, Hieronymous Emser (1477-1527), Murner and Bishop Faber of Vienna. In Italy his theology was admired by Gian Antonio Pantusa, Catharius, Bellarmine and Borromeo. In France his work against Johannes Oecolampadius (1482-1531) was noted by Willam van der Lindt (Lindanus) and Ruard Tapper of Louvain. In Spain Juan Luis Vives (1492-1540) looked to Fisher as a great humanist and Francisco de Vittoria, Alfonso de Castra and Andres Vega often referred to his writings. It was Johann Cochlaeus who was his principal ally.[1] Above all Fisher's article XXV of the *Assertio* in defence of the Papacy won approving attention. As early as 1524, Hieronymous Emser reprinted this article for its clear treatment of the texts of Matthew 16, Matthew 18 and John 20.[2] In 1532, Giovanni da Fano directed his readers to Fisher for a more elaborate discussion of Peter's primacy; and in 1536 Cochlaeus declared that Fisher had made the primacy so clear from the Scriptures and other sources that

---

[1] Surtz, *Works and Days*, pp. 384–9, 532. A. Moroni, Dizionario di Erudizione Storico-Ecclesiastica, XXV, p. 75.

[2] H. Emser, *Super his verbis 'Tu es Petrus' Dialogus...*, (Dresden : July 1524.)

it would be futile for him to repeat the task.[3] In fact, he says that if all the learned and clever men of England bent all their forces to the task, they could never refute what had been written on Papal authority by Henry VIII, Thomas More and John Fisher. Later he exclaimed, 'How many testimonies, pray, on that primacy did not the Bishop of Rochester produce against Luther's Article XXV?'[4]

The method of Fisher's article appealed to his contemporaries for in the main they too employed the same basic principles in the writings against the opponents of Catholicism. They shared the same understanding of the Church and of the ways in which revealed truth arrives in our midst. The Louvain Ecclesiastical historian, P. Polman, has outlined these similarities in his works on the methods used in Catholic writings against Luther. He describes the contemporary style of theology:

> *Since the time of the origins of Christianity up to the epoch of Luther, all the Christian polemicists, in order to resolve their debates, had appealed to the authority of their predecessors: the Fathers, the Councils and the Popes. In particular, the beliefs of the ancient Church, approved by the Fathers, always pre-empted their arguments.[5]*

And he affirms that the challenge of Luther was directed first of all at that method. He then lists the authors who, refusing to change their point of departure, met the challenge of Luther with direct reaffirmation of their traditional position. He mentions the works of Johann Eck, S. Prieras, Cardinal Tommaso de Vio Cajetan (1469-1534), Jacobus Latomus [Jacques Masson 1475-1544], John Driedo (1480-1535), M. Peresius and Cardinal Gasparo Contarini (1483-1542). All these writers affirmed a belief in the importance of tradition, rising from the guidance of the Holy Spirit in the Church which was manifestly similar to John Fisher.

In fact the similarity of their positions also embraces its problems and weaknesses, for just as with Fisher, the exact relationship between the different organs of authority was left without precise clarification. However, Polman asserts:

> *In effect, on this question it is always the entire Church, the true guardian of revelation that alone matters. All the organs are too*

[3] G. da Fano, *Opera utilissima vulgare contra le permitiosissime heresie Lutherane per li semplici.* (Bologna: 1532.) f. 38. Joannes Cochlaeus, Epistola Nicolai, sig. 2.4.

[4] Joannes Cochlaeus, *De Papa et de Unitate Ecclesiae,* sig. D 1.2. Also Surtz, *Works and Days,* p. 506.

[5] P. Polman, *L'Élément Historique dans les Controverses Religieuses du XVI Siècle,* (Gembleux: 1932) and *'La Méthode Polémique des Premiers Adversaires de la Réforme' in Revue d'Histoire Ecclésiastique,* xxv (1929) p. 471.

> *intimately linked together to be able to always rigorously distinguish one from another. The only office of the Pope and the Councils is to represent the Church.*[6]

Constantly, therefore, the method of appealing to Scripture alone was rejected, for it was the role of the Church to be guide and teacher in these matters. The habit of appealing to Scripture alone was regarded as the source of all error. Thus Polman concludes:

> *The Catholic polemicists were constantly preoccupied in establishing the existence of the authority of tradition. Despite the accounts of divergence among them on the subject of infallible authority, one can affirm that concerning essential doctrine they opposed the Protestants as a united front.*[7]

Naturally enough, following in the lines of Fisher, this dogmatic position leads to constant employment by these writers of the argument from history. Their appeal to tradition and to the consensus of past opinions is as central as Fisher's. Eck, for example, appeals to the corroboration of Patristic writings on the questions of sacramental confession, images and the sacrificial aspect of the Eucharist. Driedo works in similar fashion for the primacy of Rome as does de Castro for the Eucharistic presence.[8] The works of Gropper and Lindanus are described by Polman as 'a history nearly full of certain dogmas' and he affirms that this appeal to 'the perpetuity of the faith' was the basis for most of their arguments.[9]

Polman comments that this style of controversy, arising as it does from deep rooted convictions about the nature of revealed truth, undoubtedly led to the accentuation of theological differences between the parties involved. It gave a dogmatic strength to the point of view which saw the Reformers as heretics simply because they opposed certain long-standing traditions and it certainly removed any possibility of immediate dialogue on particular issues by underlying the central methodological differences. A mutual hardening of fundamental positions resulted.

There was also another movement among the Catholics of Europe in response to Luther which held more hope of progress towards reconciliation, for it attempted to reply to Luther in terms that were acceptable to him. Under the inspiration of the Habsburg Emperor

---

[6] Polman, *op. cit*, pp. 480–3. J. Eck, *De Primatu Petri adversus Lutherum* (1520), f. 8.11.

[7] Polman, *op. cit*. p. 485.

[8] Eck, *De Primatu Petri adversus Lutherum* (1520), ff. 48–51. Driedo, De Ecclesiasticis scripturis et dogmatibus. (1533) f. 166-172. Castro, Adversus omnes haereses, (Antwerp: 1565) f. 227-233.

[9] Polman, *op. cit*. pp. 488, 490.

Charles V (1500-1558), the *Confutation of the Augsburg Confession*
was written by Faber, Eck and Cochlaeus and it appealed largely to
Scripture. Similarly, work by men such as Gaspar Schatzgeyer (1463-
1527), Christopher de Cheffontaine (1512-1595) and François Sonnius
(1506-1576) looked for greater clarity and impact in their arguments
by starting out from Scriptural sources.[10] Unfortunately their elasticity
was not inspired by a reconciliatory motive and the highly polemical
tone which characterized the other writings of this period is also present
here. Genuine efforts at reconciliation were made under the continued
patronage of Charles V at the Diets of Haggenaut (1538), Worms (1539)
and Regensberg (1541), where considerable agreement was reached.
They eventually broke down and made way for the Council of Trent.[11]

However, for the most part, the reaction of the Catholic theologians to
Luther is very accurately reflected in the writings of Fisher. Fundamental
to their work was the emphasis on a formative and authoritative Church
tradition, and even though lesser streams showed a willingness to lay
aside that dogmatic principle, the majority of Catholics reaffirmed it
irrespective of its unacceptability to their opponents. They presented
this as their final court of appeal and effectively excluded the possibility
of dialogue.

But our real interest lies in England. Here Fisher was held in high
esteem as the foremost opponent of the Reformation; but what of his
English contemporaries? Did they simply follow in his wake, repeating
his arguments and assertions? Was Fisher as representative of England
as he was of Europe? Or, on the other hand, can we find any evidence
to suggest that for all his intellectual superiority Fisher alone does not
represent the full scope of the first response to Luther in England?

The beginnings of Lutheranism in England, especially in the
universities of Oxford and Cambridge, have been extensively studied.[12]
Early in 1521, Bishop Cuthbert Tunstall wrote to Wolsey from Worms
with a request:

> *...that your Grace may call before you the printers and booksellers
> and give them a straight charge that they bring none of his
> [Luther's] books into England, nor that they translate none of them*

[10] G. Schatzgeyer, *Scrutinium divinae Scripturae pro conciliatione dissidentium dogmaticum.* (1522). C. de *Cheffontaine. Fidei majorum nostrum defensio,* (Antwerp: 1515) F. Sonnius. *Demonstrationum religionis christianae ex Verbo Dei Libri Tres,* (Lugduni: 1564.)

[11] cf. P. Matheson, *Cardinal Contarini at Regensberg,* (Oxford: Clarendon Press, 1972.)

[12] For example: A.G. Dickens, *The English Reformation,* (London: B.T. Batsford, 1966.) H.C. Porter, *Reformation and Reaction in Tudor Cambridge,* (Cambridge Univ. Press: 1958.) E. Doernburg, Henry VIII and Luther, (London: Barrie and Rockliffe, 1961.) N.S. Tjernagel, *Henry VIII and the Lutherans,* (St Louis: Concordia, 1965.) et al.

Chapter Seven

> *into English lest thereby might ensue great trouble to the realm and*
> *Church of England as is now here.*[13]

By March of the same year Archbishop William Warham was concerned at the spread of Lutheranism in Oxford and wrote to Wolsey hoping that steps taken to eliminate it would be discreet and avoid scandal.[14] April saw Wolsey send copies of Lutheran works and a manuscript of John Wycliff (1320-1384) to Warham asking him to examine them, and on 16 April Pace found Henry hard at work on his refutation of Luther.[15] The following day Leo X (1475-1521) wrote to Wolsey suggesting a public burning of Lutheran works and, as Erasmus had predicted ten months earlier, the ceremony duly took place on 12 May, 1521.[16] This was followed two days later by a commission directing the bishops of England to search out and seize all books, pamphlets and papers written or edited by Luther and to send them to the Cardinal within fifteen days. So by 21 May, Wolsey could report to the Pope that certain proceedings had taken place for the suppression of Lutheran heresies.[17]

The ceremony at St Paul's Cross was the most significant of these proceedings and in the opinion of the Venetian ambassador thirty thousand people were present at the ceremony.[18] It was the occasion of John Fisher's first sermon against Luther. At the ceremony he had in his hands a manuscript copy of King Henry's book, the *Assertio Septem Sacramentorum*, which had been written in the preceding months and was subsequently published on 12 July.[19] Henry had first written against Luther as early as 1517 when, at Wolsey's suggestion, he had composed a treatise in defence of Indulgences. Apparently the work remained unfinished at that time, but the essence of it came to print in the opening chapter of the *Assertio Septem Sacramentorum*.[20] The main body of the book, however, was directed against Luther's *De Captivitate Babylonica* with its attack on the sacraments of the Church.

Henry's book reflected what we have seen to be the basic teaching of the Catholic Church on this very popular subject, and in the course of his argument he gives extensive quotations from Scripture and the

[13] E. Doernburg, *Henry VIII & Luther,* (Barrie & Rockliff: London, 1961) p. 8.

[14] J.S. Brewer, J. Gairdner and R.H. Brodie, Letters and Papers, Foreign and Domestic, of the Reign of Henry VIII, (London: 1862-1920,) Vol. III, pt i. No. 1193. Henceforth cited as LPFD.

[15] LPFD, Vol. III, pt i, No. 1218 & No. 1233.

[16] Erasmus to Melancthon, 21 June 1520, in P. S. Allen, *Opus Epistolarum*, Vol. IV, Ep. 1113, p. 287.

[17] J. Strype, Ecclesiastical Memorials, (Oxford: 1822) Vol. I, pt i, pp. 57-61. LPFD, Vol. III, pt I, No. 1279 & 1234.

[18] LPFD, Vol. III, pt i. No. 1273-1275.

[19] Scarisbrick, p. 153. Calendar of State Papers, Venetian. (ed. Rawton Brown, 1864.) Vol III, p.120.

[20] Doernburg, *Henry VIII and Luther,* p. 5.

Fathers. His quotations are taken from about thirty books of the Bible for a total of nearly one hundred references, evenly divided between the Old and New Testaments. There are about seventy quotations from the Fathers: one third from Augustine, one third from Jerome, Anselm and Gregory and the remainder from other familiar Patristic writers.[21] As a clear statement of popular traditional Catholic belief it was no mean achievement and it won for Henry his long desired Papal title of 'Defender of the Faith'. It is known that Thomas More helped as a 'sorter out and placer of the principal matter' and it is commonly thought that Fisher aided too. However, there seems to be no reason why Henry should not have written the work; allowing for the influence of Fisher's knowledge, method and library resources.[22]

Despite the disadvantage that it was largely lacking in imaginative presentation of Catholic teaching and that its grasp of Lutheranism was inadequate, it must have been a most effective publication and was certainly a best seller, going through some twenty editions and translations in the sixteenth century in Antwerp, Rome, Frankfurt, Cologne, Paris and Wurzburg besides England. Among these, the first German translation by Emser and Murner appeared as early as 1522. But its appeal and efficacy lay not so much in its theological content as in the fact that it was short and often unfair and, perhaps as its greatest strength, it was written by so notable a king. It could hardly have been better calculated to strengthen the humbler untrained Catholic who may have been puzzled and possibly attracted by new ideas, but it would have done little to persuade a person already in the Lutheran camp to change one's allegiance.[23]

Luther's reaction to the work was predictable and highlights vividly the traditional methodology employed by Henry:

> *The sum of the matter is this; the whole of Henry's book is based on the words of men, and on the uses of centuries and on no word of God, nor any use of the Spirit. On the contrary, the sum of my argument is that whereas the words of men and the use of centuries can be tolerated and endorsed provided they do not conflict with the Sacred Scriptures, nevertheless they do not make articles of faith, nor any necessary observances.[24]*

---

[21] Tjernagel, *Henry VIII and the Lutherans* p. 12.

[22] R.W. Chambers, *Thomas More* (London, 1935), p. 193. Scarisbrick, Henry VIII, p. 154.

[23] Scarisbrick, pp. 152-155. J.S. Brewer, The Reign of Henry VIII, (London: John Murray, 1884.) Vol I, p. 607.

[24] *Luther's reply to King Henry VIII*, trans. E. S. Buchanan (NewYork, 1928), p. 57. Also Tjernagel, *Henry VIII and the Lutherans*, p. 21.

Chapter Seven

Henry did indeed make use of 'the words of men' and 'the use of centuries' after the fashion of the times because they were held to be the work of the Holy Spirit. He made full use of the appeal to history, of the argument from prescription and thus dismissed Luther's teaching on the grounds of inconsistency with the consensus of Church teaching:

> *As if it was sufficient ground that the obstinate impudence of one single little friar should lead us to doubt those things that all the Church of Christ over the past 1500 years has believed and held to be articles of faith...his assertions are diametrically contrary to the doctrine of all the most holiest men over so many ages.*[25]

One example of this is his defence of the Catholic doctrine of the Eucharistic Real Presence where he makes an appeal to Hugh of St Victor, Eusebius, Gregory of Nyssa, Theophilus, Cyril and Ambrose, concluding that the Patristic Fathers 'teach not consubstantiation but transubstantiation.'[26]

Clearly, Henry's work was in the same mould as Fisher's and that of the majority of Catholic theologians. As with Fisher, this does not mean that he lacked arguments from Scripture; but that the emphasis of his work, the real force of his argument, lies in the teaching and tradition of the Church both as authoritative interpreter of Scripture and as a source of defined doctrine. Luther's own comments highlight how little this methodology was capable of contributing to the solution of dogmatic differences.

There is further evidence, slight though it may be, of the extent to which the method of refuting Luther pervaded the Catholic world of the early sixteenth century in England, for we also possess a sermon by an unknown author given to an unknown audience, dated about 1520, which contains a very similar attack on Luther.[27] Other aspects of this sermon, however, are more unusual and merit attention.

The theme of the sermon is the conflict between truth and falsehood described in terms of light and darkness; a conflict which first took place in heaven but, when Lucifer was banished, was then continued on earth. Christ is presented as the light of mankind who overcame the darkness of falsehood by speaking the truth. It is our duty to acknowledge him, to

---

[25] Henry VIII, Epistola Defensoria, f. 124, annexed to the 1521 version of the *Assertio Septem Sacramentorum*.

[26] L. O'Donovan, The Defence of the Seven Sacraments by Henry VIII. (New York. 1908.) pp. 30-31.

[27] British Library, MS. Harleian 311, *Sermones Latini et Anglice cum Aliis*, ff. 113–39. The only indication of authorship or identity is on f. 129 where the name Thomas Beech has been written at least ten times in the margins. This is almost certainly the name of the scribe who, at this point bored by his labour, began to amuse himself. See W. Blench, *Preaching in England in the Late Fifteenth and Sixteenth Centuries* (Oxford: Blackwell, 1964), p. 356.

hear his words, to keep them and finally to act upon them. The structure of the sermon is a prologue (f. 113-120) and three parts; the first establishing that Christ is the truth (f. 121-128), the second part that we must hear him (f. 129-135), and thirdly that we must act upon the truth with good works (f. 135-139). The pattern, the structure of the Scholastic syllogism, is an essential part of the argument and is adhered to strictly. The first section is the major premise of the syllogism, the second is the minor 'because he has all his strengthand valour of his major' (f. 136) and the third part is the conclusion which brings us 'directly to salvation' (f. 136) An applied Scholastic discipline permeates the whole of this sermon and consequently it is free from many medieval characteristics such as pictorial images or narratives, allegorical interpretations and moralising applications of Scripture and superfluity of subdivisions. Fittingly it is closely knit, adheres to its theme, and relies throughout on a literal interpretation of Scripture, on detailed quotations from the Fathers and on a use of Thomistic philosophical principles. In fact, the intellectual level of the sermon is high and though we are left to speculate as to its circumstances, it is a witness to the fact that such ability was at large in those days.

The prologue sets out to establish man's dependence on God because of the profound influence of evil within him. Man must be humble enough to acknowledge the truth of his dependence, for lack of humility causes all evil: 'Was it not a huge cloud of vanity that before clouded the mind of Lucifer that he could covet equality with Almighty God which no creature might attain.' However, in opposition to the darkness caused by Lucifer, Christ has come to bring light, and we overcome darkness by following Christ.

The author develops the first section by following the philosopher's maxim, 'describe opposites for greater elucidation' (f. 121). In a passage which is a true example of his use of the Fathers and the resources of philosophy, he presents Christ as the Truth, after St Augustine in Chapter 8 of *De Trinitate* (f. 122). Christ is the truth first of all, he says, as the eternal Truth:

> *Conceived in the most purest, glorious and blessed mind which is God, which understanding the inexplicable being of itself conceives the uncreated and co-eternal verity. He is the truth of being to everything, in that his knowledge is the cause of everything whereof it move, hath being than of itself as St Augustine declares in the said chapter…and to this agrees St Bernard in the last sermon Super Cantica saying 'The Truth of God is everything.'*

He then contrasts Christ and Lucifer as light and darkness; and as humility and pride.

> *Pride he shows to be abominable by the meekness of his incarnation…*
> *as says St Gregory in one of his homilies 'all Christ's acts are for our*
> *instruction'. Thus the darkness of vanity from man's affection with*
> *the light of verity he put away, then, man to his salvation might see*
> *the right way. (f. 124)*

However, he continues, it is clear that some men prefer darkness, either because they have hold of falsehood and not truth, or because they are vain or hypocrites and are lost in shadows. All heretics are in this first classification for 'they do not cease to confound the world with manifold errors'. (f. 125)

Luther is mentioned by name in the second part, which is concerned to show that we must give our consent to the truth and not to wrong teachings:

> *Christians, attend your soul's health and do not avert to the perverse*
> *doctrines of misbelieving wretches…and beware of such false*
> *prophets as Luther with his adherents who under cloaked colour of*
> *sane doctrine , which they say they have searched more profoundly*
> *than all their predecessors, arise with the new glosses to glorify*
> *their names…For earthly accessions to which they finally do aspire,*
> *Christian faith they fear not to subvert and will not say the truth*
> *they know in their conscience but against their conscience they rebel*
> *against the truth and by apparent sentence they induce misbelief in*
> *their audience. (f. 133)*

His diagnosis of the cause of the trouble is familiar, for quoting Jeremiah he observes:

> *Beware of those prophets who speak unto you and deceive you. They*
> *prophecy nothing but the imaginations and forgings of their own*
> *minds and not the truth of the holy Scripture. (f. 134)*

It is the misuse of Scripture and interpretations that are without humility that he sees to be the cause of error and, like Fisher, he uses the image of the harmony of Scripture to make his point. 'The blessed instrument of holy Scripture' produces harmony unless it is used by the 'bellows of fainting flattery' which 'diminishes the true harmony thereof' (f. 125). So his simple argument and exhortation is familiar to us:

> *So Christians do not believe anything else but establish you in that*
> *faith which has endured from the passion of our saviour Jesus Christ*
> *unto this time testified by all holy Doctors and approved of God by*

> *his manifold mercy shown in glorification of those which firmly hath*
> *believed it. (f. 134)*

The third part deals with the particular point of good works, which he presents as the fruits of knowing and accepting the truth of Christ. Without naming anyone, he says that many of his contemporaries do not arrive at the same conclusion because their minds are distracted by 'sensual delectation' and even though 'they daily search and investigate the truth of God contained in holy Scriptures' (f. 137), they do not admit the necessity of good works. He quotes Matthew 7:21 and James 2:14 ff on the need for good works and concludes, 'Wherefore let a good conclusion approve your premises and meritorious works commend your faith and then it shall to your soul's health.' (f. 138)

Many aspects of this sermon are not commonly found in the quoted sources of this period. Outstanding are its Christo-centric structure; its disciplined literal use of Scripture and the formative influence of a Thomistic Scholasticism. The influences of university training, such as we have seen them to be, are much more in evidence here than in the works of Fisher and the King and we are left to speculate as to the possibility of the sermon belonging to a university environment. But when it comes to dealing with Lutheranism, the sermon shows all the common characteristics of the age; an abusive polemical tone, an inaccurate presentation of the contrary position, and, from the Catholic point of view, the portrayal of Lutheranism as a black cloud to be rejected on the evidence of history, a history formed by the Holy Spirit. Even here, where many other aspects of the sermon are unusual, we find the same Catholic tactic being displayed.

The work of Richard Whytford, which we have already presented, is totally different to this sermon in style and appeal.[28] Yet his defence of the necessity of sacramental confession, against contrary opinion, is fundamentally identical. After outlining how the instruction of Leviticus 4 and Christ's cleansing of the lepers through the medium of priests in Matthew 8 are both foreshadows of the sacrament, and further quoting the authority of Peter before Ananias and Sapphira, he presents the real force of his argument which is this:

> *Our mother the holy Church therefore hath (by the inspiration of*
> *the Holy Ghost) ordained that every person that doth commit or*
> *do any deadly sin in work, words or by full deliberate consent in*
> *thought, must needfully (if they will be saved) be confessed thereof*
> *unto a priest. Since that all Christian people have received and*

---

28 Oxford Ashmolean Library, Ashmole MS, 1215.

used the same so many hundred years take you that use and custom
for sufficient authority to follow the same and put all manner of
contrary opinion clear out of mind and in no wise to hear speak or
talk thereof.[29]

The *Assertio Septem Sacramentorum*, the sermon and this handbook of Whytford together give us an indication of the extent to which this one basic approach to the Lutheran controversy was employed in England in the 1520s. Fisher was its most eloquent and learned exponent, but these works show it was used in very varied circumstances. There is no doubt about the suitability of this method to those who wished to reassert the Catholic position, for it opened the way for the admission of a great mass of evidence which was impressive even in its very bulk. It was suited, then, to those who through their upbringing, education and conviction treasured their Catholic heritage and tradition and who, above all else, were concerned to defend it from the attacks of Luther. But it was a method which of its nature militated against the development of mutual understanding and so contributed nothing, and continued to make no contribution for many centuries, to the cause of dialogue between the conflicting parties.

But have we here a complete picture of the activity in England during these opening years of the debate? The *Letters and Papers* of the reign of Henry VIII suggest that there is more to come. A letter from Henry to Leo X, dated May 21, 1521, reports that Henry not only wrote against Luther himself but thought it best to call upon the learned men of his kingdom to consider errors and condemn them. Cardinal Medici, writing to the Papal Nuncio and Bishop of Ascoli on June 7, 1521, says that the Pope was glad to find that the King had induced the scholars of his realm to draw their pens against the heretics. Further, the reported oration of John Clerk on presenting the King's book to the Pope on October 10, 1521, includes this passage:

> *There [in England] among other fast friends of the Holy See, the most*
> *conspicuous is Wolsey, a member of that college, who has caused*
> *the Pope's rescript against Luther to be published everywhere, and*
> *Luther's books to be burned, called an assembly of learned men*
> *to write against him, and supported them at his own cost for some*
> *months.*[30]

Clearly then the state campaign against Luther did not stop short at the public burning of his books but some sort of more sustained and

---

[29] Ashmolean, Ashmole MS, 1215, f. Fi-Fii.

[30] *LPFD*, Vol. III, pt I, Nos. 1297, 1333 and 1656.

academic drive, patronised by the King and Wolsey, appears to have been made. Whether they were united in this effort, or whether they patronised separate gatherings of 'the learned' is not known, but co-operation at this point seems likely.

The Register of the University of Oxford helps us here, for there is an entry under April 21, 1521, which indicates that the Cardinal clearly did call together representatives of the academics of England to his London house for a period of intense study which, according to Clerk, lasted for some months.[31] Doctors Kynton, Brynknell, Roper and de Coloribus were among those present. Do we know of any others who attended?

In December of the same year, the Oxford Convocation wrote to Edmund Audley, Bishop of Salisbury, asking that he allow the leave of absence of Edward Powel, one of the Salisbury Canons, to stand without loss of income for he had been commissioned – along with other Oxford men – to write confutations of the Lutheran heresies.[32] A later letter named him in the company of John Kynton, John Roper, Thomas Brynknell and John de Coloribus; so we may conclude with some confidence that he too was among the guests of Wolsey. Turning to the Registers of Cambridge University, we find information that indicates that Doctors Bullock, Humfrey, Watson and Ridley were sent by that university to London at the invitation of Wolsey for the examination of Luther's works during the year 1521. For lack of a precise date, however, we are left to speculate that it was for one and the same meeting.

The elected representatives of Oxford and Cambridge met under the patronage of Wolsey, and it seems also of the King, to discuss and refute the opinions of Luther. Indeed the efforts of Wolsey are not summed up by the ceremony at St Paul's Cross, but here we have evidence of a meeting of considerable importance. The fruits of this meeting are mentioned in later letters of the Oxford Convocation which speaks of works produced by their men: Powel, Kynton, Roper, Brynknell and de Coloribus;

> *Whose writings, after reading their words, we have reviewed them, ruminated upon them and appraised their merits. Nevertheless, it has seemed good to us to select the edition of Dr Powel as a principal and luminous gem.[33]*

The Biographical Register of Cambridge records that Henry Bullock wrote a work too, entitled *Contra Lutherum de Captivitate Babylonica*.[34]

---

[31] *Register of Congregations and Convocations*, Vol. II, f.60.

[32] See XVIth Century Letter Book, FF (Oxford, Bodley MS, 282) No. 87, f. 4. & No. 89, f. 46.

[33] Oxford, Bodley MS, 282, No. 89, f.46.

[34] Emden, *Biographical Register*, p. 105.

Whether the other Cambridge men ever wrote is not known for even Dodd, who has the fullest list of all the works of this period, makes no mention of them.[35] In his list Dodd provides us with the title of Dr Powel's work, *Propugnaculum Summi Sacerdotii evangelici adversus Martinum Lutherum*, and with *Tractatus contra Doctrinum M. Lutheri* as the title of the works by Brynknell, Kynton, Roper and de Coloribus.[36]

These sources also inform us of other little known writers of this period who wrote against the teaching of Martin Luther. For the sake of quality rather than quantity, however, it is sufficient to note two other writers: Richard Kiddermynster, abbot of Winchcombe, who wrote a *Tractatus contra Doctrinum M. Lutheri* in 1521, and John Batmanson, prior of the London Charterhouse, who wrote a similarly titled work.[37]

Here then, in this assembled company, is evidence of an academically based refutation of Lutheran teaching in the early years of the debate. The significance of the effort exerted in this campaign both by its promoters, Wolsey and Henry, and by its protagonists, the leading theologians from Oxford and Cambridge, should not be under-estimated and as full an appreciation as possible of this development is necessary for our balanced understanding of the state of affairs in England at this time. Unfortunately it has proved impossible to find the works produced by these scholars, with the exception of Powel's book; but even on the minimum evidence available to us we are entitled to state that initial reaction against Luther seems to have been quite widely based.[38] The disappearance of these works excludes us from a detailed analysis of this response to Luther, but first impressions would indicate fairly that, given such a wide range of writers, we can expect to find considerable differences in approach and method to the conflict with Luther. Biographical details of life-style, education and known sympathies are our remaining sources from which to draw speculative

---

[35] See C. Dodd, *Certamen Utriusque Ecclesiae*. A List of all the Eminent Writers of Controversy Catholic and Protestant since the Reformation.

[36] C. Dodd, *The Church History of England from the Year 1500 to the Year 1688*, (Brussels: 1738.) Re: T. Brynknell, p. 211, J. Kynton p. 236, J. Roper p. 209, J. de Coloribus p.231, E. Powel p.209, H Bullock p.212. Also J. Bale, *Index Britanniae Scriptorum*, Ed. R.L. Poole (Oxford : Clarendon Press, 1902.) mentions E. Powel on p. 508, and H. Bullock on pp. 159-160. J. Pitseus, *Relationum Historicarum de Rebus Anglicis*, (Paris: 1619.) names E. Powel on p. 729, and H. Bullock on p. 710. J. Tanner, *Bibliotheca Britannico-Hibernica*, (London: 1748.) lists T. Brynknell p. 126, J. Kynton p. 458, J. Roper p. 642, J. de Coloribus p. 192 and H. Bullock p. 139 with the titles of their works. These are the sources for the *Dictionary of National Biography* (London: 1885.) which gives attention to all these authors with the exception of J. Roper.

[37] G. Dodd, *The Church History of England*, p. 229. T. Tanner, p. 450. Emden, *Biographical Register*, Vol. II, p. 1047.

[38] The libraries and archives of the British Library, Oxford, Cambridge, the Vatican, the English College in Rome, Douai College, Syon Abbey and Paris do not possess copies of these works. It is not certain that, even if the works were written, they were in fact published.

The Gathering of Friends

conclusions about the contents of these books. The Oxford theologians were men held in high regard by the University. Each held positions of considerable responsibility within the University, though for the most part they appear to be men of traditional disposition and achievement.

John Roper was a Berkshire man, who was admitted to Magdalen College in August, 1482, and became a Fellow in 1483; in the course of his subsequent career he gave lectures in moral and natural philosophy and metaphysics. He took an active part in the administrative affairs of Oxford, being principal administrator of Magdalen College for two years (1492-1494) and of St George's Hall from 1510 to 1512.[39] Completing his Doctorate in Divinity in 1501, he was appointed first Lady Margaret Reader in Divinity in 1501 and was looked upon as 'one of the solid divines of the University'; he also wrote in the divorce controversy in defence of Catherine. He died in 1534.[40]

John Kynton was a Franciscan from Stamford Convent who was Magdalen College professor of theology from 1501-1509 and 'senior theologus' of the University in 1503, 1504 and 1532. He, too, was Lady Margaret Reader of Divinity for many years 'with the general approbation of the whole University', until he resigned in October 1530. He died in 1536.[41]

John de Coloribus we know as a Walloon Dominican who, after a period in Paris (1502), Lille (1503 and 1510), where he lectured on the *Sentences*, and at Douai (1508), came to England in 1511 and preached in Oxford in that year. He won favour with Wolsey, who not only appointed him to write against Luther, but also promoted him to be one of the members of his new Oxford College.[42]

It is well known that Wolsey's founding of Cardinal College was partially inspired by his wish to promote concerted efforts in the newly emerging studies of the ancient classics.[43] To this end he gathered together some of the most promising young men he could find in England and abroad, for example John Clerk, John Fryer, John Frith and others. It is also well known that in some respects Wolsey's plan misfired for, rather than serving the aims he had in mind, some of the scholars he had brought together became the chief propagators at Oxford of Lutheran teachings.

---

[39] Emden, *Biographical Register*, Vol. III, p. 1590.

[40] Dodd, *The Church History of England*, p. 209.

[41] Emden, *Biographical Register*, Vol. II, p. 1053. Dodd, *The Church History of England*, p, 236.

[42] Emden, *Biographical Register*, Vol. I, p. 470. A Wood, *History and Antiquities of the Colleges and Halls in the University of Oxford*. (Clarendon Press: Oxford, 1786), Vol. I, p. 47.

[43] For example: H.C. Maxwell Lyte, *A History of the University of Oxford*, (London: Macmillan & Co, 1886) pp. 435ff. J. Ingham, *Memorials of Oxford*, (Oxford: J. Parker, 1837) pp. 38ff.

The early days of Cardinal College and the choice of members were governed by a desire to advance the knowledge of the New Learning and, as John de Coloribus was found in this company, then he must have been at least proficient in the skills of those studies. He is said to have been held in great esteem among the Oxonians of 1525.[44]

Finally, Thomas Brynknell started his career in the school of Lincoln College, later becoming headmaster of the Magdalen College grammar school from 1502 until 1508, and then Cardinal College public lecturer in theology in 1519. His work against Luther was done:

> *To the general satisfaction of the whole university, whose common letter of praise of his works is still upon record, with the advantageous circumstance of being proper books to be read by all young divines.*

He was also a canon in both the Coventry and Lichfield Cathedrals.[45]

Well favoured by the University and holders of public positions in theology, these men were representative of the best scholars of Oxford at that time. Their work is praised in the letters of the University Convocation, and is generally portrayed as being sound. Indications point towards their being, for the most part, traditional theologians writing after the fashion of the times. However, we have some indications that the contributions of John de Coloribus may have varied from the others for his background and achievements suggest the likelihood of a different approach to this conflict. The letters of the University in fact confirm this, for when Wolsey demanded that the works of the Oxford scholars, with the exception of Powel's book, be combined into a single work, the University refused to obey, saying that the variety of methods employed in these works made a compendium edition impossible:

> *Their writings remain unpublished, yet they will edit and publish them when the order comes from your venerable authority. Why then from all the things ordered by your holy paternity was not a single book published, what was the cause? Although against Luther, one by one they wrote with great exactitude since, however, they did not do it in the same order and style it appeared that it was impossible to put together one single volume from them all.[46]*

Wolsey ordered the work of Powel to be published separately. This order was carried out and we will examine the results later.

Oxford University also spoke highly of the work of Richard

---

[44] Dodd, *The Church History of England*, p. 231.

[45] Emden, *Biographical Register*, Vol. I, p. 268. LPDF, Vol. III, pt. i, no. 570. Dodd, *The Church History of England*, p. 211.

[46] MS Bodley 282. No. 90, f. 46.

Kiddermynster: 'He wrote about indulgences with piety and erudition such that no one else can write equal to him.'[47] His reputation leads us to expect a work of sound learning for, appointed Abbot of Winchcombe in July 1488, he was one of the English delegates at the Lateran Council that took place between 1512 and 1517, and preached 'sundry times' before the Pope.[48] He was described by Henry VIII as a man of 'remarkable learning and experience', and his erudition was held in the esteem of Erasmus.[49] The reputation of Winchcome Abbey is further evidence for us to have a high regard for Kiddermynster and to lament the loss of his work. At Winchcombe the community seems to have been engaged in systematic study and lectures, covering the traditional material of Old and New Testament studies and systematic theology from the Sentences.[50] The method of study received the approval of Colet and Kiddermynster's description of his own religious house as 'another new university' seems to have had justification.[51] Coming from such a strong and apparently healthy environment, and being renowned for his active contributions there, we may rightly expect that Kiddermynster brought a unique contribution to the Lutheran debate, enabling us to be more sure of the real likelihood of a broad based response to Luther from Catholic writers in the early days of the controversy.

Erasmus' opinion of John Batmanson, the Carthusian, was very different; for Batmanson was a friend of Archbishop Lee, and he attacked the *Annotations* of Erasmus in 1519 and 1520.[52] Bale, too, is reported as having had a low opinion of Batmanson, describing him as 'supercilious and arrogant and fond of quarrelling', though he admitted he was a clear writer.[53] In all probability, Batmanson was of the extreme Catholic tradition in his method and arguments against Luther. He was appointed Prior of the London Charterhouse in 1529 and died three years later.[54]

The Cambridge contingent brought with them more varied reputations and associations. Robert Ridley was a Northumbrian and uncle of the more illustrious Nicholas, for whose education he provided. He studied for some time in Paris, eventually proceeding to a Doctorate of Divinity

---

[47] MS Bodley 282. No. 89, f. 46.

[48] Emden, *Biographical Register,* Vol. II, p. 1047.

[49] LPFD, Vol. IV, pt. iii, no. 2929. Allen, *Opus Epistolarum,* Vol. IV, Ep. 1061, pp. 162–3.

[50] G. Haigh, *The History of Winchcombe Abbey,* (London: Skeffington & Son, 1947,) pp. 161ff.W.A. Pantin. 'Abbot Kidderminster and Monastic Studies', *Downside Review,* xlvii. 1929, p. 199ff.

[51] Lupton, *The Life of Dean Colet,* pp. 90–3. Pantin, 'Abbot Kidderminster and Monastic Studies', p. 200.

[52] Allen, *Opus Epistolarum,* Vol. IV, Ep. 1099, pp. 258–9.

[53] *Dictionary of National Biography,* Vol. III, p. 414.

[54] Emden, *Biographical Register,* Vol I, p 1310

at Cambridge in 1518. He was later chaplain to Bishop Tunstall, until his death in 1536.[55] Cavendish described him as, 'a very small person in stature but surely a great and excellent clerk in divinity.'[56] He was known as a constant opponent of the Reformation but the breadth of his learning, as evidenced by the known remains of his library, should have ensured that his opposition was not narrowly based.[57]

For the Doctors Watson, Humfrey and Bullock we may turn again to Erasmus for help. This time, however, we are dealing with people he was pleased to have as his friends, for all three in fact were among the first circle of friends and admirers which Erasmus formed in his years at Cambridge between 1511 and 1516. Firstly, John Watson was admitted as a Fellow of Peterhouse in 1501, and later became Proctor (1504-1505), university preacher (1505-1506) and Vice Chancellor between 1518 and 1520, and 1530 until 1531. He travelled in Italy meeting friends of Erasmus and going as far as the Holy Land. After his return he became a Doctor of Divinity in 1517 and Master of Christ's College in the same year. He held this post until 1531 and eventually died in 1537.[58] In correspondence with Erasmus he is included among the friends whom Erasmus sends greetings and when Watson actually receives a letter from Erasmus he expresses his pleasure:

> *I value two or three pages of his writing addressed to me, almost as much as the best living that could be given to me. I can imagine you laughing and saying 'tis honest of you to add 'almost'.' I frankly confess that I do not altogether despise those material advantages; but I am so attached to them as to prefer them to good letters and the friendship of learned men, provided one has enough to live decently.[59]*

In reply, Erasmus places Watson 'among the first of his friends, remembering our delightful intercourse and those nights that passed in amusing talk of which one never tired', and he continues by expressing his pleasure that Watson has received his New Testament

---

[55] Emden, *Biographical Register,* p. 480.

[56] G. Cavendish, *The Life and Death of Cardinal Wolsey,* (London: Early English Text Society Publications,1959.) Original series No. 243.

[57] *Dictionary of National Biography,* Vol. XVI, p. 1172. Emden, *Biographical Register*, p. 480.

[58] Emden, *Biographical Register,* p. 622.

[59] Allen, *Opus Epistolarum,* Vol. II, Ep. 456, p. 329; Vol. III, Ep. 777, p. 219. John Watson to Erasmus, August 1516. Nichols, *The Epistles of Erasmus,* Vol. II, Ep. 442, p. 333. Allen, *Opus Epistolarum,* Vol. II, Ep. 450, p. 314.

with approbation, despite the fact that he holds him to be 'versed in the mazes of Scotus'.[60] Watson retorts by admitting:

> *I am not so much a Scotist as I should like to be although it is decreed that I shall not proceed further than I have done, inasmuch as I have solemnly resolved to devote whatever life is left to me to sacred studies alone.[61]*

From this Watson seems to have undertaken the style of studies envisaged by John Fisher, including both Scholastic theology and many years of Scripture study enlightened by the ideas and learning of Erasmus. In view of this, we may indeed wonder at the quality of the contribution he made some four years later to the examination of Lutheran doctrine.

Dr Humfrey is mentioned only in the company of Watson in the letters of Erasmus, although some obscure references in the letters of 1513 associate him with William Gonnell, Erasmus' host at Landbeach.[62] This is sufficient to place him in the same circle of Erasmian friends; and for us to assume that such an acquaintance did not go by without having some effect upon his academic thought.

However, it is Henry Bullock who was outstanding among all this company for he, above anyone else in England, appears as an intimate friend and companion of Erasmus, rather than a patron or admirer. Erasmus refers to him as 'most learned Bullock' and as 'my matchless friend, patron and champion', while Bullock replies with 'most learned preceptor' and describes himself as 'more bound than anyone else to you'.[63] Bullock was a Fellow of Queens' College from 1505 until 1524 and Vice Chancellor from 1524 to 1525. He gave lectures in mathematics in 1510, but with the arrival of Erasmus he studied Greek from 1511 until 1514. He gave the official oration of welcome to Wolsey on his visits to the University in 1520 and 1524 and became renowned for his Greek learning, and he was noted for his translation of De Siticulosis Serpentibus by Lucian (120-190).[64] He died in July 1526. Clearly he

---

[60] Nichols, *The Epistles of Erasmus*, Vol. II, Ep. 494, p. 453. Allen, *Opus Epistolarum*, Vol. II, Ep. 512, p. 429.

[61] Nichols, *op. cit.* Ep. 756, p. 295. Allen, *Opus Epistolarum,* Vol. III, Ep. 777, p. 219.

[62] Nichols, *op. cit.* Vol. II, Eps 268, 269, 270, 272, pp. 93–8. Allen, *Opus Epistolarum*, Vol I. Eps 274–5, p. 532.

[63] Allen, *Opus Epistolarum*, Vol. II, Ep. 449, p. 313; 456, p. 329; Vol. III, Ep. 777, p. 220.

[64] Emden, *op. cit.* p. 105. Bale, *Index Britanniae Scriptorum*, p. 159. Lucien published by J. Siberth in 1521, who also printed the oration of 1520 – the first printer in England to use Greek type. Porter, *Reformation and Reaction in Tudor Cambridge*, p. 32. J. H. McConica, *English Humanists and Reformation Politics* (Oxford: Clarendon Press, 1965), p. 59.

was at the heart of the humanist movement and learning in England and reported to Erasmus in 1516 that:

> *People here are hard at work upon Greek and earnestly hope for your arrival. The same set are much delighted with your publication of the New Testament. Good heavens, how elegant it is...*[65]

His interest was not limited to languages, for in 1517 he began a course of lectures on the Gospel of St Matthew.[66] He had already been congratulated by Erasmus in 1516 for 'having adopted the practice of public preaching...especially as you teach Christ in simplicity without any display of the subtleties of men', and this surely is an indication of his theological style, for he follows Erasmus in the course of lectures too.[67] On May 1, 1517, he writes to Erasmus:

> *I have for some months been lecturing on the Gospel of St Matthew, in which I have found more help from your short and most charming notes than from the largest commentaries of others, especially in the more difficult questions that occur.*[68]

We know nothing of his attitude of mind on being asked to write against Luther, or whether he also imitated Erasmus' reluctance to enter the controversy, but we must presume that he brought this considerable sympathy for and ability in the New Learning to bear upon the question of the defence of the Church and the Sacraments. We are left to regret the disappearance of his work, *Contra Lutherum De Captivitate Babylonica*, for it would add considerably to our detailed appreciation of the breadth and variety of the first English response to Luther, and may even give an indication of what might have been the elusive response of Erasmus to this very central question. However, his work may yet be found.

The evidence of this chapter provides us with the outline picture in which to appreciate Fisher's writings against Luther. Unfortunately, the details of his backcloth are missing and only general and sometimes tentative lines can be distinguished. It is clear however, that the expanse of this picture is greater than at first seems to be the case. Fisher's response to Luther was firm, erudite and direct. His contribution was the easily identifiable main feature of the total picture; but it was not the whole picture. Alongside the traditional answer of Catholic theology to the Lutheran challenge, which was to be found in university and parish

---

[65] Allen, *Opus Epistolarum*, Ep. 449, p. 313.

[66] Emden, *Biographical Register*, p. 105.

[67] Allen, *Opus Epistolarum*, Vol. II, Ep. 456, p. 329.

[68] Nichols, *The Epistles of Erasmus*, Vol. II, Ep. 557, p. 553. Allen, *Opus Epistolarum*, Vol. II, Ep. 579, p. 555.

alike, we can discern the outlines of different responses. The sketches of the true extent of this rejoinder begin to emerge with our knowledge of the meeting of the theologians called by Wolsey and Henry. At this meeting were gathered together men whose resources were far more varied than those so ably demonstrated by John Fisher.The conference brought together a variety of scholars: learned men of a thoroughly traditional attitude, some who received their education abroad and others who had been given greater opportunities to devote themselves to the New Learning. Together they must have represented a far wider spectrum of theological abilities and convictions than were to be found in any other setting in England at that time.

Fisher himself helped lay the foundations of this in Cambridge with his insistence on training in the use of the findings of the New Learning in scriptural and theological studies. Wolsey too had played his part in Oxford by promoting lectures in the ancient classics and appointing Thomas Lupset (1495-1530) from Paris as a teacher.[69] Consequently, the groups of representative theologians from these two universities included men whom we may justifiably suppose brought to their task of refuting Luther some of the comparatively new skills and attitudes of the New Learning. Whilst the influence of these studies appears to have been more superficial in the reputations of the Oxford men; the Cambridge theologians and Henry Bullock in particular, were so closely identified with the growth of Erasmian studies in England that a considerable influence in their anti-Lutheran writings could reasonably be expected. The work of Henry Bullock could have been radically different from that of Fisher.

Unfortunately, through lack of detailed evidence, our conclusions so far are of necessity tentative. Only the work of Edward Powel is available for study today. By reputation Powel was a traditionalist and his work does not provide us with detail of the picture furthest removed from Fisher. However, in his writings contrasts with traditional method are clearly evident, and his work illustrates the fact that even within the confines of a largely traditional formation and approach, variety of style and method were achieved. We now turn to the *Propugnaculum summi sacerdotii evangelici, ac septenarii sacramentorum... adversus Martinum Lutherum* of Edward Powel.

---

[69] Lyte, *A History of the University of Oxford*, p. 438.

Another Voice: Edward Powel

Edward Powel was the privileged member of the group of theologians who had examined and answered the teaching of Martin Luther. Under the patronage of Cardinal Wolsey and the University of Oxford, his work *Propugnaculum summi sacerdotii evangelici, ac septenarii sacramentorum, adversus Martinum Lutherum* was printed in London by Pynson in 1523.[1] Edward Powel was a Welshman, and an Oriel College man, though his education also included a number of years in Paris towards the end of the fifteenth century. His association with the College began when he became a Fellow in 1494, and although he completed his theology course in 1506, he was back at Oriel, living in rooms rented from the College, from 1511 to 1512. The College still remembers him for his contribution of a large sum of money for the re-roofing of the congregation hall, and for the decoration of the ceiling.[2]

In 1514, Edward Powel is recorded as receiving a Papal dispensation to hold three incompatible benefices, and the *Oxford Register* of A.B. Emden lists the considerable number of holdings that were his at various times; he was also a Canon of Salisbury. These are indications that the pattern of his life may have been pastoral as well as academic.[3] Powel was a traditional Catholic and a life-long supporter of Queen Catherine, voting in favour of the indissolubility of her marriage in the Convocation of 1533.[4] He spoke out strongly against the King and Anne Boleyn, and insisted upon the authority of the Church over temporal rulers. This, together with the testimony offered by a priest, Richard Arche, was sufficient for his condemnation for treason by act of attainder in November, 1534. Imprisoned first in Doncaster goal, he complained that he was badly treated and shortly afterwards was removed to the Tower of London, where he remained in the company of Thomas Abell and

---

[1] *Defence of the biblical priesthood and the seven sacraments against Martin Luther*. Copies of which still exist in the Bodleian Library, Oxford, in Cambridge University and the British Museum.

[2] Emden, *Biographical Register*, Vol. III, p. 1510.

[3] J.E. Paul, *Catherine of Aragon and her Friends*, (London: Burns & Oates, 1966) pp. 164-169.

[4] *Ibid.*, p. 179.

Richard Featherstone.[5] In 1540 he was sentenced to be hanged, drawn and quartered and he died alongside Robert Barnes, Thomas Garrett and William Jerome on July 30 in circumstances which caused Nicholas Harpsfield to comment,

> *It was a marvellous strange sight for as these (the priests) died for the Catholic religion, so were there burned three Protestants…so that our new religion as it disagreed with the Catholics so did it disagree also from other Protestants.*[6]

Besides the *Propugnaculum*, Powel was also involved in a pulpit controversy with Hugh Latimer. In 1533 Latimer preached in Bristol and, according to second-hand reports, spoke strongly against excesses in devotion to Mary and the Saints, and against indulgences and purgatory. Powel replied, along with one William Hubberton, defending traditional Catholic teaching.[7]

It was for his written work that Powel received the praise and encouragement of Oxford University. In 1521 the University Convocation wrote to Powel thanking him for his efforts against heresy. The work was also commended by the University to the King and Cardinal Wolsey. It was published in 1523 and it remains available for our inspection.[8] Powel opens his work in the most significant manner. He explains that his intention is to answer Luther by the use of Scripture alone, not because he agrees with the principle, but because he realises that only Scripture is acceptable to Luther. For the sake of dialogue and in the hope of some significant communication, he is prepared to lay aside the principle so assiduously followed by many of his contemporaries.[9] Following the pattern of Fisher, he points first of all to a distortion of Scripture as the source of error; but then he maintains that the evidence of Scripture alone is largely sufficient to correct wrong interpretations.

At times Powel does turn to the teaching authority of the Church for support, making considerable effort, first of all, to justify this on Scriptural grounds; but most importantly, throughout the work the final impetus of his arguments comes from the Scriptural evidence that he

---

[5] He wrote to Sir Thomas Arundel in April, 1534, complaining that he was without his own bed and that for lack of money he was likely to be lamed for life. J.E. Paul, *op. cit.* p. 231.

[6] N. Harpsfield, *A Treatise on the Pretended Divorce*, ed. N. Pocock (London, 1878), p. 208. Also J.E. Paul, *op. cit.* p. 236.

[7] J.E. Paul, *op. cit.* pp. 163–6.

[8] See MS Bodley 282, Eps 89 and 90, ff. 45 and 46.

[9] Edward Powel, *Propugnaculum summi sacerdotii evangelici, ac septenarii sacramentorum, editum per virum eruditum, sacrarumque literarum professorem Edoardus Powellum, adversus Martinum Lutherum fratrem famosum et viclefistam insignem,* (Pynson: London, 1523.) Tertio No. Decem. pp.3 & 4 (henceforth cited as *Propugnaculum*).

presents, and not from an appeal to tradition. Whereas Fisher was not adverse to or inept at using Scripture, but chose to act principally on the grounds of tradition, Powel conversely at times refers to the witness of tradition and defends his right to do so, but chooses to take Scripture as his final criterion wherever possible.

Further, Powel suggests that Luther's misuse of Scripture is down to a severe lack of humility, which takes him far from the imitation of Christ. Not only does Luther's pride distort his view of Scripture, but it also places him alongside John Wycliffe (c.1320-84), making him incapable of giving due respect and obedience to the Pope. This lack of obedience, in Powel's view, is the heart of the controversy, the source of heresy and of all social discord. Consequently, the denial of papal supremacy is the first problem tackled by Powel; with the hope that by using Scripture alone he may bring clarity to the problem.

He opens his defence of Papal primacy by stating that there is a basic pattern which is common to the three successive stages of man's history: the stages of natural, divine and evangelical law. The natural law, he claims, applied from the time of Adam to the time of Moses when the divine law succeeded it. The evangelical law of Christ incarnate is the perfection of all preceding order. Throughout all three stages, however, Christ is presented as head of mankind, along with a representative of Christ present as a visible leader among men. Under the natural law, as a result of the fall of Adam, man was in need of a leader of knowledge and wisdom who would be high priest, 'for repeated propitiatory offerings and sacrifices'. The first manifestations of this need being fulfilled were already visible in Adam, when he named the animals in Genesis 2 and in Melchisedech, King of Salem and high priest of God referred to in Genesis 14 and 18. These examples are cited to show that it was not only fitting, but also a fact of the natural law condition that there was a single head of the people.

Then the Mosaic Law brings new clarity, for God appoints Aaron to be the visible religious head on earth and confirms his choice with miracles, indicated in Numbers 16 and 17.[10] He emphasised that there

---

[10] Powel, *Propugnaculum,* p. 9. Fisher uses a similar appeal to miracles as proof of the authentic work of God, for example in *Corpus Christi,* Prefactio III. However, the notable difference between them is that, here and again later on, Powel refers only to miracles reported in the Scriptures, whereas Fisher appeals to the wealth of medieval miracle stories and revelations, for example the revelations of Hildergardis and of Mechtildis. This aspect of Fisher's work caused Dr Lewis some amazement, 'that one of the Bishop's great learning and good sense could be carried to so an extravagant degree of credulity as seriously to quote and transcribe them as proof of the verity of Christ's body in the Sacrament of the Eucharist'. Lewis, *The Life,* Vol. I. p. 313.

is indeed a foreshadowing of the New Covenant in the Old. He points to the sacrifices of the Old Law as foreshadowing Christ, and to the 'provision of the synagogue that foreshadowed and afterwards was succeeded and by the confirmation of the Church.' [11] The evidence of the Old Testament is admissible, therefore, because there is an immediate correlation between the two; but this is summed up for Powel not so much in terms of foreshadowing, but rather by the words of Christ in Matthew 5:17. 'Do not think that I have come to set aside the law or the prophets. I have come not to abolish them but to complete them.' Consequently, the priesthood we see established by God in the person of Aaron is perfected under the New Law in Christ, and the divinely appointed Peter works miracles which are evidence of this superiority. If Aaron was appointed by God, so much more is the fulfilled high priesthood of Peter *iuris divinae*, for the words of Christ that nothing would disappear from the law could not be true if the high priesthood of Aaron was not continued and perfected.

The contrasts drawn between night and day in Romans 13:12, between the two daughters of Abraham of Galatians 4:21, between the Old and New Laws of 2 Corinthians chapter 3 are used as bases for expounding the fulfilling of the priesthood of the Old Law into a New Testament reality of greater perfection. Powel argues against Luther's claim that the Old Testament prefigures the perfect priesthood of Christ by referring to Hebrews 13;8, 'Jesus Christ is the same today as he was yesterday as he will be forever' , and by asserting that Christ was always the head of the synagogue and of the Church. Alternatively, just as under the Mosaic Law Aaron and his successors were his divinely appointed vicars, so too under the New Law the role of vicar is maintained in a new and more perfect form. He has no doubt, therefore, that under the headship of Christ there is a vicar appointed by divine authority.[12] By holding the papacy to be of human origin and a Babylonian captivity, Luther has strayed far from Scriptural truth.

Powel's appreciation of the relationship between the Old and New Testaments is significantly different from Fisher's. Whereas Fisher takes the principle of foreshadowing as an opportunity to argue from detailed similarities between Moses, Aaron, Christ and Peter, Powel looks more to the overall patterns of Old Testament life, bringing the Old Testament together in its proper context, and then points to its main features as foreshadowing the New Testament. He shows greater appreciation

---

[11] Powel, *Propugnaculum*, p. 10.
[12] *Ibid.*, p.13.

of the Old Testament as a reality and a covenant in its own right, and consequently does not treat it as material to be manipulated into detailed and particular arguments and proofs.

Having established the existence of a New Testament high priesthood of divine appointment, Powel then examines the New Testament texts to show that it was Peter who was appointed to that position. He points to the cry of Jesus on the cross 'It is finished [consummated]'[13] as heralding the New Covenant. He then sets about establishing the point that before his death Christ made clear his intention of choosing Peter, and after his death he did in fact appoint Peter as his Vicar on earth.

Before his passion, Christ made this intention clear by changing Peter's name in John 1:42; by the promises made to Peter as reported in Matthew 16:18; by his prayer for Peter preparing him for his future tasks in Luke 22:31,[14] and the incident of the temple tax in Matthew 17:24. This is sufficient for Powel to remove any doubts concerning the identity of Christ's intended leader of his Church on earth.

Concerning the actual bestowal upon Peter of this office with accompanying authority, Powel turns to John 21:15ff. for his scriptural evidence. He asserts first of all that the triple question and answer is to show that the Church is begun, developed and complete in its triple form and Peter is appointed its leader.[15] Then he attacks Luther's interpretation of the triple charge given to Peter which applies it to the service exclusively of doctrine, life and natural goods for the whole Church. Powel rather interprets the Latin and Greek text as indicating not only the care and attention required on the part of Peter, but also as bestowing on Peter the authority to govern, and so the honour and dignity to be given to him by the rest of the Church.

Such an appeal to Scripture, such an argument based on the textual detail and authority of the scriptural text alone is typical of Powel's work. However, this is the only occasion on which he makes any explicit reference to contemporary linguistic and interpretative achievements. So even though we find no evidence to connect him with the New Learning, and the absence of any extensive use of Greek in his work suggests an ignorance of the language, he was at least in touch with the intellectual

[13] Vulgate: *consummatum est;* John 19:29. See also Mark 15:37 and Matthew 27:50.

[14] Powel insists that this prayer is for Peter in his apostolic role after the death of Christ before his passion and is not concerned with his denials of Christ before his passion. The denials were a momentary weakness, quickly repented and not a falling from faith. Powel, *Propugnaculum,* p. 15.

[15] In passing he points out that Christ also asks about Peter's love and not his faith whereas, he argues, Luther attributes all to faith. Powel, *Propugnaculum,* p.16.

movements of the day and was quite ready to employ them for his own ends.

He continues his defence of the Papacy by turning to the Acts of the Apostles and outlining the ways in which the divine and evangelical authority of Peter was exercised, particularly with reference to Matthew 16:18 and 18:18. He offers well known texts, substantially the same as those used by Fisher at this point: namely the election of Matthias in Acts 1:15, the Pentecost sermon in Acts 2:14, the speech before Annas in Acts 4 and the incident of Ananias and Saphhira in Acts 5.1. The evidence of miracles is again invoked as reported in the Acts of the Apostles, particularly chapters 3 and 9, and these witness to the power and authority given to Peter. Powel suggests that anyone denying Peter supremacy and that of his successors, cannot escape the charge of putting God's integrity into question.[16] In this way, Powel seeks to defend the primacy of Peter and his successors.

This first section of Powel's work gives us a good appreciation of his style and method. As the book progresses, the clarity and precision with which he pursues his aims become obscured by a rise in the level of polemic and a greater insistence on a point-by-point refutation of Luther. In this section, however, we can see most clearly how he attempts to work from Scripture alone, from a strict literal interpretation, without recourse either to external criteria of interpretation or any other authority. He achieves a good measure of success both here and throughout the work, for his appeals to Patristic interpretations are rare, and only under a special section does he make appeal to the tradition of the Church. This early section of his work received special commendation from the University Convocation, and certainly it is pervaded by a clarity and unity that is the hallmark of a well-trained and disciplined mind.

Powel attempts to maintain this method of refutation throughout the rest of his work. As we shall see, at times he falls well below this standard; but as each item of controversy is introduced, he attempts an argument based principally on the evidence of his reading of Scripture. It would serve little purpose to follow him in detail throughout his book as we have already seen the pattern of his work and that at its most effective. One or two further points need to be observed. In defence of Catholic teaching on the Eucharist and Penance he again accuses Luther of misusing the Scriptures. Even though his defence opens with the claim that Greek and Latin interpreters have taken John chapter 6 as applying to the Eucharist, he does repeat his claim that, although this support is

---

[16] Powel, *Propugnaculum*, p.23.

available to him, his argument is based on the scriptural texts alone. The sixth chapter of St John, he says, is to be understood as Christ's promise to institute the Eucharist. It is not to be understood, as the Jews did, as some carnal sense, but in a spiritual and sacramental sense.

In the more detailed points of the Eucharistic controversy, such as the withholding of the chalice, Powel tries to show the impossibility of arguing from Scripture by ridiculing the method; he asks whether it is lawful for women, or gentiles, to receive the Eucharist, for neither were present at the Last Supper. At this point Powel begins to uphold the right of the Church to change various less important customs of Church practice, and conscious of the principle involved, he immediately initiates a defence of the Church's authority to do so, arguing as far as he can from Scripture alone. In the course of this argument, however, Powel wanders far beyond acceptable uses of Scripture in his eagerness to adhere to his chosen method. Here we begin to see some of the shortcomings and weaknesses of his ability in the use of Scripture and the overall assessment of Powel's work must bear in mind these lapses.

To begin with, Powel maintains that the Scriptures report four General Councils held in Jerusalem before the dispersal of the Christian community, and he offers these as evidence of the Church's right to formulate doctrine and teach with authority. The first of these Councils, he claims, was the election of Matthias in Acts chapter 1; the second was the election of the deacons in Acts chapter 6, arguing that these changes made for the good of the Church could only have been accepted by a General Council; the third Council is reported in Acts chapter 15 and was concerned with the initiation question about circumcision; the fourth Council is described as being held immediately before the dispersion in order to establish uniformity of faith. The only scriptural reference given for this is a verse 9 of Psalm 47: 'The rulers of the nations assemble with the people of the God of Abraham'. Many aspects of this theme appear to be taken from the then prevailing traditions rather than established facts. The outcome of this fourth Council, for example, is said to have been the Apostles creed, of which each article was composed by an Apostle: it was a theme often seen in late medieval manuals.[17]

The work of these Councils he upholds as being achieved under the guidance of the Holy Spirit, and Luther's opposition to the pronouncement of Councils stems from his lack of docility to the Spirit at work in the Church. Throughout the history of the Church, heresies have been met and defeated by Councils: the Nestorians, Arians,

[17] Powel, *op. cit.* p.36.

Another Voice: Edward Powel

Sabellians and Jacobites were all separated from the Church through the pronouncements of Councils.[18] Therefore, Powel concludes that the Scriptures testify against Luther's rejection of conciliar teaching as authoritative, for it is clear that the Holy Spirit guided the work of the first Councils and has continued to do so in all subsequent Councils of the Church.

This question about the source of Church authority is of major importance, and it is a little surprising to see Powel content to rest his case so far on such flimsy evidence. His interpretation of the events in the Acts of the Apostles and his lack of concern for historical accuracy show how easily he allowed his desire to defend Catholic teaching to lead him to distort the evidence he had presented. As his work progresses, he comes near on many occasions to switching his argument to the grounds of authority and tradition. In this section on the authority of the Councils he is struggling to avoid that temptation and the struggle is a bitter one, for it is clear that his ability in the use of the Scriptures does not enable him to cope with such broad themes as Church authority in general. He is certainly capable of quoting Scriptures in debate over particular points, as can be seen clearly in his defence of Papal primacy, but he does not appear capable of drawing from the Scriptures valid support for a theme as vast and inclusive as that of the guidance of the Holy Spirit in the Church both in her foundation and subsequent growth.

In the course of his work, Powel shows only a limited detailed appreciation for the findings of contemporary linguistic and biblical studies. He gives us no reason to suppose that his own education had included any absorption of the New Learning, and furthermore, some of the lapses in the standard of his work are almost definite indications that he did not deeply understand the ideals and tenets of biblical humanism. His thoughts on the origins of the Apostles Creed, for example, give notice of the extent to which his training had been deeply traditional and had not really prepared him to accept the challenge of Luther's theology in the manner in which he chose to do so.

In many ways, then, Powel's work is more notable as an attempt than as an achievement. At least here was one person who for the sake of mutual understanding was prepared to leave the mainstream Catholic response to Luther and to set out on a radically different course. The measure of his success may not be very great, but the significance of his intention should not be underestimated. The definition of the Church

---

[18] Powel, *op. cit.* p.35.

171

with which Powel concludes this section is an indication of how readily he would have countered Luther with traditional Catholic arguments if he had wished to do so. He concludes that the authority of the Church, founded on the abiding presence of the Holy Spirit that leads it into all truth, demands humble obedience and any person who opposes this principle is automatically outside the truth.[19]

Probably aware of the weaknesses of his defence of the Church's authority so far, and conscious of how close he had come to switching his ground from Scripture to authoritative tradition, at this point Dr. Powel inserts an independent section in which he attacks Luther's principle of Scripture alone, and defends the traditional pattern of argument against heresy used by the Catholic Church.[20] In this we see Powel on an equal footing with Fisher and other contemporaries; the arguments used are of great similarity and so this brings to light both the greater precision and learning of Fisher and the inadequacies of Powel's work on certain central issues. Subsequent to this he has less success than Fisher in reaching a statement about the relationship between Scripture and tradition as sources of revelation; he mentions the negative norm, that teaching must not contradict Scripture, but this is only in passing and nowhere does he make a positive statement on this topic. He certainly argues for the inadequacy of Scripture in supporting many accepted doctrines and practices by pointing to various long accepted aspects of faith which are not to be found in Scriptures: the language of dogma, St Augustine's use of the term persona in Trinitarian theology and the use of the terms *unigenitum* and *consubstantialem* in the Nicene Creed; along with customs such as the observance of Sunday, Lenten fasts, mixing of the wine and water, the use of images and the building churches towards the east. These at the time were accepted parts of the Church's belief that have no foundation in Scripture. The Apostles Creed itself, he says, is not of scriptural origin and, predictably, quotes St Augustine concerning the Canon of Scripture. In this manner he maintains the insufficiency of Scripture in defending the accepted essentials of faith and the Church traditions and customs as a clarification of the relationship between Scripture and tradition.

So, it is that these inadequacies in Powel's work bring to light the superiority of Fisher, for Fisher shows considerably more ability and elasticity in his handling of this crucial relationship between Scripture and tradition. Powel quickly resorts to a statement of bare faith in

---

[19] Powel, *op. cit.* p.38.
[20] Powel, *op. cit.* p.40.

the Church; but Fisher, for all his unrelenting and bitter attack on his opponents, goes to far greater lengths to account for his faith in Church authority and to reconcile it with the informative importance of the Scriptures. Not only does Fisher seem to have been more sensitive to the anxieties of the protesters about the role of the Church, but he also had more understanding of good Scriptural knowledge and the hopes which they engendered. Powel, on the other hand, despite his noteworthy readiness to attempt some fresh approaches to Lutheran teaching, here reveals himself to be less able to read the implications of Luther's work, and less able to respond to them adequately at this crucial level.

At first sight, the time Powel spent studying in Paris might have seemed to be a reason for expecting a display of different talents in his work. This now has appeared as a false expectation, for while Powel achieves certain notable variations from the majority of Catholics, the scope of these differences is not sufficient to cause us to search for a radically different formative influence in his intellectual training. Brief study of the University of Paris at the turn of century when Powel was there does not reveal any startling indications of a potential major influence in Powel's academic formation.[21] In fact, in many ways similar to the universities in England, Paris presents a picture of the official university, being largely conservative in its teaching and strictly orthodox in its academic decisions. We have evidence, for example, of a strongly worded condemnation by the faculty of theology in 1497 of some theological opinions about devotion to Our Lady and the Immaculate Conception given by Jean Grillot.[22] Much later, in 1519-1521, the Faculty again issued a most traditionally composed condemnation, this time of Luther's teaching. This document identifies individual items of Luther's teaching with heresies of the past, and once classified they are formally rejected.[23] Similarly, knowledge of books in use and books printed at the turn of the century also suggest that traditional studies were the pattern of the day, with the Bible and the Sentences identified as the two books essential for theological studies.[24]

---

[21] A. Renaudet, *Préréforme et Humanisme à Paris pendant les guerres d'Italie 1494-1517*, (Paris : Librairie D'Argences, 1953). He comments 'Up to the middle of the first year of the century they remained scholastics… So, a generation of logical determinists was formed.' p. 366. Also A. L. Gabriel, *'Les étudiants étrangers a l'Université de Paris au XV Siècle'*, in *Annales de l'Université de Paris*, No.3, 1959, pp.377-388.

[22] P. Feret, *La Faculté de Théologie et ses docteurs les plus célèbres*. (Paris: 1894-1097) Vol. 5, p.138. 'The Faculty allows nothing to pass that does not conform to true doctrine.'

[23] See *Determinatio Theologicae Facultatis Parisiensis super doctrina Lutheriana*, published by Josse Bade (Ascensius) in *'Martin Luther and the Sorbonne 1519-1521'*, *Bulletin of the Institute of Historical Research*, Vol. XLVI, No. 113, May 1973. pp. 28-40.

[24] Renaudet, *Préréforme et Humanisme*, pp. 29, 368 f.

Only gradually does the new style of Biblical studies seem to have found its way into the University, through the influence of Jocodius Clichtove (1472-1543) and Jacques Lefèvre d'Étaples (c.1460-1536), and through changes brought about by Standonck and Mair at Montaigu College in the first ten years of the sixteenth century. But this was after Powel's time in Paris.

The only comments on the theological studies of Paris which seem to have relevance to Powel's work are very general comments that the Faculty in Paris, by tradition, gave considerable emphasis to the study of the Bible. Such studies are known to have dominated the Faculty in the Middle Ages, and we also know that on July 28, 1502, the Faculty published an edition of the Bible.[25] However, the general pattern of these studies was not exceptional and the Bible that was published was without any new contributions in textual criticism or commentary.[26] The picture of a traditional Faculty, giving emphasis to the study of the Scriptures, as yet not enlightened by humanist learning, corresponds to the work produced by Powel, whether that Faculty did have a large influence on his or not.

There is another feature of Powel's book that is of considerable interest. In the course of his study on Penance, Powel charges Luther with having misrepresented both Catholic doctrine and practice concerning the role of faith in the working of the sacrament. He accuses him first of distorting Catholic doctrine and insists that Catholic teaching upholds the principle that faith is basic to all sacraments. This point is supported by our findings from parish handbooks and sermons.[27] A little later on a similar statement about the necessity of faith appears, directed more to the defence of Catholic practice, which Powel sees as misrepresented by Luther.[28] It is difficult to know how much importance to give to these and subsequent comments by Powel. He is concerned to defend both Catholic teaching and practice in the parishes. The details of his University career and the number of parish benefices he held open up the possibility that at some time he may have been engaged in an active parish ministry; but that must remain speculation. His defence of the teaching of the Church about the nature of the sacraments, the need for faith in Christ and, as we shall see, for true repentance receives support from the sermon material we have examined, but there always remains

[25] H. Denifle, 'Quel livre servait de bas à l'enseignement des maîtres en théologie dans l'Université de Paris,' *Revue Thomiste*, II, 1894, pp.157-8. pp 160-1.
[26] Renaudet, *Préréforme et Humanisme*, pp. 368, 407. The Bible was published without any Greek and with little improvement on the commentaries of Hugh St Cher and Lyra.
[27] Powel, *op. cit.* p. 86.
[28] *Ibid.*, p. 89.

an insurmountable gap between propositions about the content of teaching, the actual teaching in concrete situations and the final practice of any individual or community. Powel is very clear, however, that an accurate representation of the teaching given to Catholic congregations and of their personal piety be adhered to. The picture he maintains is more healthy than is often imagined.

Further, he gives an example of the prayer of the repentant sinner, showing that pious Catholicism is not without a true appreciation of Christ.

> *Hear me Lord in your justice. Christ indeed is the justice of his Father and of us. Of his Father since he is to judge the world; and of us since he has died for our sins, there is with him therefore abundant redemption. (Echoing the De Profundis.)[29]*

Underlining the Christo-centricity of such piety, he continues by describing Christ as 'Our most innocent Abel slain for us; our Noah who saved the world on the wood of the cross; our Moses who fasted and prayed for us; our Absalom; our Jonathan who gave his life for us; our Samson who broke the bonds of sin.'

> *As St Paul has said, for our justification he [Christ] gave to man all that was necessary – his blood to wash us, his body to redeem us. In his passion justice and peace have met each other.[30]*

His insistence is on the place which Christ occupies in the Catholic teaching and the piety of his day. Powel maintains that it is to Christ and to the promises of God that the Catholic looks first of all, and he objects strongly that Luther would portray this priority otherwise. Finally, he attacks Luther again for suggesting that in Catholic teaching a muttered penance is sufficient for forgiveness without any reform of life. This, he insists, is simply untrue.

This contribution by Dr Powel, the insistence upon a correct presentation of Catholic teaching, could have been a major factor in the Lutheran-Catholic debate. It is an issue on which great clarity has been achieved in recent decades, but the atmosphere of the contemporary situation, as it developed, negated any impact that may have been made by works such as Powel's. There was a manifest need for correction in the representations of Lutheranism by Catholics and of Catholicism by Lutherans, and it is interesting to find a determined effort at this by one of the contemporary contributors.

---

[29] Powel, *Propugnaculum*, p. 96.
[30] *Ibid.*

We are told that Powel enjoyed a considerable reputation as a preacher, and no doubt we see something of his preaching style in his devotional passages on the role of Christ in the economy of forgiveness.[31] The late medieval flavour of these passages is immediately evident, with their over-elaborated analogies and pictorial Scriptural references. We would expect Powel's spiritual writings and sermons to fit into the contemporary patterns, for he has shown himself to be a traditional Catholic both in his education and in the underlying nature of his work. On this level he must stand as a point of comparison with Fisher and as such we have seen that he highlights the quality of Fisher's work when considered in its contemporary setting. Weaknesses in the use of sources, especially the Scriptures and early Patristic writings, appear less frequently in Fisher than in Powel, for the greater depth of learning of Fisher and his continual application to academic work made him more sensitive to the progress being made in those areas. Powel, on the other hand, worked well within his limits, using Scripture in a disciplined manner after the fashion of Aquinas, Lyra and their schools. But as soon as these limits were reached, as with the problem of textual accuracy or under pressure in the debate about the authority of Church tradition, then Powel was not able to make genuine progress but lapses into assertions which spring more from faith and conviction than from the evidence he offers.

The original contribution made by Powel to the campaign against Luther was his decision to argue on the grounds of Scripture only. In this he appears to have been alone, but there are several indications to show that, while his is the only surviving work of this kind, there was a more widespread movement in Catholic theological circles to take seriously the . importance of Scripture and the significance of the New Learning. While Powel's work in itself can only be given limited approval, it points the way to two important conclusions.

Firstly, Powel's attempted response to Luther highlights both the nature and shortcomings of traditional Scriptural studies. The pattern of University education which we saw to have shaped Fisher's training would appear to be behind Powel's writings also. He had an extensive knowledge of Scripture, especially the New Testament, and was capable of quoting Scripture in a disciplined manner in support of any article of faith. The shortcomings of the studies likewise emerge, for Powel, more so than Fisher, seems largely unable to approach the New Testament with any freshness or an overall grasp of broad Scriptural themes. In

---

[31] J. E. Paul, *op. cit.*, pp. 168f.

other words, as patterns of education would lead us to expect, the study of Scripture was dominated by an apologetical frame of mind which sought to find support for already held statements of faith. When the very root of that faith was attacked, then Powel was not truly equipped to approach Scripture to discover or rediscover a source of faith there. Furthermore, Powel demonstrates that he was not deeply conversant with the achievements of the New Learning, especially with regard to textual detail and authenticity. The instruments of study that were being developed in humanist circles were not employed by Powel, nor, to a large extent by Catholic apologists.

Secondly, however, Powel's desire to answer Luther on the basis of Scripture alone means that he was aware of the vital role that Scripture was playing in the theological events of the time. Powel was not alone in this awareness, for many of the current developments in Catholic theological studies originated in the desire to integrate the New Learning into the systems of education and debate. The initiatives of Fisher at Cambridge, of Wolsey at Oxford and the work of Colet and Kyddermynster are all indications that among some Catholics there was an unhesitating acceptance of the importance of Scripture studies, not just as they were traditionally carried out, but as renewed and enlightened by humanist learning. While the achievements of these initiatives were limited, their original intentions were clear, that the New Learning was to be brought into the service of Catholic theology. We are left to speculate that Bullock's unfound work could have been one of the more fruitful products of this liaison.

The crucial difficulty with this project, which emerged in the heat of the early Lutheran controversy, was the relationship between Scripture and Church tradition as sources of dogma and teaching. The increased importance given to the Scriptures, the exciting sense of discovery that the New Learning engendered, soon led to a direct challenge to the legitimacy of much Church teaching, and so this issue became central not just in the development of University studies, but in the whole radical Lutheran-Catholic conflict. This was the point at which both Powel's and Fisher's works appear at their most incomplete and it is only through subsequent development and clarification of the issues involved by both sides that the considerable theological agreement that exists today has been achieved.

Powel's work, which had behind it the praise and support of Oxford University, adds to our picture of the Catholic response to Luther. Powel's willingness to undertake a discussion with Luther based on

Scripture alone is a radically new feature in our picture of the age and adds some colour and richness to the features of traditional Catholicism. It is against this background that we must appreciate Fisher's own work, and Powel's contribution enables us to be more aware of both the strengths and weaknesses of Catholic theology and education. Fisher was certainly its foremost spokesman, but it is now quite clear that he was not its only exponent and some of the other voices that were raised had different contributions of their own to make, contributions which were not just weak echoes of Fisher's voice, but which added variety and breadth to the total Catholic response to Luther.

Conclusion

W illiam Rastell gives us this report of John Fisher's final statement of faith:

> He believed directly in his conscience and knew by his learning precisely that it was very plain by the holy scriptures, the laws of the Church, the general council and the whole faith and general practice of Christ's Catholic Church from Christ's ascension hitherto, that the King was not, nor could be, by the law of God, supreme head of the Church of England.[1]

By 1535 the issues of the controversy had changed, the nature of the opposition had altered and the outcome of the struggle was now life and death; but in many ways the attitude and posture of John Fisher had not changed. He was adamant in that year as ever in his defence of the truth of the Roman Catholic tradition of Christianity; his courage and readiness to fulfil his duty as a leader were unabated, and his appeal to the full range of the Catholic heritage was as prompt and detailed as it always had been. The course of events which brought Fisher through the controversies of Henry's annulment and then divorce proceedings to the crisis of the supremacy constituted the longest sections of his biographies, and we shall not repeat their words.[2]

Throughout the period from 1527 to 1535 Fisher portrayed all his characteristics of mind and behaviour that we could have expected of him. Scarisbrick summarises his role in the divorce controversy thus:

> He wrote at least seven books on Catherine's behalf (so he himself maintained) and their clarity and range of learning are remarkable. He had an eagle eye for the essential and decisive, his command of sources was staggering...Having declared himself an opponent of Henry from the very beginning in 1527, he sustained his opposition for eight years... That Henry should have had this indefatigable bishop fulminating on his doorstep (and in this Fisher was very different from the silent More) must have been an insult so

---

[1] Van Ortroy, *Vie*, Vol. XII, p. 254, quoting W. Rastell's *Life of More*, from BL, Arundel MS 152, ff. 309–12.

[2] M. Macklem, *God Have Mercy*, (Oberon Press: Ottawa, 1967), 68–209. E. E. Reynolds, *op. cit.* (New York: Everyman's Library, 1963), pp. 129–96.

provocative that we can only marvel that ultimate retribution was delayed until 1535.[3]

The final end came after a year of imprisonment. On the morning of his execution on July 22, 1535, he was awakened by the prison officer at 5.00 am and told that his execution was to be at 10.00 am. He promptly asked to be allowed to sleep a few more hours.[4] This same calmness was shown in his final words:

Christian people, I am come hither to die for the faith of Christ's Catholic Church. And I thank God hitherto, my stomach hath served me well, so that hitherto I have not feared death. Wherefore I desire your help and assist me with your prayers, that at the very point and instant of my death's stroke and in the very moment of my death, I then faint not in any point of the Catholic faith for any fear, and I pray God save the King and the realm and hold his holy hand over it and send the King a good counsel.[5]

This remarkable peace of mind displayed by John Fisher sprang from the knowledge that throughout his life he had worked to the best of his ability, faithful to his deepest convictions and at no point could he hold against himself any serious charge of negligence or dishonesty. The intense spiritual training to which he had been subject since his earliest years also equipped him well to face death. Deep in the heart of medieval spirituality was the insistence that death must be faced constantly, not in any morbid, destructive manner as would be likely today, but with a positive frame of mind convinced that the situation of a person's confrontation with death reveals the deepest truths and dependencies of his condition; and therefore provides most fruitful instruction in the priorities of daily living.

The foundation of this strength of spirit had been laid in his youth when, as we have seen, Fisher was immersed in an ecclesiastical context which by means of its education, sermons and spiritual exercises established him in a mode of belief and devotion which, in the course of his life, went from strength to strength. During his time of isolation imprisoned in the Tower, Fisher's attention returned significantly to the same themes and concerns that had occupied him before the outbreak of the controversy fifteen years previously. His life was coming to its personal climax in death and Fisher's temporal horizons became drastically reduced. It was as if he acknowledged that his part in the battle

---

[3] Scarisbrick, *Henry VIII*, p. 223.

[4] Van Ortroy, *Vie*, Vol. XII, p. 263.

[5] *Ibid.*, p. 265.

Conclusion

of Church affairs was over and his task was now no longer public and the result of his office of bishop, but private and personal – the salvation of his soul. Consequently not a word of apologetics emerged from his prison cell, but he devoted himself to spiritual writings concerned with the preparation for death by a good living faith.

We have already observed how the two works produced by Fisher in the Tower sum up many of the themes and stylistic points of the Middle-Ages. The *Spiritual Consolation* he wrote is an exhortation to repentance, motivated by a meditation on the closeness of death, and marked by an insistence on hope and trust in the mercy and forgiveness of God. The *Ways to Perfect Religion* similarly outlined the path to be taken by the individual who wishes to de devoted to a religious life. Again, the attitude of mind displayed is positive in that love alone will produce true 'joy and pleasure' and the method of presentation used characteristics of the age that were rapidly passing.[6] In the light of our examination of Fisher's theological works, however, the most notable feature of these last writings is that they make very little reference to the role that is to be played by the Church on the path of the individual to perfection. After the crucial importance given to the Church in the economy of salvation in his theological works and the centrality of commitment to her as an authoritative instrument of God's work, the different emphasis of these spiritual writings is a vivid indication of how much Fisher's comparative freedom from the commitments to public office permitted him to turn his attention once again to the more intimate desire of his spirit.

A long prayer, composed by Fisher at this time, illustrates these points. It comes to a conclusion in this way:

> *Wherefore, dear Father, when thou hast strictly commanded me thus to love thee with all my heart and thus would I right gladly do (but without thy help and without thy Holy Spirit I cannot rightly do) I beseech thee to shed upon my heart thy most Holy Spirit by whose gracious presence I may be warmed, heated and kindled with the spiritual fire of charity and with the sweetly burning love of all godly affections, that I may steadfastly set my heart, soul and mind upon thee and assuredly trust that thou art my loving father and according to the same trust I may love thee with all my heart, with all my soul, with all my mind and all my power. Amen.*[7]

During this time in prison, then, Fisher was devoted to intense personal growth, which was to be achieved by a total dedication to prayer,

---

[6] John Fisher, *The Wayes to Perfect Religion*, 1535. Copies in the Rylands Library and the Mayor collection and reproduced by the Early English Texts Society.

[7] Reynolds, *op. cit.*, p. 299.

repentance and spiritual exercises. It is only for the sake of confession that Fisher complains of his isolation in the Tower, and at this stage of his life separation from the other aspects of the visible life of the Church did not seem to hinder him in the least.

Two remarks arise from this: first of all, this almost spontaneous movement of Fisher into spiritual writings is a measure of his dedication as a bishop, for it suggests strongly that Fisher was not a polemicist by nature. The fact that he sustained an involvement in deep controversy for so many years is an indication of his immense strength of character and dedication as a bishop. Secondly, the fact that Fisher along with More appear to have found themselves almost at home in a prison cell, at least as far as their spiritual lives were concerned, is a measure of how much the medieval style of spirituality sprang from and moved towards a monastic experience. The lack of a genuine lay spirituality is one of the evident weaknesses of the pre-Reformation period which found a response in the work of Erasmus.

The purpose of this study has been to examine the life and works of John Fisher firstly in order to understand them in their contemporary setting and secondly to use them as an occasion for examining the state of Catholic theology and its preparedness, at many levels, to face the theological challenge of Lutheran teaching. In many ways we have seen Fisher to be representative of the period. In his education, at school and university, he enjoyed the best that the age could offer; he continued his study with exceptional dedication and considerable awareness, welcoming intellectual innovations, and he spoke with a learned and determined voice on behalf of Catholicism in England when he offered his first replies to Luther.

Taking Fisher as thus representative, we have outlined the dominant features of the early education available to the aspirant cleric in England in the later part of the fifteenth century. The formation of young clerks, being in the hands of the clergy of the large cathedrals, abbey churches and minsters, was based on a firm grasp of the essentials of the faith; rehearsed, repeated and memorised in the cause of literacy in English and Latin. A rigorous discipline, both of mind and behaviour, was held at a premium and enforced by uncompromising means with the result that any young boy who enjoyed and endured being a pupil at one of these schools would certainly have emerged with a sufficient ability in Latin and English to continue his education by further reading if he so desired. Evidence of the ability and books of the parochial clergy towards the end of the fifteenth century suggests that such limited standards of literacy and learning were being achieved.

The foundations of knowledge of the faith laid down in these collegiate schools received backing and reinforcement from the pulpits of the parish churches. The attentive listener to sermons would hear the articles of the creed, the Ten Commandments, the sacraments and the seven virtues and vices presented as the basic material of sermons with great variety of style, skill and success. The continual urging of the preacher appears to have been towards constant reform of life, in clear adherence to a simple trusting faith in Christ and the Church, and in an exercise of continued repentance brought about by an awareness of sin and use of the sacraments. The main insistence of many sermons centred upon the love and forgiveness of God for those who turn to him; and upon the way in which the spiritual life of the individual was initiated, nourished and guided by the life of the Church. It is the Church who mediates the saving grace of Christ in the manner of a servant of Christ, a necessary and unique servant. Only in conjunction with the Church can the individual be sure that his faith is genuine and that he is on the path to salvation. The main points of growth offered to the individual by the Church are the sacraments, and a great deal of sermon time was given over to explanation of the sacraments, especially the importance of a correct and regular reception of them.

Generalised comments about a topic as intangible as preaching are never satisfactory, for unknown factors such as the individual abilities of the clergy and the attentiveness of the congregations are often the decisive ones. Yet the patterns of the strengths and weaknesses in this preaching emerge and find some correspondence in later events, whether by pure coincidence or by connection. Many of the shortcomings of the preaching material which we have examined correspond to areas of challenge and weakness in later years. As remote preparation for the conflict with Lutheran theology, the preparatory training offered by the Church to its young clerics and to its congregations shows weaknesses in the key areas of Church authority, of individual experience of faith rather than devotion, and of the Church as the community formed and guided by the Spirit rather than the provider of the sacraments for the individual. Little or nothing appears to have been said about quite why the Church was the authoritative guide for the Christian believer, about the source of the Church's authority to teach and about how this related to the individual's own thinking or reading of Scriptures. Similarly, nothing was said about how this role of the Church was fulfilled, about the criteria of authority or about the function or importance of the Pope. Little use was made of St Paul's writings as a source of spiritual growth and it is more the spirituality of the *Imitation of Christ,* with insistence upon self-discipline and unworthiness than an awareness of incorporation into the living Christ, which is offered in this sermon material.

These are weaknesses that appear with hindsight, but nevertheless they were contributory factors in the growth of the Protestant challenge and in the ability of Catholics, simple or learned, to meet that challenge. Fisher himself continued his education and intellectual development for many years; but for many, both clergy and lay people, the content of these sermons was the limit of their consideration of the teachings of their faith. As such we can say that it was firm in some essentials, lacking in other topics which were soon to become essential, and limited to the traditional in the means towards holiness offered to the individual. In sum, the sermons appear to be evidence of a traditional faith and way of life being taught and encouraged faithfully and thoroughly, but with a limited enthusiasm and not fired with the excitement that innovation and fresh inspiration can produce.

The picture of theological study in the universities at this time is not radically different from this. Fisher's own career centred upon university life, and embraced the beginnings of many important changes. But in his early years at Cambridge he was inserted into a pattern of education which as far as we can perceive was traditional, systematic and, like the sermon material, largely uninspiring. Even though suffering from a lamentable lack of source material, we are able to make tentative conclusions about the nature of this university training. It would appear to have been strong in the rigour of its intellectual discipline. Long years of preparatory study and priority given to the classical exponents of Scholastic theology assure us of this. It was strong in its emphasis on the literal use of the Scriptures and robust in its insistence upon the ability to argue in systematic detail in defence of any given statement of faith.

Equally evident, however, are the weaknesses of the long years of applied study conducted in the late medieval universities of England. The most obvious shortcoming was the lack of variety and innovation both in the content and method of teaching, for in the years of Fisher's engagement with philosophy and theology, from 1483 until 1501, there was little to suggest that the changes in pattern and methods of learning which were being established in some parts of Europe were having any impact in England. Clearly these influences did arrive eventually, and

Fisher played an active part in their advent, but as yet they were not in sight. This lack of innovation should not be taken as a total lack of activity. It was symptomatic of this period in which the old was being supported by thorough and detailed study, but neither renewed nor seriously challenged by the new.

The method of disputation, chosen by the universities as their theological tool, carried with it serious limitations. By its nature this method is analytical and insists that the strength of any thesis is derived from the strength of its constitutive parts, brought together to form a logical whole. By breaking down a thesis into its essential propositions its strength or weakness can be determined, its necessary consequences examined and judgement of its acceptability given. But such an analytical procedure, and the accompanying frame of mind, sometimes miss the overall impact of propositions, and are not always able to grasp radical and wide ranging theses which demand a definite shift of viewpoint. The traditional method of refutation used by Catholic writers, arising as it did from this philosophical disposition, concentrated on a detailed examination and rejection of opponents' works, literally phrase by phrase. The underlying impact of the work of Luther, for example the creative insight at the heart of his writings, was never really perceived in a positive way by Catholic writers who were drawn away from it by their urgent desire to oppose his more detailed propositions.

The same strengths and weaknesses of this method can be seen also in the uses made of the Scriptures. As we have remarked in the context of Dr Edward Powel's work, there was a detailed and thorough knowledge of the Scriptures abroad in this period, and a readiness to use both the New and Old Testaments in a literal, disciplined manner in theological disputation. However, this use would appear to be limited by the habit of apologetics which saw the Scriptures as an excellent means of defending dogmatic propositions. The Scriptures were the first range of armour to be brought to the defence of the faith; a defence which was to be carried out statement by statement until each detail of Catholic teaching had been safeguarded from attack. But the ability to approach Scripture as a source of theological inspiration, as a source from which to discover new depth and understanding of faith seems to have been lacking. A freshness of approach, taking away the dominance of apologetics and replacing it with a broader appreciation of Scripture as a source of revelation was needed. When this sort of innovation did arise, it is not surprising that poorly equipped Catholics found it difficult to react competently to the phenomenon, for it gave rise to the tensions between Scripture and Tradition which we have seen were to be left largely without any final solution.

The lack of non-printed evidence of activity at Cambridge University at the time of Fisher's theological studies means that we are left with an incomplete picture. Printed material, which has survived to our day, no doubt represents the more stable elements in the studies carried out by Fisher and his contemporaries. The oral and note work which students undoubtedly undertook probably was far more varied and may even have contained elements of controversy, change, unease and reaction. But that is as yet speculation. The picture which the printed evidence presents to us is a method of training that was heavily emphatic of system and discipline, strong in a limited use of resources, especially the Scriptures, and generally ready to give a rigorous though unimaginative defence of statements of faith by disputation. The weaknesses of the approach though are also evident. The number of years of study, for example, was not reflected in the breadth of material or methods embraced, which contributed to the heaviness and lack of elasticity of much of the subsequent Catholic writings. The absence of genuine literary and linguistic skills in dealing with the Scriptures rendered the fruit gained from these studies pale and insignificant in comparison to later achievements.

It is out of this context of training and preparation that the major of the first Catholic response to Luther emerges. These writings show many aspects of the educational perception adopted: mainly in the general curriculum patterns, teaching methods and academic approaches that were employed. The limits of university provision do, for the most part, become the limits of their responses. Fisher displays greater learning and precision than his contemporaries but they, for their part, show signs of being able to approach the controversy with individuality and some originality. The true extent of the response to Luther has begun to emerge in this study. The variety of replies to Luther that flowed from a traditional background and theology must be complemented with the work of the Cambridge theologians. These Doctors, especially Dr. Bullock, seem to have been immersed in the humanist New Learning and their presence serves to remind us of the awareness that did exist among some leading Catholics of the importance of modern Scriptural studies. Fisher was not able to make this bear dividends in his apologetical writings, but the Cambridge theologians may well have done so. At least the awareness and possibility were there, even if only in small measure.

Conclusion

Our detailed examination of Fisher's work shows the pivotal concepts of his theology are the Church, the Holy Spirit and the Truth and the way in which they are locked in close relationship. In this Fisher is representative of the traditional schools of Catholic theology, all of which seemed content to rest their case on the statement that the Spirit of Christ is with the Church, and therefore what she holds and teaches is the truth which must not be opposed. But an equally vital second step of the statement, one which Fisher brings out more clearly, is the importance between the *ecclesia docens* and the *ecclesia discens* (the teaching and the learning Church). He is quite adamant that this distinction, which is the distinction between priest and people or hierarchy and laity, was founded by Christ, intended for all time and is to be strictly upheld as essential for the correct ordering of the Church. This differentiation becomes an almost active-passive distinction, for while the people have the right of believing and giving assent, they do not have the right of dissenting from their legitimate teachers as long as they are not suspect of heresy.[8] The activities which are proper to lay people are those of offering themselves to God, for which they are correctly called a 'royal priesthood' and of publicly bearing witness to Christ; not by preaching the Gospel which is the task of the ordained ministry, but by life and example. The teaching and preaching in the Church is the explicit task of those ordained to do so and those so appointed.[9]

One result of this distinction is that Fisher's writings encompass two objectives. First, he wished to defend the lay people from false teaching and secondly, he wished to preserve the true teaching of the Church in those theological circles where controversial teachings were being discussed and disputed. Fisher saw these as two different tasks, for what is permissible in theological controversy is often out of place in a pastoral context. Only sure and true doctrine should be placed before the people and not the issues of controversy. He went even further when he said that the appeal by a teacher or scholar to public opinion, of which he accused Luther, was regarded by every intelligent man as foolish, according to Seneca's apposite saying 'popular favour is sought by evil artifices.' [10]

The first of these objectives Fisher executed in his anti-Lutheran sermons, which are comparatively short, very direct and unequivocal condemnations of Luther. He endeavoured to give clear guidance to his congregation not only about the truth of their traditional faith, but also

---

[8] *Defensio*, 11. 3.

[9] I Peter, 2:9. *Assertio*, Art. 16.

[10] *Assertio*, 11. 1.

about the thorough wickedness of Luther who was only misleading them. He only touches upon the intricacies of the theological controversy, being intent more upon establishing the utter reliability of the Church and her teachings. Luther's opposition to the Church was self-condemnatory, for he lacked the qualities of humility and obedience which all must show to the legitimate teaching of the Church. Fisher sought to build up for his audience the reasons why the Church, especially in the person of the Pope, should be obeyed and trusted, and so he was more interested in supporting and reinforcing the established authority of the Church than in a detailed refutation of Luther's theses. He sought to serve his flock as a dutiful bishop by leading them to recognise the truth of their inherited adherence to the Church, and in that way defended them from the dangers inherent in teaching that was contrary to it.

Fisher's theological writings in defence of Catholic teaching are somewhat different. Unlike the sermons, they are marked by a scholarly strictness in the use of the sources in their systematic analysis of Luther's writings, and they are offered not to the public but to those who by their qualifications are able to take part in the debate. Fisher employed every resource at his disposal in his conflict with Luther. On the detailed points of their debate, Fisher calls upon very possible support, drawing from his vast knowledge of patristic and scholastic writings and upon the text of Scripture. In doing so he was not particularly selective, and spared no thought for the final length of his work, as in these circles the habit of the day was to be detailed and meticulous rather than incisive and brief. His works then are long and tedious, impressive in the unrelenting and systematic pursuit of error, outstanding for their range and detail of learning and memorable for the depth of personal commitment to faith that they display. But they lack any liveliness, inventiveness or boldness of approach, persisting to the end with laborious refutations of even the smallest consequence of Luther's stance.

Fisher's intransigent approach to Luther can hardly be a point of criticism, except that it may have obstructed his accurate appreciation of the content of Luther's writings. Certainly, a total lack of communication was one of the characteristics of the Catholic-Lutheran controversy, but by the time Fisher joined in the debate positions were already hardened into outright opposition and most of the opportunities for negotiation had been lost. One of the key points on which Fisher refused outright any latitude to Luther was the appeal to Scripture alone as the definitive source of doctrine. It must have been quite clear to Fisher that this principle was central to Luther's theological method, and that it was opposed to the Catholic position as it had evolved to date. The true use of the Scriptures, insisted Fisher, could only be guaranteed by conformity with the interpretation of the Church, otherwise there was no steady criterion for interpretation and gross inconsistencies would appear in the understanding of Scripture.

There is sufficient evidence in the life of Fisher for us to be quite clear that, despite this connection between the Scriptures and Church authority, he cannot be criticised for any lack of appreciation of the importance of Scripture and good Scriptural studies. During his life at Cambridge Fisher showed great interest in the linguistic achievements of the New Learning. As we have seen, he went to considerable personal effort to benefit himself from the newly available knowledge, and he spent a great deal of time promoting these studies in the University. His support and enthusiasm for Greek and Hebrew studies are beyond doubt, and Fisher is rightly held as one of the champions of the humanist New Learning in England. Yet even here, where his enthusiasm is aroused on intellectual grounds and where he can see great possibilities ahead in Scriptural studies, there is another factor at play too. This gives rise to an ambiguity in his attitude to Greek and Hebrew studies and to revised biblical texts, for when the conflict is engaged, his loyalty and commitment to the Church and all her traditions become more important to him than his undoubted love and regard for learning. So he makes a limited use of his linguistic skills in his controversial writings, almost as if he regarded them as a luxury that could not be indulged while the conflict was to hand.

This struggle of John Fisher to bring the New Learning into the service of Catholic theology must constitute one of his sad inner conflicts. Not only did he personally not achieve sufficient learning in these studies in time to achieve his desired alliance, but he lived long enough to see his attempts at the University lead in a direction that he could not have wished. His desire was that learning should be in harmony with the proclaimed teaching of the Church, for then the high regard which he had for all genuine scholarship could rejoice in the approval of the legitimate authority of the Church. Although at times it must have caused pain and possible confusion in Fisher's heart, it is clear that for him the findings of scholarship were not the ultimate criterion of truth. No matter how coherent an argument or how convincing a proof, the final arbiter of truth was the Church: and the Church speaking ultimately not through her Doctors, but through her Bishops. For the most part Fisher believed that all true learning would correspond with the teachings of the Church and so the measure of truth was normally conformity with the teaching proclaimed by the Fathers and Doctors of the Church. But at times a more concrete criterion is required, and then Fisher states quite clearly that it is the Councils of the Church together with the Pope that are to be obeyed, not because of the claims of their learning, but because of the presence of the Holy Spirit. So the findings of scholarship are held in constant interplay with the judgement of the Church hierarchy and together this is the *ecclesia docens*; but of the two, the legally appointed hierarchy is undoubtedly the ultimate guide.

Fisher was a scholar of considerable ability and reputation; he was a man of true learning and devoted to the study of theology. This ultimate submission of his mind and will to the authority of the Church was an expression of his deepest faith and personality. It is this same commitment that brought his life to its end against his undoubted feelings of loyalty to the king and country, whom he prayed for with his last breath. But, as we have observed, this was not a commitment to the Church that rested on a blinkered or self-deceptive view of the Church. Fisher was keenly aware as any man of the shortcomings of the Church, both in Rome itself and in England. He condemned with vigour and courage the corruption which he observed in Church life and he worked by example and project to renew her life. As was consistent with his understanding of the Church, Fisher's attentiveness to the need for reform centred on the requirements of the clergy, especially on the need for improved standards of preaching. Unlike some of his contemporaries, however, Fisher took steps to effect reformation in this area and nearly all his initiatives at Cambridge were inspired by pastoral motives. It was his idea that, equipped with better learning and more able to handle the resources – especially the Scriptures and the Fathers – the priests who emerged from Cambridge would be ready and able to offer an improved standard of preaching and instruction to the faithful. This, together with a continual reform in life style, would be sufficient to bring about a revitalisation of the Church in England.

Fisher's constant and often heartfelt attacks on the bishops and priests of England to reform their way of life in conformity to the standards of Christ were similarly inspired by his concern for the faithful. Once given good example by cardinal, bishops and priests, then standards of the lay people would rise as surely as night follows day. And Fisher was quite sure as to how this was to be achieved: by a faithful observance of the already existing laws of the Church.

Conclusion

In these proposals for reform, Fisher stood in the company of some of his contemporaries, most notably John Colet. Many critical eyes were being cast at the affairs of the Church, and some constructive steps and proposals were being made, but in no sense could these initiatives of Fisher be considered radical. It is quite clear that he was a reformer in the broad sense of that word, but whether or not he was getting to the heart of the Church's problems is quite a different matter. It is a fascinating speculative question whether the reforms proposed and carried out by Fisher, Colet and others would have been sufficient to strengthen the evident weaknesses of the Church if political events had not taken the turn they did. Fisher's reading of the situation was that radical solutions were not necessary, and that there were sufficient resources within the structures of the Church to bring about a movement of renewal, given the changes of heart and learning that he advocated. Yet the challenge of Luther's radical theology would still have had to be faced and the standards of theological training which we have seen to be operating at that time suggest that, unless the contribution of Henry Bullock and his Cambridge friends represented a genuine and mature meeting of Catholic theology and New Learning, there was not sufficient breadth or room for manipulation in Catholic theological circles to avoid a major conflict and subsequent split.

But the years before the Reformation have been our interest. This study presents John Fisher as a leader in this period. It presents him as leading first of all in the desire for reform and in the pastoral life of the Church. The example he gave as a bishop in his diocese was a clear indication of what he was urging upon his fellow bishops and priests. He strove to serve the needs of the Church and its people to the best of his ability. When controversy became the order of the day, this book again presents him as a leader, for he spoke out with a voice that rose above the rest, speaking clearly and definitely the statements and defence of his faith. But it has also been the aim of this study to demonstrate that while Fisher was a leader in this controversy, he was not alone in his defence of Catholicism. Others in England spoke out too and it is a mistake to imagine that Fisher was more or less isolated in ability and readiness to defend the cause. The full breadth of the Catholic response is still unknown, but the outlines are clear and reveal a deeper and far reaching response to Luther in the early days of the controversy.

This book has also sought to bring out the comparative strengths and weaknesses of Catholic theology as it moved into conflict with Luther. In some areas of theological activity Catholics were well educated and prepared. The strengths of late medieval theology were present and readily employed. In other areas, though, little progress had been made and the weaknesses of the writings of Catholic theologians can be traced back to the shortcomings in their training and university life. This was especially true of the renewed linguistic studies, for the incorporation of these into Catholic theology involved particular dilemmas, some of which were not easily to be resolved.

With this in mind, John Fisher appears to bridge two ages. His formation and early education place him firmly within the embrace of the medieval Church, and he never lost his admiration for its scholastic theology, and his total commitment to its spirituality. Yet at times he appears quite as much at home in the next era, denoted by an interest in revised classical Latin, Greek and Hebrew studies, for he supported and promoted these studies with enthusiasm and had a warm and sympathetic relationship with Erasmus. In fact he gives us a number of indications that he was often seeking to reconcile these two influences: to bring together the new and the old. But events did not grant him sufficient time to achieve that ambition, for it fell to him to devote all his learning and scholarship to the defence of his faith. Yet we are left with the impression that (noteworthy though his achievements were in this controversy) this was not the natural, nor the most suitable outlet for his talents. By instinct Fisher was a scholar and a spiritual man, not a polemicist It may be that his life would have produced greater theological fruit had history allowed him time and place to follow his instincts and, with suffering and effort, bring together all that was best of medieval theology with the vital contribution of the Renaissance. Had such a meeting been achieved, it would have given joy to his heart and hope to his successors.

Afterword

ince 1976, when the thesis of Vincent Nichols came off the loom, a considerable amount of research has been completed that has reviewed the years of the English Reformation in general, and the life of John Fisher in particular. Consequently, our understanding of this important period in English history has been revised and our knowledge about Fisher has been extended. This work, in many respects, vindicates the appeal made by Archbishop Nichols in his first chapter for a more balanced approach to be made in our assessment of the early sixteenth century and the characters that occupied the stage of events, numbered among whom was Bishop John Fisher.

It is the purpose of this chapter to augment the detailed study done by Vincent Nichols with more recent work that has contributed to our knowledge of Fisher and his life and times. This will not only confirm the achievement of the Archbishop, when he was a young priest, it will also provide the reader with a firmer grasp of the developments in research that have subsequently taken place in supplying evidence to show that the late medieval English Church was in need of reform, but far from moribund. I give particular attention in this introduction to the revisionist scholars whose work has successfully encouraged a changed perception about how we view the early sixteenth century. This revisionist approach has inevitably experienced something of a reaction in the last decade as a new generation of scholars has entered the field of historical research, and this needs to be recognised[1]. However, it has been my particular focus to establish a correlation between the material in this book, completed originally in 1976, and the subsequent work that has been achieved. Inevitably, within a single introductory chapter, the issues raised have to be selective and are limited. I have further interpreted my brief within the limitations of identifying certain key points raised in the main body of the text, and then providing some account of the subsequent research that pertains to them; rather

[1] For example, the work being done by Alec Ryrie at Durham: see his *The Age of Reformation: The Tudor and Stuart Realms, 1485–1603* (Harlow: Pearson, 2009) and his edited *Palgrave Advances in the European Reformations* (Basingstoke: Palgrave MacMillan, 2006). Or, at the University of California, we have Ethan H. Shagan, who has written extensively on the period and is engaged in various editorial work: *Catholics and the Protestant Nation: Religious Politics and Identity in Early Modern England* (Manchester University Press, 2005).

than exploring a detailed account of the extensive investigations and academic debates that have taken place up to the present day. Such a task would require a book in itself.

The text following this introduction is as it was delivered to the examiners in 1976 with some slight modifications: I have made a few small changes to the text to avoid repetition, changed the style of the footnotes and inserted some references. The Latin quotations in the original document have been translated into English, for which I thank Abbé Germain Marc'hadour for his valuable help. The early sixteenth-century quotations have been linguistically represented in modern English, though I have retained the currency values of the period: for example, in Chapter One, with the Will of Robert Fisher, multiply the amounts by one thousand to acquire an approximation of current-day values.

We are aware that it is often the case that it is the victors who write the history, and this is particularly pertinent when we consider the English Reformation. The development of printing in the early sixteenth century provided the means by which ideas could be disseminated and polemical debate could be engaged: it also offered an opportunity for the power of propaganda to be manifested. The monarchs of the Tudor dynasty were particularly good at using the mass media of their time to advance a particular interpretation of their actions. In many respects the propaganda of the time has shaped our understanding of the period, but fortunately our perspective has been modified in recent years by the investigations into other areas of life than the polemical printed words that featured so strongly in the debates between Catholic and Protestant exponents.

In 1987, Christopher Haigh edited a collection of essays that were published under the title of *The English Reformation Revised*.[2] It was noted that much of our perception about the English Reformation period had been influenced by the 1563 writings of John Foxe in his *Actes and Monuments*.[3] This was a work written to promote the Protestant cause in England by describing in some detail the Catholic cruelties that were alleged to have occurred during the Reformation period. The great study of the English Reformation by A. G. Dickens tended to reinforce the position adopted by Foxe. This position assumed that the Reformation in England rescued the country from a corrupt and at times persecuting Roman Catholic Church and established a reformed, sound Church

---

[2] Christopher Haigh (ed), *The English Reformation Revised* (Cambridge University Press, 1987).
[3] John Foxe, *Actes and Monuments*, Ed. G. Townsend, (London 1843.)

of England that was based upon scripture and Protestant principles.[4] However, Haigh contends in his introduction that 'revisionist attitudes and recent researches have combined to challenge the 'Foxe version' of Reformation history endorsed by Professor Dickens.' Geoffrey Dickens was an good British historian, given to precision and detail, and his work still stands with enduring authority, but he never appears to have questioned the inherited wisdom that tended to demonise the Catholic inheritance that was gradually extinguished in England, apart from recusance, as the sixteenth century progressed.

The revisionism identified by Haigh in the 1980s has continued and deepened with a whole range of researched studies conducted by an international array of academics, particularly in England.[5] As in chapter 2, where Vincent Nichols describes the local spirituality of the Abbey church of Beverley in Yorkshire, other historians have focused upon provincial initiatives taken by local bishops and harvested the evidence derived from wills and other surviving documents that suggest a more vibrant and healthy state for the Catholic presence in England on the eve of the Reformation than was previously thought. For example, a rich description of lay spirituality in the York diocese following the episcopate of John Thoresby (1352-73) is provided by Jonathan Hughes.[6] Also, Eamon Duffy's substantial study into Catholicism in medieval England established two clear principles. Duffy draws a picture from an extensive investigation into the wills of people, as with the will of John Fisher's father in this work, and the state of the ordinary parishes of England to demonstrate that by the eve of the Reformation the argument that there was widespread dissatisfaction with the Catholic Church cannot be sustained.[7] For one thousand years and more England had been Catholic and indeed had proved to be a devoted and loyal country to its Catholic heritage, derived largely from the papal mission initiated by Gregory the Great and delivered by Augustine of Canterbury in 597. In the Middle Ages the country featured two of the major pilgrimage sites of Europe: those of St Thomas Becket in Canterbury and Our Lady of Walsingham in Norfolk. And it should be remembered that, with the exception of a few Jewish and possibly Muslim minority groupings, every person born

---

[4] Arthur Geoffrey Dickens, *The English Reformation*, (London: 1964.)

[5] Numbered among the English scholars who have contributed to our revised perception of the Tudor period are: Jack Scarisbrick, Eamon Duffy, John Guy, Richard Rex, Brendan Bradshaw and David Starkey. There are also clusters of scholars in North America and in the rest of Europe.

[6] See Jonathan Hughes, *Pastors and Visionaries*, (Boydell Press: 2002.)

[7] Eamon Duffy, *The Stripping of the Altars: Traditional Religion in England c.1400-c.1580*, (Yale Univ Press: New Haven and London, 1992.) The work was later amplified with a particular study of the village of Morebath. See: *The Voices of Morebath, Reformation and Rebellion in an English Village*, (Yale Univ Press: New Haven and London, 2002.)

in England was baptised into the Catholic sacramental system, which cared for the people from the cradle to the grave, and beyond.

Secondly, Duffy argues that the Reformation in England was by no means a popular development. The revisionist reading of the spread of the Reformation suggests that it was a slow, localised influence that took a considerable length of time to seep into the religious landscape of England. Apart from the dramatic reaction to the religious reforms expressed by the Pilgrimage of Grace in the north of England in 1536 and the Western Rebellion later in 1549, which may have had other motivational grievances than purely religious ones, assessment of support for, and reaction to, the Reformation cause has tended to divide the country into several interest groups.[8] In the country districts it may be suspected that the Reformation was very reluctantly embraced, and in many cases it was purely superficial in terms of its loyalty and expression. The intellectual élite in the universities were probably divided, as were the bishops. The main support for the aspirations of the reformers were to be found among the merchant classes of London, especially those dealing with the Hanseatic League, and sections of the aristocracy in the royal court, particularly those associated with the Boleyn faction. Susan Brigden has completed a very interesting study that traces the tensions between reformers and conservatives in these spheres as the battle for the soul of London was engaged. As she observes,

> *The people of England found themselves caught up in a Reformation, not at first of their making, but in time made by them. Religious choices were demanded most immediately from the Londoners, because in London the English Reformation began, and the capital was 'the common country of all England.' Maybe as many as one in twenty of the population of England found their home in London in the mid-sixteenth century, at least for a time. The power of the City's religious example was immense. There the new faith was first and most powerfully evangelised; there, under the eyes of the government, conformity to the royal will was most imperative.* [9]

It was in this religious and political turmoil that John Fisher and Thomas More lived, and they were cast as two of the leading exponents that defended the traditional faith of England, a defence that eventually cost them their lives. It was little wonder that Fisher preferred Rochester and More preferred Chelsea to the vitriolic and sycophantic life of the royal court, with all its machinations and confabulations.

[8] D. M. Palliser, 'Popular Reactions to the Reformation' in Haigh (ed), *The English Reformation Revised*, p. 94f.

[9] Susan Brigden, *London and the Reformation*, (Oxford University Press, 1989.) p. 2.

Afterword

In our general description of the work of the revisionists, other important points have come to light and are worthy of mention. A convenient but misleading suggestion is that the Protestant influence was exclusively the influence for reform that was being expressed, whereas the Catholic exponents were fundamentally reactionary and conservative. Opinion now would recognise that the issue of the need for some kind of reform in the Church was held generally as an undisputed matter. Many Catholic writers at the time, particularly those who had been influenced by Christian humanism, were calling for reform. For example, the Dutch Christian humanist and priest, Desiderius Erasmus (c.1466-1536) believed in Church reform and a greater accessibility to the Bible for all, stressing the importance of conscience, inner belief and living in charity. He sought to promote purity in religion and faith, and was not hesitant in mocking the absurdities that religion can manifest.[10] Unlike John Fisher and Thomas More, Erasmus was a reluctant controversialist, and it took some time to encourage him to enter the fray. In the event, although Erasmus expressed many of the ideas adopted by the later reformers, he remained loyal to the Catholic Church; appalled by the developments that the Reformation communities appeared to be adopting, once they had separated from the Church. None of these great Catholic heroes actually lived to see the more extreme measures that were eventually manifested in the English Reformation, which was probably a mercy for them.

The humanist scholars within the Catholic Church, who embraced Renaissance values and thinking, were numerous, and indeed included most of the popes of the period. It would, therefore, be a distortion to see the conflict as simply being between reactionary Catholics and new-thinking reformers.[11] The tension in the early years was not around the question of whether or not reform should take place, but about how it should take place: Should the Catholic Church reform itself, or were more drastic measures necessary? The Renaissance popes in particular were cultured men who were not strangers to the new learning and supported it with their extensive patronage of the arts and architecture. The Italian principalities of the time featured several universities that were pioneering the new learning. It was not therefore pressing that the papacy should add to the academic provision that already existed.

---

[10] In 1509, at the house of his friend Thomas More, he drafted his work *In Praise of Folly*, which was a sharp satire about human actions and careers, while promoting the theological message of being a fool for Christ.

[11] Diarmid MacCulloch has observed, 'Humanism was a way of approaching and the acquisition and ordering of knowledge, not a coherent movement of thought.' (sic) In his essay 'England' in Andrew Pettegree, *The Early Reformation in England*, (Cambridge Univ Press, 1992) p. 170.

Afterword

Several English bishops had been educated at these Italian universities and Cardinal Wolsey emulated the papal architectural interest in his construction of Hampton Court.[12]

The early reformers clearly originated from within the Catholic Church: most of them being priests, friars or monks. The process of attitude-change towards the Catholic Church, which happened relatively quickly, remains interesting. From the frustration of failing to effect reforms within the Church, some reformers reached the view that the Church was an institution beyond reform. This changed view quickly stimulated a theological rethink about the nature and status of the Catholic Church, and questions relating to authority were then raised. The Catholic Church came to be seen as not having simply failed in its divine commission, but having become transposed into the instrument of the anti-Christ. The process by which the papacy became demonised had begun, and this gained a particularly strong focus in England.

When Martin Luther penned his 95 theses for disputing abuses in the late October of 1517, he was attacking the most visible, outgrown and obvious areas for reform. This need for reform was a shared opinion among the Christian humanists who had arisen within the Catholic Church. Some of them were to form the main body of reformers that emerged. However, the humanists who remained within the Catholic Church, particularly John Fisher, Desiderius Erasmus, John Colet and Thomas More, formed a responsive and critical audience for the protesting reformers.

A further point, addressed by the archbishop in his first chapter, was the issue of a sacred/secular divide, so familiar today, that simply did not feature in England before the Reformation. There were tensions between common and Canon Law, rivalries between the monasteries and the various guilds engaged in trade, and friction between the various pressure groups in the royal court. It may be suspected, however, that there was nothing particularly critical or new about this state of affairs in English society. Furthermore, it is difficult for us to imagine how deeply the Church was woven into the fabric of everyday life as it was

---

[12] Cardinal Christopher Bainbridge (1464-1514) of Durham (1507) and York (1508) attended Ferrara and Bologna. Charles Booth (d. 1535) of Hereford (1516) and priest at Beverley (1501) attended Bologna. John Clerk (d. 1541) of Bath and Wells (1523) attended Bologna. William Knight (1476-1547) of Bath and Wells (1541) attended Ferrara. Edward Lee (1482-1544) of York (1531) attended Bologna. Richard Nix (1447-1535) of Norwich (1501) attended Ferrara and Bologna. Richard Sampson (d.1554) of Chichester (1536) attended Perugia and Siena. John Stokesley (1475-1539) of London (1530) attended Rome. Cuthbert Tunstal (1474-1559) of London (1522) and Durham (1530) attended Rome and Padua. See: Andrew Allan Chibi, *Henry VIII's Bishops*, (James Clarke & Co: Cambridge, 2003) p. 263. Table 3.

Afterword

lived five hundred years ago. We are conditioned by the sacred/secular divide: a dichotomy which is clearly present in modern western culture. One should be disciplined in abandoning present-day assumptions when attempting to visit the Church of the early sixteenth century. Religious symbols, featuring Christ or the saints – either in motif or image – decorated every street and thoroughfare in London and the cities. Church buildings dominated even the smallest of villages and towns. Chapels served educational establishments and guildhouses of the trades wherever they were established. All were staffed by one or more priests, as there was no clergy shortage. The Church employed most of the intelligent people of the time for its religious and civil services. Because reading, writing and languages were taught through Church institutions and because the Church, through the universities, had access to most areas of law, service in the Church frequently meant work for its functionaries in most departments of civil and indeed court life.

The influence of the Church was not only manifested in terms of its structural and occupational presence, but also in other key aspects of life. Time was measured ecclesiastically: people went to market, celebrated their pageants and established their annual temporal rhythms according to the Church's calendar. The principal festivals of Christmas, Easter and Whitsuntide were the major reference points for other festivals of more local significance, with Rogation-tide in the Springtide to bless the crops and All Saints/All Souls tide in November to commemorate loved ones commended through death. These holy days remain in the English language as 'holidays'; in name if not in religious observance. The English language benefited considerably from the deep influence of the Church. Many ecclesiastical words were in common parlance and many place names were given to villages and towns that still evoke the religious importance of the time. People greeted each other and parted with the blessing: 'God's day' for 'good day' and 'God be with ye' for 'goodbye'.

Chapter Two of the archbishop's study took us to the University of Cambridge and explored the time that Fisher spent there and the educational curriculum, based on the scholastic *Trivium and Quadrivium*, that he undertook in his intellectual formation.[13] Initially, Fisher went to Michaelhouse under the tutorship of William Melton, a priest and also a Yorkshireman, and he achieved his Bachelor degree

<hr/>

[13] More recent material on Cambridge University and the curriculum can be found in Damien Riehl Leader, *History of the University of Cambridge*, Vol 1, to 1546, (Cambridge Univ Press: 1989) and also John Twiggs, *History of Queens' College Cambridge 1448-1986*, (Boydell Press: Cambridge, 1987.)

in 1488 followed by his Master degree three years later. The university colleges at this time were religious foundations and organised very much as semi-religious houses. The notion of academic discipline and discipleship were closely related concepts. Fisher was quickly elected a Fellow of the college and a Proctor of the university. Having been called to accept holy orders as an expected condition of his involvement in the higher studies of the university, he was ordained a priest in 1501. The practise of creating academic clergy at the universities continued long after the influence of the English Reformation had successfully taken hold of these establishments, but fundamentally it declared the vocational aspect of learning and more particularly, in Fisher's case, a dedication to the Queen of Sciences: theology.[14]

Melton was preferred to be the Chancellor of the cathedral church of York and after his departure, according to Thomas Bailey's biography of 1655, Fisher was elected the Master of Michaelhouse by the Fellows.[15] It was at this time that he became acquainted with Lady Margaret Beaufort, countess of Richmond and mother of King Henry VII, being appointed her confessor. The friendship that was sustained between them lasted to the end of her life and was fruitful in the endowments she showered upon the university at Cambridge, in no small measure establishing the two new colleges of Christ's and St John's.[16]

Commentators on the Renaissance have detected a degree of antipathy between the scholastic tradition that dominated both Oxford and Cambridge in the early sixteenth century and the philosophical principles of Renaissance humanism, or to use its contemporary term, the *litterae humaniores*. This tension was also detected, possibly more strongly, in the continental universities. As Richard Rex has observed,

> *The privileging of the classical past and the awareness of the decline of classical culture in what were seen as the Middle Ages played their part in the vociferous humanist critique of medieval academic life and style which arose in the fifteenth century and intensified*

---

[14] In the nineteenth century, John Henry Newman was admitted to Holy Orders in the Church of England when he was a Fellow of Oriel, to serve his title at St Clement's, Oxford (deacon, 13 June 1824; priest, 29 May 1825).

[15] Thomas Bailey, *The Life and Death of the Renowned John Fisher, Bishop of Rochester*, (London: 1665, reprinted for P. Meighan, Bookseller at Gray's Inn Gate, Holbourn in 1739) p.9.

[16] See Malcolm Underwood, 'John Fisher and the Promotion of Learning' and Christopher Brooke, 'The University Chancellor' in Brendan Bradshaw and Eamon Duffy, Eds. *Humanism, Reform and the Reformation*, (Cambridge Univ Press, 1989.) p. 25f and 47f. Also the biography on Lady Beaufort by Michael K. Jones and Malcolm G. Underwood. *The King's Mother. Lady Margaret Beaufort. Countess of Richmond and Derby. 1443-1509.* (Cam,bridge Univ Press. 1992.) Review by Guy Bedouelle in *Moreana*, Vol. 32, No. 121, March 1995, p.91.

in the sixteenth. Humanists sneered at the 'barbarous' style of the scholastics.[17]

This tension should not be overemphasised, however, because the scholastic tradition employed a curriculum design and method that were intrinsically classical in origin. It should be noted that educational development in Europe has historically been based on foundation principles. In other words, a basis is established upon which further learning may be developed. This was essentially the function of studying the Trivium and the Quadrivium. Courses in the universities only adopted a subject-based focus once the basic techniques of analysis and expression had been achieved. So it initially did not matter whether or not one was studying Common Law, Canon Law, Political Science or Theology, because a traditional basis was important. Knowing how to think logically, express oneself clearly, and argue persuasively were skills that had general application in all fields of law, political science and theology. The same principle applied in the world of art and architecture where the new generation of painters still had to learn the rudiments of their craft. They continued to attend schools under a master who taught them his technique that they then elaborated, but they also were equipped with the ancient skills of design, mathematical proportion and compositional technique. The approach was applied to those studying good letters for whom the acquisition of competent grammar, rhetoric, and ancient philosophy, in the Trivium, and arithmetic, geometry, music and astronomy, in the Quadrivium, remained fundamental in providing a knowledge base upon which they were taught to think clearly and express themselves lucidly in their oratory, disputations and determination. For the humanists, however, the scholastic inheritance was a means to an end rather than an end in itself, and educational frustration could clearly be encountered if the focus on fundamentals was never developed.[18]

Trying to comprehend the philosophical complexity of Renaissance humanism is no easy task. Several reasons can be advanced to explain why this is the case. The humanist movement originated in Italy and then spread throughout Europe, but in its transmission it was adopted in various places with different emphases and nuances. Its comprehensiveness as an influence established its principles mainly in the realms of art,

[17] Andrew Pettegree (ed.), *The Reformation World* (London and New York: Routledge, 2000). See Richard Rex, 'Humanism', ch. 4, p. 53. Also Richard Rex, *The Theology of John Fisher* (Cambridge University Press, 1991), ch. 1, 'Humanism and scholasticism in late fifteenth-century Cambridge', p. 13f
[18] *Moreana*, Vol. 32, No. 122, June 1995. Thomas. M. Finan, *Collected Works of Erasmus*, Vol.11, p. 80, Theology and humanism.

architecture, philosophy, statecraft and theology. Further, its development in the different localities where it was established was variable. How can we describe its influence? Fundamentally it was a movement born of the Renaissance: that remarkable period when classical design, ancient sources and the respublica, or statecraft, occupied the interest of intellectuals and artists throughout Europe. The preoccupation with giving attention to classical sources was not done just to represent those points of inspiration in the 16th century. It was a radical movement that went back to the roots of classical culture to gain momentum by which it could be catapulted into new ways of thinking for the future. The rebirth was manifested in an outpouring of new approaches in architecture, art, philosophy and a renewed interest in the principles of government.[19]

It was Kenneth Clark who, some forty two years ago when political correctness was not our moral arbiter, coined the phrase 'man – the measure of all things' in his personal view of Civilisation. He was echoing the question of the psalmist: 'what is man that you think of him; mere man that you care for him? Yet you made him inferior only to yourself; you crowned him with glory and honour.' (Ps. 8.4) It was a pertinent observation about the development of Renaissance humanism and he explored the way in which perceptions about human nature and humanity in general became the main focus of the genius that arose in that period. The important point that Clark was making was that the preoccupation of philosophers, artists, architects and the theologians was to focus on what understanding humanity as being made in the image of God meant. The world of Renaissance art demonstrates the point well, where human scale and physical perfection were graphically represented. In Clark's words,

> It was the first authoritative statement that the human body – that body which, in Gothic times, had been the subject of shame and concealment, that body which Alberti had praised so extravagantly – could be made the means of expressing noble sentiments, life giving energy and God-like perfection. It was an idea that was to have an incalculable influence on the human mind for four hundred years.' [20]

There are two outstanding examples of this artistic presentation that are given theological expression: both are in the Vatican. The first is a painting by Raffaello Santi (known as Raphael – 1483-1521) and is called *The School of Athens* (c.1509).[21] It is situated in the papal apartments in

---

[19] See Gareth Bennett, *To the Church of England*, 'The Impact of the Reformer on Religious Thought,' (Churchman Publishing Ltd: Worthing, 1988.) p. 21f.

[20] Kenneth Clark, *Civilisation* (London: BBC Books, 1969), p. 125.

[21] Raphael, *School of Athens*, in the Stanza della Segnatura, Vatican Palace, Rome c.1509.

a room once used as a library and is, therefore, a celebration of learning. The painting depicts a scene that gathers together the great men of antiquity and creates a picture in which poets, sages, philosophers and theologians share, and indeed dispute, their respective knowledge and wisdom. To say the least, the participants are focused on their task. The basic theme is about the transmission of God-given knowledge, in this case, through the reading of books, ancient texts and scientific discovery. The meaning of the work receives Christian reinforcement when one's glance moves to its associate painting on the opposite wall, known as the *Disputa*. There we find an assembly of saints, bishops, popes and theologians from the past contemplating and discussing the nature of the Blessed Sacrament, which is displayed in a magnificent monstrance on an altar. It is a graphic reminder that the creative word was made flesh and dwelt among us in human form. A remarkable fact is that both these paintings were commissioned at the command and expense of Julius II (1443-1513), the 'warrior' pope, which makes the point that the much maligned popes of the Renaissance were also people of some culture.[22]

The second example is by Michelangelo Buonarotti (1474-1564) and it is the magnificent and celebrated painting that adorns the Sistine Chapel roof in the Vatican: a work also commissioned by Julius II and begun in 1508. Again the central theme of the massive work is the creation of man and the stories of creation and the Fall. However, the whole work is supported by a framework that includes sibyls and classical motifs, and remains an outstanding example of Renaissance humanism. More searchingly we may ask, what is happening with this inclusion of what are basically pagan allusions in Christian art? The humanist theologians would answer that we are dealing here with the revelation of prevenient grace. The mediaeval scholastics may have searched to discover God at the end of a logical syllogism, the humanists sought God in the motivation that inspired the ancient philosophers and all who pursue the quest for the truth. Christianity is a revealed faith and God reveals himself in mysterious and wonderful ways that are not always confined to ecclesiastical structures. It was this new approach that refreshed the academic halls of Cambridge, particularly under the competent guidance of Fisher. Fisher emphasised prevenient inspiration of the Holy Spirit in the pursuit of learning, while retaining a great respect for mediaeval scholasticism.[23] In a sense, Fisher defies categorising easily

[22] For more detail, read Andrew Graham-Dixon, *Renaissance* (London: BBC Books, 1999), pp. 181–3.
[23] Diarmid MacCulloch, *Reformation, Europe's House Divided, 1490-1700*, (Allen Lane Penguin : London, 2003) p. 112, John 6:44, Philippians 2:13.

Afterword

into the particular loyalties that then existed, consequently some see him as a conservative reactionary, whereas others see in him an educational innovator. This point has been discussed by Brendan Bradshaw in an essay that explores the life and character of Fisher.[24] Fisher the theologian, however, was not interested simply in the revival of classical values but in a new approach to Biblical Christianity. His focus was the recovery of biblical studies that were supported by the Church Fathers and by an expertise in New Testament knowledge, especially in Greek.[25] It was Fisher's outstanding competence as a theologian that made him so formidable an opponent in the debates that ensued, particularly as the doctrines of sola scriptura and sola fide became enunciated. Under Fisher's considerable influence, Cambridge was a bulwark of Catholic defence as the English Reformation began to be realised from 1527. It was ironic that once Fisher's presence had been removed in 1535 the university became increasingly occupied by the new men who promoted the cause of Protestant reform.[26]

Of course the influence of Christian humanism, which seems to have been absorbed by the Catholic Church without too much difficulty, was not well received by everyone or in every place. The protests against the use of pagan references were vociferous, for example, in the preaching of Girolamo Savonarola (1452-98), a Dominican friar with a lean and hungry look, who found the pagan allusions and nudity of the perfect human form in art to be too much. The puritanical measures that he inspired resulted in bonfires of vanities in Florence, where books and works of art were destroyed. But his protest was not really about reform; it was a challenge to the Catholic Church about its embrace of pagan influences. The Catholic Church considered these references to be acceptable in a society without a sacred/secular divide and a Church that respected the presence of prevenient grace. Be that as it may, once the Reformation adopted more extreme characteristics, and the influence of Calvin began to be felt in England, the universalism of Christian humanism began to evaporate.

> *The prophet of Geneva had made it abundantly clear that salvation was no longer a prize to be won. No paltry act of man, in his fleeting passage on earth, could possibly atone for the moral catastrophe of the Fall. The humanist concept of the dignity of man was shattered;*

---

[24] Bradshaw and Duffy, Ed. *Humanism, Reform and the Reformation*, Chapter 1, p.1.

[25] Bard Thompson, *Humanists and Reformers, A History of the Renaissance and Reformation*, (William B. Eerdmans Publishing Co: Michigan., 1996.) p. 347.

[26] Richard Rex, *The Tudors* (Gloucestershire: Tempus Publishing, 2003), p. 109.

> *no son of Adam could ever please God by his own design or*
> *inspiration.*[27]

The reformers increasingly turned their back on the classical references in Christian humanism in favour of purely scriptural study. It came to be an issue that provided a point of difference between Catholic and Protestant emphases. In his study of the clerical profession, Anthony Russell made the following observation:

> *The English Reformation was much more than the establishment of*
> *national independence from Rome in ecclesiastical matters; it was*
> *also a reaction against the poor quality and abuses of the medieval*
> *clergy and the assertion of secular authority over the ecclesiastical*
> *corporation. In terms of the clergyman's role, it represented a*
> *challenge by the laity to the clerical estate of the medieval church.*[28]

In what is in many respects an excellent piece of work, Russell regrettably asserts one of the most enduring and resilient myths about the English Reformation that has ever been perpetrated: the matter of clerical laxity and abuse, which Archbishop Nichols addresses in chapter 3. Again an appeal is made in that chapter for a more balanced assessment to be made. In the life of the Church throughout history it seems to be an unavoidable fact that among the clerics of the Church there will be some who disappoint. When this happens, those clergy who are worn out by the demands made upon them and become 'burnt out' attract the sympathy of the faithful; those clergy who become eccentrically deranged can be a source of amusement; the bad ones are a focus for scandal. However, it would seem that the proportion of scandalous clerics is comparable, if not less, to those who are given to their weaknesses in other professions. The reality that great treasures of the Church are kept in earthen vessels is carried in the minds of those who are ordained, and they know how unworthy they are of the dignity that is given to them. Otherwise, there would be no need for an ex opere operato doctrine by which the sacraments of the Church are not conditioned by the worthiness of those who administer them.[29]

The question of anticlericalism was addressed by Christopher Haigh and he has demonstrated that disenchantment with the clergy was not a paramount issue that contributed to the demand for reform. He comments:

---

[27] John Morgan, *Godly Learning*, (Cambridge University Press, 1986) p. 23.

[28] Anthony Russell, *The Clerical Profession*, (London: SPCK, 1980) p. 28.

[29] *Catechism of the Catholic Church*, (London: Geoffrey Chapman, 1994) 1128. p.310.

Afterword

> *If we seek the origins of the Reformation, we shall find them not in any general 'anticlericalism' but in the aspirations of particular interest groups: the common lawyers who coveted ecclesiastical litigation and Court politicians who aimed to make or salvage careers by taking advantage of the king's concern for the succession. Nor need we hope to find 'anticlericalism' an explanation for easy acceptance of religious change, since we now know that enforcing the Reformation was a much more difficult task than was once thought.*[30]

The religious orders of monks, friars and nuns conducted their worship and works of mercy to the extent that they had virtually dominated the social security system of many cities, towns and regions. They provided the first hospitals, schools and places for the care of the elderly, besides managing successful agricultural interests in sheep-rearing, farming, bee-keeping, beer-making and dairy products. Some religious foundations, which were already ancient by the early sixteenth century, had become incompetent or inefficient. It was in fact Cardinal Thomas Wolsey who first began a reform of the religious foundations in the early 1520s. Following his appointment as papal legate in 1518, Wolsey drew up plans for Church reform, including the creation of 13 new bishoprics, but the proposals remained intentional and were not carried through. He did, however, manage to dissolve some thirty religious houses between 1524 and 1529, using the funds raised to support educational foundations. Thereby he provided a blueprint that would be used more extensively later by Thomas Cromwell, when he was appointed vice-gerent in Spirituals with powers equal to the former legate, in the dissolution of the monasteries.

The position and status of the clergy in the medieval Church was a demographic phenomenon. To give some idea of the scale of the Church's engagement within society, it was possible that as many as one fifth of the working population of England was involved occupationally in ecclesiastical commitments to society. To represent this in present-day terms, you could put together the entire civil service along with the workers of our banks, our building societies, our schools and our doctors to create a comparative scale of social involvement. An enduring problem for the time was that there were so many people holding the benefit of the clergy, which produced a commensurate proportion of bad

---

[30] Haigh (ed), *The English Reformation Revised*, ch. 3, 'Anticlericalism and the English Reformation', p. 73.

clergy.[31] John Fisher alluded to this in his commentary on the Penitential Psalms when he observed reflecting upon the early Church 'In that time were no chalices of gold, but then was many golden priests; now be many chalices of gold, and almost no golden priests.'[32] Fisher was applied in improving the quality of the clergy in his diocese and articulated this desire when he observed, 'All fear of God... cometh and is grounded in the clergy; for if the clergy be well and rightfully ordered, giving good example to other of virtuous living, without doubt the people by that shall have more fear of God.'[33]

A further germane consideration arises when the development of the monastic foundations is explored. Most of the religious orders were based upon a rule that emphasised the three principles by which their daily life was organised: these principles were prayer, work and study. The emphasis upon study meant that monasteries became centres of learning besides houses for prayer, providers of agriculture and sources of social provision. The monasteries, along with the universities, were the main outlets for library provision and schools were established within them by which their scholars could gain literacy and equip themselves as monastic candidates for future occupation in the civil service.[34] Hence the enduring title of a clergyman as a 'Clerk in Holy Orders'.

Furthermore, many of the cathedrals in England were staffed and managed by religious orders. As the mother church of a diocese, the cathedrals were expected to be centres of excellence not only in terms of the worship performed in them, but also in terms of the learning they provided. This applied also to the cathedrals under the control of the secular clergy. William Melton's appointment from Michaelhouse to be the Chancellor of York was to a post in which his teaching capacities could be extended to include clergy in-service formation. Cathedrals by the late mediaeval period had also become centres of study and theology where the writing of chronicles and spiritual manuals for the clergy flourished. A notable example of this activity was to be found in the theology school established at St Albans, which had achieved a national reputation as early as the end of the thirteenth century. The cathedrals

[31] Like Chaucer, Thomas More could laugh at the antics of clerics in *A Dialogue Concerning Heresies*, and as early as his *Utopia* (1516) he had expressed the view that there were too many of them. See, Richard Marius, *Thomas More* (Fount: London, 1986) Ch. 23. In *Utopia*, 'They have priests of extraordinary holiness, and therefore very few', *Complete Works*, Vol 4, p.227.
[32] J. S. Phillimore (ed.), *Commentary on the Seven Penitential Psalms*, by John Fisher (London: Manresa Press, 1915) p. 40.
[33] *Ibid*, p.38.
[34] James Kirk (ed.), *Humanism and Reform: The Church in Europe, England and Scotland, 1400–1643* (Blackwell: Oxford, 1991), chapter by Claire Cross, 'Monastic Learning and Libraries in Sixteenth-Century Yorkshire'.

were an important resource for education by which those who had the time to give to learning could support the clerics working in the parishes.

For the clergy, courses were provided in preaching and pastoral techniques when definitive texts, such as the Sentences of Peter Lombard, were explored. Few of the clergy who worked in the parishes of the vast dioceses were educated to university graduate level. However, they had to possess two basic competences to do their work. They first had to have literacy skills, particularly in reading and writing; and secondly, they had to have a basic command of late mediaeval Latin in order to perform their sacramental functions. It would be misleading to consider the clergy as either incompetent or ignorant by the standards of the early sixteenth century, and we may assume that some formation must have been provided that would qualify them to receive the benefit of the clergy. Preparation for preaching and the provision of sound doctrine remained a priority of the academic endeavour for the clergy and schools were available to promote this: an outstanding example of which was the school formed by William of Wykeham at St Mary's, Winchester.[35] It is interesting to note in passing that when the Church of England reinstated its provision of theological education preparing clergy for ordination from the early nineteenth century, following the medieval pattern, it established its theological colleges in cathedral cities.[36]

The practice that appears to have some justification for concern and criticism was that of pluralism, by which individuals could collect clerical appointments and their incomes. This practice was common throughout the medieval period and was not restricted to national boundaries or indeed parochial appointments. The papacy used its right of appointment to English posts, particularly bishoprics, to fund its own bureaucracy. Consequently it was not surprising to find a number of Italians receiving incomes from English dioceses. Notable among these were the appointments of Giovanni de' Gigli to the See of Worcester in 1497, followed by Silvestro de' Gigli in 1499 and Giulio de' Medici in 1514 (*in commendam*); later he was to become Pope Clement VII in 1523 and was succeeded by Geronimo Ghinucci. Another notable, Lorenzo Campeggio, was appointed Bishop of Salisbury in 1525 and retained it until he was deprived of the See following the appointment

---

[35] Helen Spencer examines the development of preaching in her book, *English Preaching in the Late Middle Ages*, (Clarendon Press, 1993). See also Susan Wabuda, *Preaching During the English Reformation*, (Cambridge Univ. Press, 2002), especially the first chapter.

[36] Durham College was founded in 1831, Chichester in 1839, Wells in 1840, Lichfield in 1856, Canterbury in 1860, Salisbury and Exeter in 1861, Gloucester in 1868, Lincoln in 1874 and Ely in 1876.

of Nicholas Shaxton in 1535.[37] The associated abuse with pluralism was absenteeism, because clearly omnipresence and bi-location are not graces conveyed with holy orders. Assistant curates or suffragan bishops would be appointed, at a reduced stipend, to look after the pastoral responsibilities in the absence of the person who held the appointment. It may have been the case that these appointees competently performed their duties; however, this practice had been viewed as questionable for some considerable time. Later, the issue of pluralism attracted the interest of the Reformation parliament that met in the 1530s, which sought to curtail the payments that were being made to foreign interests. However, it is important to note that the reformed Church of England did not in fact seek to stop the practice, it merely curtailed payments to foreigners. The Enlightenment cynics of the eighteenth century were still complaining about its continued presence among the privileges of the Church of England. It was not until the creation of the Church Commission in the Reform Acts of the 1830s, and particularly the Pluralities Act of 1838, that pluralism and absenteeism were finally forbidden. In the Catholic Church the issue of bishops and their residence was considered by the Council of Trent and consequently the practices of pluralism and absenteeism attracted the frown of the Council Fathers, but papal discretion and dispensation in the matter was interestingly retained.[38]

John Fisher's loyalty to his diocese of Rochester and his devoted application in spiritual and pastoral matters is well documented.[39] His care for the clergy extended to the publication of a major work on priesthood in 1525, *Sacri Sacerdotii Defensio*, that was not only a defence of the sacerdotal order against Lutheran criticism, but also a statement about the dignity of the vocation. The archbishop returns to the work of Fisher in the diocese in chapters 6 and 7, where he also considers the theology of Fisher and his interest in reform. More recently, an extensive amount of research has been completed by Richard Rex, who examines Fisher's work as a Christian humanist and specifically his written works against Luther and Oecolampadius.[40]

Fisher's presence as a bishop was significant from several points of view, and these were not limited to his intellect or competence. He was appointed to Rochester in 1504 at the age of 35 by Henry VII, by

[37] *Crockford's Clerical Directory*, Diocesan list of Episcopal Succession.

[38] Michael A. Mullett, *The Catholic Reformation*, (London : Routledge, 1999) pp. 45 and 55.

[39] Stephen Thompson, 'The bishop in his diocese', in Bradshaw and Duffy (eds), *Humanism, Reform and the Reformation*, p. 67ff.

[40] Rex, *The Theology of John Fisher;* also an unpublished Oxford PhD thesis by Stephen Thompson on the *Tudor Episcopate*.

any standards a young age for such a preferment. Fisher went on to deliver the encomium at Henry VII's funeral. What this meant in time was that by the late 1520s, when the religious disputes were gaining force in England, he was still physically vigorous and also possessed considerable experience. In this respect he was very much of the old order and an appointee of Henry VIII's father: a fact that did not necessarily warm him to the new king, who appears to have been determined to appoint his own men into his service. Fisher's appointment as adviser to Catherine of Aragon and his loyal support of her during the annulment debate did little to improve his position with Henry VIII. On the annulment question, he countered the Levitical prohibition with the Deuteronomic requirement.[41] His popular respect among the people and his international intellectual reputation had little influence on a monarch who by 1530 was becoming determined in the exercise of his will. By 1531, the saying that 'the wrath of the king meant death' was beginning to be manifested and it increased under the influence of the Boleyn faction at court. Fisher's position was proving personally dangerous, and it has even been suggested that an unsuccessful attempt was made to poison him during his stay at Rochester House in the February of 1531.[42]

It is a fascinating historical question to try to comprehend why the Catholic episcopal bench did not mount a stronger resistance to the reforms that were proposed in the Southern Convocation of 1532. Fisher remained singular in his opposition, though William Warham (c.1450-1532) of Canterbury does seem to have summoned some belated opposition before his death later in that year. An explanation may be found in the initial foray that was mounted against the Catholic Church in England and which was centred upon the matter of ecclesiastical jurisdiction made in a charge of *praemunire*. The critical question that was emerging in England was about who ruled in England: King or Pope? The charge of *praemunire* was an accusation that the perpetrator was disloyal to the king and country in favour of a foreign power. Already by 1532 treason was replacing heresy as a religious offence. It was a clever but cruel strategy on two counts. First, there was no reason to think that the bishops were disloyal to the monarch, even if they had taken an oath of allegiance to the Pope at their consecrations.[43] Secondly, the interference of the State in Church matters was contrary

---

[41] Rex, The Tudors, p. 60. Lev. 20:21; Deut. 25:5. Also, Rex, *The Theology of John Fisher*, p. 172.

[42] Giles Tremlett, *Catherine of Aragon*, (London: Faber and Faber, 2010.) p. 340.

[43] Interestingly, Thomas Cranmer, whose nomination to Canterbury had been accepted by Clement VII, in 1532 was canonically consecrated and took the papal oath.

to the provisions made in the *Magna Carta* of 1215.[44] None the less, the action taken against the Church with the charge of *praemunire* effectively silenced the episcopal bench at a stroke, because any bishop who sought to defend himself by an appeal to Catholic Canon Law would expose himself to the suspicion of treason. It then transpired that, after the clergy of the Catholic Church in England technically transferred their allegiance from Pope to King, firm steps were quickly taken to abandon the application of Catholic Canon Law in the realm. There were rich pickings to be had by lawyers as elements of Canon law were transferred to common law practise. But this development left the nationalised Church of England in something of a quandary as to how it would continue to manage its internal, ecclesiastical affairs without any authorised legal code. Consequently, from 1532, the clergy were subject to the crown and a new code by which their behaviour and their ministries were to be regulated was eagerly sought.

A select committee of 32 men, constituted in equal proportions of clergy and laity, was formed by parliament to complete the reform of Canon Law in England. With the changes of personnel and the chances of the time, it took no less than twenty years and many revisions to complete the *Reformatio Legum Ecclesiasticarum*, which was duly presented to the last parliament of Edward VI in March 1553. Surprisingly its adoption failed in the Lords, thanks to the mysterious intervention of John Dudley, the Duke of Northumberland. Edward VI died shortly afterwards and the *Reformatio* never secured the status of royal assent, though it was later adopted for use in the Church of England.[45]

When parliament began its legal assault on the Church, Fisher had reacted in forthright fashion,

> *My Lordes, you se daily what bills come hither from the common house and all is to the distruction of the Churche, for Godes sake se what a realme the kyngdome of Boheme was, and when the Churche went doune, then fell the glory of the kyngdome, now with the Commons is nothing but doune with the Churche, and all this me semeth is for lacke of faith only. (sic)*[46]

Nor did the complacency and compliance of the other English bishops escape criticism. When Fisher was later in prison he received a delegation of conservative bishops and he reprimanded them for their co-operation

[44] This point was argued by Thomas More at the conclusion of his trial. See E.E. Reynolds, *Roper and Harpsfield, Lives of Thomas More*, (Everyman's library: New York, 1963) p. 45.

[45] See James C. Spalding, *The Reformation of the Ecclesiastical Laws of England, 1552*, (Sixteenth Century Essays & Studies, Northeast Missouri State Univ. Vol. XIX, 1992.)

[46] Edward Hall, *The Triumphant Reigne of Kyng Henry The VIII*, (London, 1904) 2:167. Hall was a member of the Reformation Parliament.

with Henry's designs for the Church, 'it would better become us all to stick together in repressing the violences and injuries which daily are obtruded upon our holy mother the Catholic Church, whom we have all in common, than, thus divided among yourselves, to help on the mischief.'[47] Thomas More sharpened his quill with enthusiasm as he also lingered in the Tower to write a reprimand, by likening them to the sleeping disciples in Gethsemane.[48]

Andrew Chibi has produced a very interesting and detailed study of Henry VIII's bishops and in his book he argues that the king was very careful to balance his episcopal appointments between the conservative and the reforming interests, albeit that from 1530 all appointees had to agree to support what had become the divorce issue to secure their selection. Henry himself remained conservative in religious matters all his life and by appointing new men like John Stokesley (1475-1539) for London, John Longland (1473-1547) for Lincoln, Richard Nix (c.1447-1535) for Norwich, Cuthbert Tunstal (1474-1559) for Durham and Stephen Gardiner (c.1483-1555) for Winchester he could keep more extreme Protestant sympathisers in check. It should also be remembered that the measures taken against foreign interference applied as much to the followers of Luther, Calvin and Zwingli as it did to the papacy. [49] The sharp reprimands of Fisher and More to the bishops did not pass unforgotten, however, and the point has perceptively been made that later the Marian bishops, which included some of the remaining former conservative bishops appointed by Henry, made little effort to elevate the cults of the martyred Fisher and More.[50] A notable exception to this was the Marian bishop Reginald Pole (1500-1558), and it was left to family, friends and acquaintances to perpetuate the sanctified memory of these two saints in biographies.

In chapter Six, consideration in some detail is given to the theology of John Fisher. By far the most outstanding recent study of this aspect of Fisher's life is to be found in Richard Rex's *The Theology of John Fisher*, published in 1991 and containing various dimensions of Fisher's involvement with, and competence in, the Queen of Sciences. The chapter also relates Fisher more closely with the other great theologians of the time in England: Erasmus and Thomas More. When England was still staunchly Catholic in its religious disposition, it was to Fisher

---

[47] Bailey, *The Life and Death of Bishop Fisher*, p. 180.
[48] *The Complete Works of Thomas More*, (Yale University Press: 1976) *'De Tristitia Christi',* Vol 14, Part 1. p.259, 357.
[49] Chibi, *Henry VIII's Bishops*, p. 105.
[50] MacCulloch, 'England', p. 184.

and More that the country turned to lead the defence against Lutheran incursions, which were taking place by the printed word or the presence of Lutheran preachers. The association between Fisher, More and Erasmus had been a long one and it was strengthened by their shared humanist interest. Both Fisher and More had been for a time tutors to the young Henry VIII, and they had encouraged and supported Henry in his 1521 written work in defence of the Catholic Church, *Assertio Septem Sacramentorum*.[51] More was invited in 1528 by Cuthbert Tunstal, the conservative bishop of London who was later translated to the Palatine See of Durham, to accept a mandate to read and refute heretical works. This was a remarkable invitation in the sense that More technically was not a theologian, but a lawyer who knew his Bible and the early Church Fathers well. Tunstal himself was a good theologian, so it speaks volumes in the confidence people had in More in this respect that the invitation came from him. Fisher remains, however, the outstanding theologian in England who could enter the lists, which he did with characteristic enthusiasm.

Chapter Six also discusses in some detail the substance and methods employed by both Fisher and More as they replied to the charges and refutations assembled by the reformers on the continent. The collective works of both of them exceed by far the written canon of William Shakespeare and much of this material remains the subject of further research for the future. Part of the difficulty in coping with the written material is that both men had a detailed and thorough approach to their subjects of debate, consequently their work is lengthy, repetitive and indeed pernickety. This has proved to be a delight for scholars of linguistics and a challenge to historians and indeed theologians. We may also add that people who encounter the vehemence of their language for the first time can be shocked at their lack of moderation, but these were disputants who were not prepared to take prisoners and indeed they gave as good as they received from the Protestant side.

In my view, one of the most accessible works of Thomas More that indicates superbly his competence as a theologian and his skill as a lawyer – a potent quality in debate – is his *Letter to Bugenhagen*, written in late 1525.[52] The work illustrates well the style of debate explained by the archbishop in this book. Catholic and reformist factions within the royal court, in the universities and the city of London were becoming

[51] Richard Rex, 'The polemical theologian', in Bradshaw and Duffy (eds), *Humanism Reform and the Reformation*, pp. 109f.

[52] A view shared by Richard Marius in his biography, *Thomas More* (London : Fount, 1986.) pp. 326f.

more pronounced. It was in this context that Johannes Bugenhagen (1485-1558), the Lutheran Pastor of Wittenberg, had dispatched his printed commendation of Lutheranism in the summer of 1525 under the title of a *Letter to the English* (*Epistola ad Anglos*). On February 11, 1526, there was a public burning of heretical books at St Paul's Cross, in London. On this occasion John Fisher preached and, during the proceedings, the arrested merchants who had smuggled the books into England were subjected to an act of symbolic penitence.[53] The English Channel was no longer proving an adequate defence against the influence of mass production and the effective communication that the printing press achieved.

Previously, in the August of 1525, More had met with John Eck, a Catholic polemicist in Germany, and had been fully briefed about the events that were taking place under the new, reformed administration in Wittenberg and it was probably at this point that he received a copy of Bugenhagen's letter, and he promptly composed his reply.[54] However, after completing his response he laid it aside and it was not published until long after his death in 1568. The title word of 'letter' is misleading. It is in fact a twelve thousand word essay, which takes Bugenhagen's letter point by point and goes on to provide a devastating critique of Bugenhagen's commendation. More's reply also has the advantage of preserving Bugenhagen's original letter almost entirely, so thorough was More's response. Both More and Fisher adopted the same technique in their apologetics: examining the reformers' statements in detail, and then dismantling them in the light of their scriptural knowledge and familiarity with the early Church Fathers. It was a powerful approach, even if it was not persuasive for the Protestants, and included both elements of parry and thrust in the conduct of debate.

Both Fisher and More knew that in the conflict it was critical to probe the weaknesses of the Lutheran position where it thought it was the strongest, which brings us to the vital theological position posited by Lutheranism embodied in the *sola scriptura* doctrine. It was in dealing with the authority of scripture that the significance of the early Church Fathers was to be found. *Sola scriptura* declared that only Holy Scripture, particularly the New Testament, carried authority in determining the teaching, and confirming the religious practices, of a

---

[53] The suppression organised by Wolsey between 1526-1529 would seem to have been a modest affair designed to dissuade. In fact, More allowed the merchants of the Hanse notice of a day before his raid on their premises. See *Journal of Ecclesiastical History*, Craig W. D'Alton,' The Suppression of Lutheran Heretics in England' (Vol 54, No 2. April 2003.)

[54] *Complete Works of Thomas More*. (Yale University Press, 1990), Vol 7.

true Church. This position diminished the importance of the Church's tradition and the Councils of the Church that had been held throughout its history, ironically including the first Council recorded in the Acts of the Apostles. Fisher and More defended the ongoing activity of the Holy Spirit in the life of the Church, which had been expressed in the teachings of the early Church Fathers and its Councils. Why was this so important?

The Catholic writers underscored the point that Holy Scripture carried only the authority it had been given by the Church that had approved its Canon in the West by 397 at the Council of Carthage. The interesting point was that Luther himself appears to have been somewhat selective about what New Testament books were truly acceptable: suspicion settled on the Epistle of James, suspect because of its support of righteous works; and the Apocalypse, because it did not refer directly to Christ and his teaching. Fisher and More, with Erasmus on the Continent, argued for the living, oral tradition that had eventually informed the written books that were to be placed in the New Testament as we know it. As John Guy has perceptively commented, and his words would apply to all three theologians:

> When More attacked the reformers, he knew that the vital terrain was not papal authority, but catholic tradition. The reformers rejected tradition, but More argued that Catholic tradition had prevailed since the time of the Apostles. There were two types of Christian revelation: one written (Scripture), the other unwritten (oral), and More pointed to an oral tradition which had been handed down from the Apostles and safeguarded by the Church.[55]

Archbishop Nichols explores in some detail the authority and primacy of the Papacy, particularly its role in defending the Church from error. More recently, however, attention has focused upon the essential role of the papacy in securing the unity of the Church, which carried a special and important function for Europe at the time. Certainly, for Fisher and More, the threat of disunity that appeared to be created by the reformers, particularly from the Lutheran experience in Germany, was a greater problem than the corruptions that needed to be resolved within the Church. They suspected that, like Pandora's box, once opened things would never be the same again and loyalty to the Pope was vitally important in maintaining the unity of the Church, the Body of Christ.

In chapter Seven, the contemporaries of John Fisher are given consideration. In England, we should remember that for most of the

---

[55] John Guy, *Thomas More*, (London : Arnold, 2000) p. 117.

1520s the position occupied by Fisher and More on the Lutheran question was the official national position held by royal support and authority. It is only to be expected, therefore, that quite a number of academics and theologians at that time would have identified themselves with what the bishop and the lawyer had to say. Furthermore, there was frequent contact with the humanist coterie on the Continent who was not persuaded by the reformers. In connection with this, chapter 9 is exceptional and distinctive in its exploration of the work of Edward Powel, and it constitutes a contribution to our body of knowledge on the subject. The archbishop's assessment of Powel is balanced and fair; admitting areas in Powel's approach that leave things to be desired, but also placing him on the list of support that was being extended to the traditional position by the scholars of the time. Powel's great contribution to the debate was his Christ-centred emphasis, to which subsequent centuries and Councils of the Catholic Church have gradually given greater attention in dealing with religious matters of discord. The information provided in this chapter on Powel remains an important contribution that has been made to our knowledge of the tensions of the time.

Ever since their joint Canonisation in 1935, John Fisher and Thomas More have remained closely associated with each other, and this association is appropriate. Together they both provide two important lungs that breathe a very special life into the Church. A life that recognises the importance of intellect in the particular scholarship of both men expressed in their distinctive roles: theologian and statesman, bishop and layman, Canon lawyer and common lawyer, pastor and father. But they also share much: their joint loyalty to a monarch, who ultimately showed them little loyalty in return; their devotion to a kingdom not of this world, and a willingness to render to God the things that are God's; their love of learning and enjoyment of a good debate; their preparedness to live in, and die for, the Catholic faith and their shared comprehension of the Catholic Church that includes the community of history, the Church expectant and the Church triumphant. The centuries that form their historical afterlife have brought to light the true value of these saints who, even if some historians may still have reservations about aspects of their lives, are remarkable in the clear witness of their deaths.

In the first decade of the twenty-first century, historians have shown an increased interest in writing biographical reassessments of the key figures of the time. This has been particularly true of the character of Henry VIII whose transfiguration from enlightened Renaissance prince into royal tyrant has never ceased to fascinate.[56] George. W. Bernard has given specific attention to the people who resisted the influences of Protestant reform in his book *The King's Reformation*, and continues the process of reassessment in his capacity as Editor of the *English Historical Review*.[57] In many of the books that appear, however, John Fisher receives passing mention, but really no in-depth treatment.

It may be fair to claim that between John Fisher and Thomas More it is the latter that has received the lion's share of attention when it comes to research and general interest. This is for two basic reasons. First, there was the popular dramatisation of Thomas More in Robert Bolt's 1960 play, *A Man for All Seasons*, later made into an award-winning film in 1963, that has proved to have worn well over the past fifty years. Second, from the early 1960s an international community of friends and scholars under the auspices of the *Amici Thomae Mori* has organised conferences and published an academic journal, *Moreana*. The journal continues to be published from the Catholic University in Lille. However, John Fisher has not been without his friends, and the historiography produced about him is considerable: with the notable works of T.E. Bridgett, Fr. Van Ortroy, E.E. Reynolds and M. Macklem being well known. We can also mention the considerable labours of the French scholar, Jean Rouschausse, and the recent extensive studies produced by Richard Rex.[58] Fisher has also featured frequently in the pages of *Moreana*. We can now, of course, add this present work by Vincent Nichols to this historiography.

This brings us to the final chapter of Vincent Nichols' *opus*: the final act. We find John Fisher and Thomas More inevitably brought even more closely together in terms of their arraignment, confinement and trials. Both were summoned to Lambeth Palace for interrogations in connection with their refusal to sign the oath attached to the Act of Succession that had been passed in 1534, which exposed them to the charge and penalty of misprision of treason. On April 13th Fisher considered the oath, but in conscience he could not subscribe to the Act in its entirety. Both Fisher and More found difficulty with the preamble to the Act in which the King is styled the Head of the Church in

[56] David Starkey, *Henry: Virtuous Prince* (London: Harper Press, 2008). A further work, *Henry: Model of a Tyrant*, is anticipated in October 2012. Lucy Wooding, *Henry VIII* (London: Routledge, 2008). David M. Loades, *Henry VIII: Court, Church and Conflict* (National Archives, 2007). Michael Graves, *Henry VIII* (Harlow: Pearson Education, 2003).

[57] G.W. Bernard, *The King's Reformation: Henry VIII and the Remaking of the English Church* (New Haven CT: Yale University Press, 2005).

[58] Jean Rouschausse, 'La Théologie de John Fisher: Une étude anglaise revue en France', *Moreana*, Vol. 32, nos. 123–4 (1995), p. 31. A list of biographical work on John Fisher can be found in Bradshaw and Duffy, *Humanism, Reform and Reformation*, p. 18, n5.

England. Insofar as the preamble had been added by Thomas Cromwell after the Act had been passed, both Fisher and More questioned the legality of requiring them to subscribe to it as if it had been integral to the Act. When directly requested to swear the oath accepting the Act, Fisher refused and was then sent directly to the Tower of London. The obstinacy of More delivered the same fate and both eventually found themselves confined to the Tower. At first they had a degree of liberty by which they could contact each other but, fearing exposure to the charge of conspiracy, caution counselled that they reduce such comforts. In any event, extra restrictions were gradually introduced over the summer months that increased their solitary confinement.

Both men had alluded to the oath as a double-edged sword, in the words of Fisher:

> *My Lords, you present before me a two-edged sword; for, if I should answer you with a disacknowledgement of the King's supremacy, that should be my death; and if I should acknowledge, perhaps contrary to my conscience, that would be assuredly unto me worse than death.*[59]

This use of the allusion by both men carried the threat of collusion as their impending trials became a reality. So the initial liberties were forbidden and indeed the estate and belongings of Fisher were sequestrated by the crown.

Fisher was officially attainted by a special Act passed by parliament in November 1534 and this measure also deprived him of his episcopal see as from 2 January 1535, and enacted that, 'the King our sovereign Lord, his heirs and successors, kings of this realm, shall be taken, accepted and reputed the only supreme head of the Church on earth of England, called Anglicana Ecclesia.' We may strongly suspect that this was a statute that was designed to dispose of Fisher and More. The two men, confined to their cells in the Bell Tower, were subject to further interrogations as the legal preparations were put in place for their trials.

Several attempts were made to persuade them to change their minds, even resorting to deception. For example, Fisher received a conservative episcopal delegation that included Stokesley of London, Gardiner of Winchester and Tunstal of Durham, who in vain tried to get him to join them. Then a more devious tactic was employed. Each of the men were told that the other had agreed to subscribe to the oath, in the hope that they would change their mind, but the ploy failed. Also the shadowy

---

[59] Bailey, *Life and Death of Bishop Fisher*, p. 166. See also Cecilia A. Hatt, 'The Two-Edged Sword as Image of Civil Power for Fisher and More', *Moreana*, Vol. 45, no. 175, p. 67.

character of Richard Rich, the Solicitor General, was also sent to Fisher and, as with More, the lawyer offered hypothesis and secrecy to elicit a response that could later be used at their trials. It was probably the case that Fisher proved to be an easier target than More in the legal webs that were woven, More employed his right to silence and obviously was more familiar with legal practice. Fisher appears to have been much more transparent in speaking his mind.

On 20 May 1535, the new Pope Paul III created Fisher a Cardinal, probably in an attempt to provide the ailing bishop with some security and even possibly to please the King. Whatever the reasons, the gesture backfired and the papal honour rather sealed the fate of Fisher. The situation had not been helped by the Pope's predecessor, Clement VII (1478-1534), threatening excommunication for Henry in July 1533 and again in March 1534. The threat should not have occasioned surprise for Henry, but by this stage his relationship with the papacy, and Clement in particular, had reached a point when schism seemed to be inevitable.

Accounts of the trials and execution of John Fisher and Thomas More are now well documented, so appropriately we provide here a summary of them.[60] The trial of Fisher began on 17 June, 1535, and it did not take long to complete. It was considered that there was sufficient evidence against the bishop to preclude any lengthy proceedings. The Ambassador of Charles V, Eustache Chapuys (1490-1556), was present at the event and reported that Fisher was informed, when he attempted to defend himself, that he was there not to dispute, but to hear the sentence of his death. The bishop was found guilty and condemned to be hanged, drawn and quartered. He was finally given an opportunity to speak after sentence had been pronounced. Four days later the means of his death were commuted to beheading and he was spared the journey to Tyburn, with the execution taking place on Tower Hill instead. His final words contained no malice and great charity.[61] After beheading, his body was buried unceremoniously in the churchyard of All Hallows by the Tower, with the head being displayed on Tower Bridge.

Thomas More's trial at Westminster Hall followed on July 1. His was a more difficult case to prosecute, not least because of his considerable

---

[60] See J. Guy, *A Daughter's Love: Thomas and Margaret More* (London: HarperCollins Fourth Estate, 2008), pp. 256–64).

[61] 'I am come hither to die for the faith of Christ's Catholic Church, and I thank God hitherto my stomach hath served me well thereto, so that yet hitherto I have not feared death; wherefore I desire you help me and assist me with your prayers , that at the very point and instant of death's stroke, and in the very moment of my death, I then faint not in any point of the Catholic Faith for any fear; and I pray God save the King and the realm, and hold his holy hand over it, and send the King good counsel.'

familiarity and competence with the law. He faced no less than four counts and a total of eight charges, and was acquitted on the first three counts.[62] It was the final count, which alleged that More had denied parliament's authority to declare the King supreme head of the Church in England during a visit of Richard Rich to More's cell on June 10, that proved fatal. Richard Rich's perjured evidence sealed More's fate. He was found guilty and given the same sentence as Bishop Fisher, commuted to beheading. Execution took place on Tower Hill on July 6, and More's last words were, 'I die the King's good and loyal servant, and God's first, suffering death in and for the Faith of the Holy Catholic Church.'[63] His body was buried in a mass grave in the church of St Peter ad Vincula within the Tower precincts and his head displayed on Tower Bridge.

The year following their deaths, Catherine of Aragon died on 17 January 1536, at Kimbolton and, after a modest funeral, was interred within an equally modest tomb in Peterborough Abbey on 29 January. On 19 May of that year Anne Boleyn was executed for treason and her body was placed in the same mass grave as Thomas More. Erasmus died on 12 July of the same year in Basel. Thomas Cromwell, the loyal servant of the King's wishes and effective architect of the English Reformation, was beheaded for treason after five years on 28 July 1540.

We may ask how were the executions of these men viewed on the Continent? The question is a pertinent one as Fisher, along with More, was widely read and respected on the continent as a humanist bishop and theologian. In the northern climes and districts, where the Reformations had taken hold, the news would have been received with considerable surprise and possibly joy. The executioner's axe had removed two of the most dangerous intellectual figures to their cause and their departure would have received little regret. Henceforth, the time of writing extended and learned diatribes of defence and attack diminished, and the ink flowed more fluidly in the direction of recording the merits or cruelties that had allegedly taken place on both sides. In Catholic Europe there was a deep and profound shock, for ultimately blood is thicker than

---

[62] Count 1. Maliciously denying the King's title of supreme head of the Church in England. Count 2. More had corresponded with the traitor Fisher. Count 3. More had used hostile language regarding the Act of Supremacy. James Monti, *The King's Good Servant*, (Ignatius Press: San Francisco, 1997) p. 420 ff.

[63] An account of More's death was reported, probably at the instigation of Erasmus, in a Paris newsletter on the 4th August, shortly after the execution. The last words are usually but incorrectly related as 'I die the King's good servant, but God's first.' However, in the newsletter the French word used is *et*, not *mais*. "*qu'il mourait son serviteur et de Dieu premièrement.*" Gerard B. Wegemer & Stephen W. Smith, *A Thomas More Source Book*, (Catholic University of America Press: California, 2004) p. 352. More was alluding to the tribute money incident in Mark 12,17.

Afterword

ink and speaks more profoundly. Henry VIII's reputation never really recovered from what had taken place, and he shortly found himself ruling in a realm that increasingly became more insular and nationalist in its attitude to European affairs.

In the rest of this work Archbishop Vincent Nichols provides us with a considered and detailed study of various vicissitudes relating to John Fisher's life. His study provides the reader with substance to a character and a life that for many has been vague and unknown. Like most great men, Fisher was a complex person subject to the difficulties and trials that his time experienced. The archbishops' pages provide the reader with new insights about the life and witness of a truly remarkable man. His public life and office brought him into the company of the high and mighty, and his devoted service to God and king was dutifully applied. It is perhaps appropriate that he has the last word. Alluding to the story of the beseeching widow before the judge, in Luke's gospel, he observes:

> *Take heed what the importune and never ceasing labour in a great and necessary cause doth profit and avail. It is written, 'Incessant labour' by the way of intercession 'overcometh all things'. So, merciful Lord, thou desirest to have us opportune in our prayers...*[64]

John Kevin Eastell
Les Verchers sur Layon
France

---

[64] John Fisher, *The Penitential Psalms,* Psalm CI (Part 1), in Phillimore (ed.), *Commentary on the Seven Penitential Psalms,* p. 9.

Abbreviations

Allen, *Opus Epistolarum*	P S Allen, *Opus Epistolarum Des Erasmi Roterodami*
Assertio	*Assertionis Lutheranae Confutatio*
BL	*British Library*
Corpus Christi	*De veritate Corporis et Sanguinis Christi in Eucharistia adversus Iohannem Oecolampadium*
Defensio	*Catholica adversus Lutheri Babylonicam Captivitatem Defensio*
Documents	*Documents relating to the University of Cambridge to AD 1500*
DS	*Doctrinal of Sapience*
EC	*Exonatorium Curatorum*
EETS	Early English Text Society
Emden, *Biographical Register*	Emden, *Biographical Register of the University of Cambridge*
IPP	John Myrc, *Instructions for Parish Priests*
Lewis, *The Life*	J Lewis, *The Life of Dr John Fisher, Bishop of Rochester in the Reign of Henry VIII*, 2 vols
Literature	G R Owst, *Literature and Pulpit in Medieval England*
LPFD	Brewer, Gairdner, Brodie, *Letters and Papers, Foreign and Domestic of the Reign of Henry VIII*
Magdalene	*De Unica Magdalena libri tres*
MC	*Manipulus Curatorum*
Opera	*John Fisher, Opera, quae hactenus inueniri potuerunt, omnia*
Powel, *Propugnaculum*	Edward Powel, *Propugnaculum summi sacerdotii evangelici, ac septenarii sacramentorum, editum per virum eruditum, sacrarumque literarum professorem Edoardus Powellum, adversus Martinum Lutherum fratrem famosum et viclefistam insignem*
PS	*Penitential Psalms*
Priesthood	*Sacri Sacerdotii Defensio contra Lutherum*
QS	*Quattuor Sermones*
Quinqua	*Preface to the Sermons of 11 Feb 1525 on Quinquagesima Sunday*
SS	*Speculum Sacerdotale*
Surtz, *Works and Days*	E Surtz, *The Works and Days of John Fisher*
Van Ortroy, *Vie*	P Van Ortroy, *Vie du bonheureux martyr Jean Fisher, Cardinal Évêque de Rochester* (ob 1535)
VCH Yorks	W Page (ed) *Victoria History of the County of York*

Index

(Note: In the early sixteenth century there was no established standard of English spelling; it tended to be phonetic in its application, and this obtained as much to proper names as to other words. Much depends on the sources that scholars use. This variation is reflected in this index and its reference to proper names in the main text.)

Index

Index

Index

Select Bibliography

Works of John Fisher:-

Sermons:

Treatise concerning the fruitful sayings of David the King and Prophets in the Seven Penitential Psalms. Wynkyn de Worde. 1509. To be found in the Bodleian and Rylands Libraries and J.E.B. Mayor, E.E.T.S. Extra Series, XXVII, pp. 1-267.

This Sermon was compiled and said, the body being present of King Henry VII. A Eulogy, May 1509. To be found in the Bodleian, Rylands and Mayor, pp. 268-288.

Funeral Sermon for Lady Margaret, Countess of Richmond and Derby. June 1509. To be found in the Bodleian, Rylands and Mayor, pp 289-310.

Hereafter ensueth two fruitful sermons, made and compiled by John Fisher for the feast of All Saints, William Rastell, for P. Treverys, 1532. To be found in the Bodleian.

A sermon preached upon Good Friday. Mayor, pp. 388-428.

The sermon made against the pernicious doctrine of Martin Luther, on May 12th, 1521, Wynkyn de Worde. To be found in the Bodleian, Rylands and Mayor, pp. 311-348.

A stern address against faults of clergy, to London synod, in the presence of Cardinal Wolsey, 1519-1520. Van Ortroy, X, pp. 255-259.

A sermon upon Quinquagesima Sunday concerning heretics, which then abjured for holding the heresies of Martin Luther, T. Berthelet, 1526. In the Bodleian.

Select Bibliography

Spiritual Writings:

Tractatus de necessitate orandi. De orando Deum et de fructibus preces, 1521. In Bodleian and Rylands.

A Spiritual Consolation to Sister Elizabeth, 1535. In the Bodleian, Rylands and Mayor, pp. 349-363.

The Ways to Perfect Religion, In Rylands and Mayor, pp. 364-387.

Theological Writings:

De Unica Magdalena, libri tres, Feb, 22nd, 1519. In Bodleian and Rylands.

Eversio munitionis quam Iodocus Clichtoveus erigere moliebatur adversus unicam Magdalenum, June, 1519. In Bodleian and Rylands.

Confutatio secundae Disceptionis per Iacobum Fabrum, Sept, 1519. Bodleian.

Convulsio calumniarum Ulrichi Veleni Minhoniensis, quibus Petrum nunquam Romae fuisse cavillatur, 1522-1523. In Bodleian.

Assertionis Lutheranae Confutatio, Jan, 2nd, 1523. In Bodleian and Rylands.

Assertionum Regis Angliae de Fide Catholica adversus Lutheri Babylonicam Captivitatem Defensio, June, 1525. In Bodleian and Rylands.

Sacri Sacerdotii Defensio contra Lutherum, June, 1525. In Bodleian and Rylands.

De Veritate Corporis et Sanguinis Christi in Eucharistia adversus Iohannem Oecolampadium, Feb, 1527. In Bodleian.

Opera quae hactenus inveneri potuerunt, Omnia. Wircenburgh apud Georgium Fleischmannum, 1597. In Bodleian.

Select Bibliography

Contemporary Sources:

Manuscripts, Cambridge Baker Manuscripts, Vol. 8, f. 92-93.

Oxford XVI Century University Letter Book, FF, MS Bodley 282. No. 87-90.

Register of Congregations and Convocations of University of Oxford, Vol.II, f, 60.

Sermones Latini et Anglici cum Aliis, MS Harleian 3118, f. 113-139, 'Si veritate dico vobis quare non creditis mihi.'

Printed Sources :

Cambridge Grace Book A. Ed. S.M. Leathes, Cambridge, Deighton, Bell & Co., 1897.

Colet John:-

Ennaratio in Epistolam S. Pauli ad Romanos, London, Bell & Daldy. 1874.

Ennaratio in Epsitolam S. Pauli ad Corinthios, London, Bell & Daldy. 1874.

Opus de sacramentis ecclesiae, London, Bell & Daldy. 1867.

Opuscula quaedam theological: letters to Radulphus on the Mosaic account of the creation, together with other treatises, London, Bell & Daldy. 1867.

Two Treatises on the Hierarchies of Dionysius, London, Bell & Daldy. 1869.

Doctrinal of Sapience, London, Caxton, 1489. (Manual.)

Exonatorium Curatorum, London, P. Treveris, 1530. (Manual.)

Fisher Robert, The Last Will and Testament in *Testamenta Eboracensia.*

A selection of Wills from the Registry of York, Surtees Society, Vol. III. 1864.

Harpsfield Nicholas, *A Treatise on the Pretended Divorce between Henry VIII and Catherine of Aragon,* London, Camden Society Publications, N.S. XXI. 1878.

Select Bibliography

De Monte Rocherii Guido, *Manipulus Curatorum,* Hamburg, 1481.

Myrc John, *Instructions for Parish Priests* from Cotton MS, Claudius Aii. London, E.E.T.S, Series. No. 31.

Oxford University Grace Books I and ii, Ed. H. Bateson, Cambridge University Press, 1903-1905.

Powel Edward, *Propugnaculum summi sacerdotii evangelici, ac septenarii sacramentorum, editum per virum eriditum, sacrarumque literarum professorum Edoardus Powellum, adversus Martinum Lutherum fratrem famosum et Viclefistam insignem,* London, Pynson, 1523.

Quattuor Sermones, London, Caxton, 1489, (Manual).

Speculum Sacerdotale, Ed. E.H. Weatherley, London E.E.T.S. Original Series, No. 200, (Manual).

Whyteforde Rycharde, *A werke for householders or for them that have the gydyinge or governaunce of any company,* from MS Ashmole, 1215, Wynkyn de Worde, 1530.